STATIONS ALONG THE WAY

STATIONS ALONG THE WAY

THE SPIRITUAL TRANSFORMATION
OF FORMER HITLER YOUTH LEADER

URSULA MARTENS
and
MARK SHAW

To order additional copies of this book, contact:
Xlibris LLC
1-888-795-4274
www.Xlibris.com
Orders@Xlibris.com
609269

CONTENTS

Book IV

He alone, who owns the youth,
gains the future.

—Adolf Hitler,
1935 speech at the Reichsparteitag

My program for educating youth is hard. Weakness must be hammered away. In my castle of the Teutonic order, a youth will grow up before which the world will tremble. I want a brutal, domineering, fearless, cruel youth. Youth must be all that. It must bear pain. There Must be nothing weak and gentle about it. The free, splendid beast of prey must once again flash from its eyes. That is how I will eradicate thousands of years of human domestication . . . that is how I will create the new order.[1]

—Adolf Hitler, 1933

Nazi indoctrination was
able to miseducate and
misuse a whole generation of
young people, a generation that,
on the whole, felt happy and
empowered under the Third Reich,
but one that also came to realize,
in the words of one former young
man, that they were "used up
and destroyed as a generation
by Adolph Hitler."[2]

—Klaus P. Fischer
Nazi Germany: A New History

The war progresses—safety from Allied bombs and then Russian troops is all-consuming.

One also has to consider Martens's postwar life in America, with a sequence of lovers and husbands, and the overwhelming pressures on GIs, wives, and families—experienced firsthand in Hispanic, black, and—incredibly—in Jewish communities. Her turbulent years reach well into the 1960s, when the US was undergoing its own wrenching legal and social changes in civil rights laws and in public attitudes.

As Martens describes her lifelong journey, from reveling in *Mein Kampf* as a teen to finding a measure of personal salvation in the reading of the Torah decades later, she provides a unique perspective—a view from the ground up—of the cataclysmic events of the twentieth century—the rise of the Nazis, the Holocaust, WWII, and an American in transition.

—Gene Policinski
Executive Director
First Amendment Center
Nashville, Tennessee

ACKNOWLEDGMENTS

While the author's name appears on the cover of this book, the story within is a collaboration all around. Without the help of others, and of the Holy Spirit guiding our lives, *Stations along the Way* would have never been published.

I am most grateful to Ursula for trusting me to tell her story, one that is both disturbing and inspiring at the same time. She is very courageous in exposing for the first time a previous life in Germany during World War II and beyond since doing so is inherent with risk. Bless her, and may the Good Lord guide her path in the coming years.

My thanks go to Seymour Englander, a superb writer in his own right, for contacting me about this amazing story. Without him, there would be no book.

To my wife, Wen-ying Lu; our beloved Labrador, Black Sox; my daughter, Marni Morrison; and my two granddaughters, Allison and Lucy, whom I never knew existed until two years ago, thank you for the love and support. To Gene Policinski, a true defender of free speech and independent thinking, thank you for writing the Foreword.

Readers of the manuscript at various stages are thanked for their comments and suggestions. These include Sally Boone, Shawn Hermanson, and Hugh Campion.

Thanks are extended to line editor Kristina Howard. She improved the text while not disturbing the true nature of Ursula's "voice" throughout the book.

At Tate Publishing, I wish to thank Janey Hays, Christina Hicks, Leah LeFlore, Katja Nichols, Melanie Harr-Hughes, Rachael Sweeden, and Judy Abell for their belief in the book and its production. I am most blessed to be associated with these loving people.

Above all, I thank the Holy Spirit for giving me the chance to help Ursula tell her remarkable story. I am truly the most blessed man on the face of the earth.

INTRODUCTION

In September 1941, Adolf Hitler and the Nazi Party ordered all Jews to wear the Star of David, thus marking them for persecution and extermination. Today, this same sort of branding occurs based on gender, nationality, religious belief, ethnicity, race, sexual orientation, or simply because people are different.

In the infancy of the twenty-first century, it seems that little has changed regarding the elements of prejudice, discrimination, fear, anger, and hatred, our worst enemies. People are still singled out, still subject to ridicule, to banishment, and to being scorned by those with little toleration. In 2010, more than 1,200 anti-Semitic incidents occurred in the United States, including many where physical violence was the call of the day. In October 2010, several gang members in New York brutally beat and brutally tortured two boys and a thirty-year-old man after posing the question, "Is it true that you are a fag?" During spring 2011 in Boulder, Colorado, a man was convicted of chasing down a Nigerian University of Colorado student and punching him in the face after an alcohol-induced fight filled with racial slurs, including use of the word *monkey*.

To blunt this sad state of affairs, our only hope is awareness through education, and one essential element of education is to learn from the past regarding what triggers human mistreatment, including words that dent the very soul of those being castigated. This is where biographies are most relevant, for each one permits us a peek into the past where we may observe a true slice of history, where we may learn from others who were eyewitnesses to similar disturbing conduct. Such is *Stations along the Way*, Ursula Martens's biography; one not focused on a celebrity but instead a common person whose story is so compelling that it shocks our sensibilities and makes us realize that unless we stop the cycle of prejudice and hate, mankind is doomed.

To be certain, there has never been a biography such as this one; it is, for several reasons, an autobiography within a biography, a literary hybrid of sorts. Why? Because after this author carefully listened to Ursula's heart-wrenching stories as she spoke about her life experiences during a visit at her modest Los Angeles home, read this petite, soft-spoken, former Hitler Youth leader's private papers, and sorted through priceless family photographs, it was apparent that the only plausible changes to her story were punctuation, grammar, and clarity. To do otherwise, in my opinion, to change one letter or one word of what she either had written in her diary or had told me during multiple interviews, would be akin to blasphemy since any distortion on my part of Ursula's remarkable story is unfair to her and to you, the reader.

Since those Germans who witnessed the horrors of World War II and the Holocaust are gradually passing from this earth to the next life, Ursula's unabridged, unvarnished, clear perspective and testimony to one of the most critical times in world history is essential to learning from the past. Most important, the chronicle of what occurred inside Germany as Hitler's grandiose plans to rule the world unfurled is told by weaving together plain facts and the most pertinent of human emotions. To her credit, Ursula lets us experience what she experiences, the joy of early childhood, confusion about Hitler's intentions during her formative years, ethnic prejudice, blind devotion, hatred, clarity regarding the true purpose of Nazism, and guilt, all while living in Germany. And then we experience the emotions of racial prejudice, love, forgiveness, and finally self-forgiveness when she moves to the United States after the war. To date, no book has followed the path taken by a former Hitler Youth leader as she struggles in America following years of indoctrination by the Nazi regime.

To our good fortune, Ursula serves as a teacher, a messenger sent from the past, one who may educate, inform, illuminate, and enlighten us for one special reason—so that we may understand the parallels between what happened seventy years ago and what is occurring in today's upside-down world. The same sort of propaganda that Hitler leveled at the Germans is being leveled at people all over the world through a media bent on exaggeration, sensationalism, and downright untruths. The intent, the same one Hitler used, is fear. It is designed to embalm us in negativity so that the division between the haves and the have-nots widens and war may continue to escalate around the globe.

As it was in Ursula's time in Germany and in the United States after the war, independent thinking is the casualty, the right to choose based on the facts, on education instead of the forced feeding of hysterical globs of doom preached daily by those, among others, representing

URSULA MARTENS AND MARK SHAW

the ultraconservative right wing of the Republican Party or the far left wing of the Democratic Party. Each has an agenda; each wants to bulldoze people into believing that unless they support extremist ideas or opinions, the world as we have known it will never be again. Examples of this disturbing behavior, this extremism, abound as pointed out weekly by the Southern Poverty Law Center, a nonprofit civil rights organization dedicated to fighting hate and bigotry and to seeking justice for the most vulnerable members of society. Recently the center reported several disturbing statements, including ones by Kansas state Republican representative Virgil Peck ("If shooting those immigrating feral hogs works, maybe we have found a [solution] to our illegal immigration problem"), New Hampshire state Republican representative Martin Harty ("I wish we had a Siberia so we could ship [the mentally ill] all off to freeze to death and die"), and blog columnist Debbie Schlussel ("[Muslims] are animals, yes, but a lower form than a dog").[3]

The latter statement is just one of many today singling out Muslims for persecution just as Jews were the favored target during Hitler's insanity. Others include Republican presidential candidate Herman Cain's promise that if elected, he would never appoint a Muslim to his cabinet for no other reason than objection to the Muslim faith, and the comments made by former NPR commentator Juan Williams as reported in the *Washington Post* in October 2010: "When I get on a plane, I got to tell you, if I see people who are in Muslim garb and I think, you know, they are identifying themselves first and foremost as Muslims, I get worried. I get nervous." In California, the SPLC reported, two elderly Sikh men were shot to death by assailants who mistakenly thought they were Muslims.

Former House Speaker Newt Gingrich actually connected the hatred of Jews during the Hitler madness to modern-day feelings toward Muslims when he said that locating an Islamic center near ground zero in New York City was similar to permitting the Nazis to erect a monument near the US Holocaust Museum. Former Fox television program host Glenn Beck swore that at least 10 percent of all Muslims, nearly 160 million people, were terrorists thus branding them as the enemy much as Hitler had done with the Jews. He then took his disturbing conduct one step further by comparing the unfortunate young people gunned down by a madman in Norway with the Hitler

Youth due to the youngsters being at a "political camp." Norwegian prime minister Jens Stoltenberg called Beck's comments "ignorant and extremely hurtful."

Even comments such as those from Democratic California congresswoman Maxine Waters ("I'm not afraid of anybody. This is a tough game. You can't be intimidated. You can't be frightened. And as far as I'm concerned, the 'tea party' can go straight to Hell") indicate insensitivity to others as do statements such as those by actress and liberal political activist Susan Sarandon who called the Pope "a Nazi." Irreverent name-calling appears to be the call of the day with extremists attempting to top one another with disturbing rhetoric.

To illuminate how Ursula Martens's story reflects such abhorrent conduct seven decades ago, it actually begins where Daniel Jonah Goldhagen's bestselling book *Hitler's Willing Executioners: Ordinary Germans and the Holocaust* leaves off. A devoted member of the eight-million-strong Hitler Youth, Ursula allows us to put a more complete face to one of the millions of ordinary Germans, in this case a child, one who contributed to the rise to power of Adolf Hitler and the Third Reich, ultimately resulting in the extermination of more than six million Jews. Ursula not only experiences the horror of World War II, the guilt and shame of later understanding how she was used by Hitler as a youth leader in his quest to create a master race to rule the world, but also a metamorphosis transforming her from a young person whose innocence was stolen, who worshipped the swastika, and who believed Hitler was her god, to an adult seeking to shed the guilt and shame stalking her very being while searching for a true spirituality to guide her path.

To be certain, indoctrination, brainwashing, and the irreverent comments, or action that follows, in any form is wrong, and it must be stamped out. While considering the impact of Ursula's story, perhaps it makes sense to recall the prolific words sometimes attributed to Albert Einstein: "The world is a dangerous place to live, not because of the people who are evil, but because of the people who don't do anything about it." To this end, in *Manual for Living: Reality*, author Seth David Chernoff tells us, "We must learn from those before us in order to recall key lessons and understandings from previous lifetimes . . . [since] we have neither the time nor the energy to experience every lesson through our own volition."[4]

As you will learn, Ursula Martens, through her experiences, is telling us to "do something about it" before it is too late based on the "key lessons" we may garner from her story, one pockmarked with incidents where people are singled out for being different. When the reading is complete, the important question is a simple one: "Are you listening?"

AUTHOR'S NOTE

For those who may wish to understand what important events are occurring as Ursula's story unfolds, historical preludes for each chapter are located in the appendix. Included are relevant texts regarding not only Adolf Hitler's ascent to power and a chronicle of the war years but extensive background information concerning the formation, and subsequent growth, of the Hitler Youth movement.

PROLOGUE

When I later looked back at the little girl who was born on March 28, 1929, I realized that without knowing it, the Ursula Martens of my youth was somehow trained to hate before I was ten years old. But I had learned the word *hate* even before that—"I hate this or that food, I hate it when my parents go on vacation and leave me at some youth camp, I hate my teacher, I hate going to school" and on and on.

I didn't really *hate* these things, but nobody made me think about what that word meant, and so as time passed, my feelings grew to "I hate fat people, tall people, rich people, and poor people." Finally, it became "I hate the mentally retarded, hate the Jews, hate the gypsies, and hate anyone that's against us Germans."

During the beginning of the war, my family still had a membership in the church, and I had to take religion as a class in school. One of my teachers was a dear old lady named Ms. Pabst. She was a typical-looking teacher, with gray hair in a bun, and glasses. She had a sister who was also a teacher. They lived not far from us, and I saw them every morning walking to school together. The sisters shared an apartment, and it was known that neither of them had ever been married.

Some of the other girls and I hated Ms. Pabst's class; we were constantly disrupting it. Not only did we make fun of her name, but every time she would try to talk to us about Jesus, I spoke up and interrupted the class by asking stupid questions. Of course the other kids liked it because it was fun when "Ulli made trouble for the teacher."

Kids soak up everything, and I had been indoctrinated, though I didn't know it at the time, to be very wary of any Jews. One day, when Ms. Pabst started talking once again about Jesus, I got up and asked, "What is so important about him? He was a Jew." She tried to explain, "No, he wasn't a Jew, he was born in Jerusalem." I said, "Of course he was a Jew" and I kept repeating, "Jesus is a Jew, Jesus is a Jew, Jesus is a Jew, Jesus is a Jew!" Soon others joined in, and we got louder and louder. Pretty soon all the kids in the class were joining in chanting "Jesus is a Jew! Jesus is a Jew! Jesus is a Jew."

Ms. Pabst tried to restore order, but she couldn't. Her face was all flushed. I could tell she was scared and angry that she had lost control of the class, but she didn't call anyone for help. Fear must have kept her from it. We should have all been reported and punished. But Ms. Pabst and other teachers knew they would be punished instead of us. From then on she never again talked about Jesus or anything having to do with him. She turned the class more toward religious history. This made me feel good since we no longer had to deal with this Jesus guy, another Jew I hated. Or even God. I was really sick of them since I had my own god, Adolf Hitler. He was all I needed.

BOOK I

CHAPTER ONE

Station: Kröpelin/Karow, Germany (1929–1934)

I was brought into the world by my mother, Annemarie Martens. My father, Willie, anxiously awaited the arrival. Five years earlier, sister Evamarie (everyone called her Evie) preceded me. That was it; no other sisters or a brother.

Because Father was a stationmaster, the one responsible for every phase of running the train station, including being a mechanic, office worker, selling tickets, and making sure the trains ran on time, our family occupied the entire spacious top floor over the railroad station in Kröpelin, a town near Rostock in the district of Bad Doberan. It was bordered to the north by the Baltic Sea and surrounded by lush forests, sparkling lakes, and green farmland. Most people there, Mecklenburgers as they were called, had a reserved, unemotional character. This was depicted in a song written by Fritz Reuter, a well-known writer. He was from the state of Mecklenburg and wrote all his stories, songs, and poems in Low German, a dialect mostly spoken in the rural parts of the country. In other regions of Germany, it was often not understood.

The song tells a story about the feudal times in Mecklenburg when people were given small parcels of land by the rich nobleman in exchange for total loyalty. During one of his rare visits, the nobleman, accompanied by his daughter, admired an oak tree that had grown unusually large. When he asked one of his subjects how it had grown so tall, a very handsome young farm boy stepped forward and said, "You and your beautiful maiden daughter have never done anything for us or even cared. Just like the tree, we had to fend for ourselves and grow strong so we could survive." The rest of the somber song tells how the maiden fell in love with the young man, but the main point of the story was meant to show that the people of the region encountered tough times but survived anyway. That is how it was with our family since Father worked hard to keep us from wanting.

Father was six feet tall and had brown hair and brown eyes. He was rather subdued at times, never prone to be silly even though he had a good sense of humor. Mother was a beauty; everyone said so. She had blue eyes, and her golden-blond hair was curly because of the permanent waves that were popular then. Mother visited the beauty shop at least twice a month, something we could afford due to Father's sufficient salary. Mutti (what most kids called their mothers when I was young) had somewhat of a sharp, curved nose inherited from her father, one that she thought was ugly. I did not. She had a nice figure on a slender frame and never had a weight problem. Mother dressed well, always seeking to look her best. Father sometimes called Mother *mukie*, or *muk*. This meant bunny. Later, she took up the game of bridge and won some tournaments. She was so proud of that.

Like many German families, affection was not shown, especially in public. Everything was quite formal, polite, reserved. But at an early age, I met a dainty woman named Tante Loteisen. She was not a relative but instead leased the restaurant in the Kröpelin train station where Father was stationmaster. Older than Mother, Tante was big and busty with a halo of beautiful white hair piled into a bun. She had a beautiful black dress with a high collar and long sleeves. I loved that dress.

Although she walked with a cane, I remember her seeming regal and bigger than life. Tante never had children, and I guess she adopted me as her own. She would always lift me into her arms and squeeze and kiss me. This made me feel so loved since Evie was usually everyone's favorite.

My parents taught us that hugging and kissing, any physical contact, was inappropriate in the presence of others. I cannot remember seeing them hug or kiss each other, and the older I got, the more awkward physical contact became. But Tante was my first experience of unreserved affection. She was a true blessing, and I never forgot how she treated me and made me feel.

Father and Mother were also very strict about sweets, allowing them only on holidays. But every time we visited Tante, she gave us a piece of hard sugar candy. It tasted so good, and I couldn't wait until we visited her again so we could have some more.

Evie and I were instructed that religion was very personal and was not talked about freely. When no one was in the restaurant, Tante would sit in a rocking chair in the corner of the railway station holding a Bible. I guess she was also the first spiritual person I ever knew. Sometimes when she was reading that Bible or knitting, Evie and I would run in and try to surprise her. She'd pretend to be frightened, and we'd all laugh.

Tante may have read the open Bible on her lap because of her Lutheran faith, but even though our family was Lutheran (most everyone in our part of Germany was), Mother and Father never read the Bible to themselves or to Evie and me. We were not religious at all and never attended Christmas services on a regular basis.

My middle name was Waltraud, and for the grandparents' sake, I must have been baptized. I went to church with them, but I don't remember it meaning much to me. The middle name may have been after a cousin, I am not sure.

Later on, I wondered if these memories of my very early years were mine or stories my mother told me later on in life with photos to make them become so real and alive. But memories are memories, so it really doesn't matter. No matter, but later I thought that being around Tante and her Bible was the first time God started chasing me, something He did my whole life.

In very late 1932 or very early 1933, Father was transferred to Karow, a village instead of a town but with a more important railway station. Here trains passed through heading in many different directions. There was a lot more traffic, with many passengers changing trains.

More stations were to follow, but I never felt displaced or unhappy by the constant moving. I greeted our arrival at each new station much as we eagerly awaited each train we heard coming down the track, just out of view. Perhaps this helped prepare me for the even greater travels, each a life-changing experience, which were to become so central to my life.

The station in Karow was an impressive-looking two-story structure, built of gray brick with a tile roof. Often, doves built their nests up there. Father captured many of them and those birds, baked and served with sour-cream gravy, provided many a delicious meal for us.

There was a cobblestoned street running in front of the station. A balcony the length of the building was part of our large apartment above the station. It had a spacious attic with plenty of room to play on rainy days. During summer, when no trains were pulling in, Evie and I were able to run and play in a garden on the other side of the tracks. The garden was quite large, with room for several fruit trees, many flowers, and plenty of vegetables for every season.

In one shady corner, Father built a lovely shed. We called it our garden house. At times when we were surprised by rain, we hid in there. Mother had helped paint it, and she sewed colorful drapes for the windows. Friends came to visit, and they all sat on garden chairs around the table. It was quite a lovely place and so peaceful when trains were not breaking the silence even though the noise did not bother us after a while since we were used to it.

Evie and I had our own little garden plots that we took care of. Because she was older, her flower and vegetable beds looked much nicer than mine. One time when I wanted to borrow some garden scissors and hadn't realized that she had just raked her place clean, she yelled at me, "Stop! Don't walk on my land!" I was scared and told her I just wanted to borrow the scissors. With that she threw the scissors at me. They opened in flight, and half of the pointed side landed in my thigh. I screamed and pulled the scissors out, but there was blood where the cut was. Looking at Evie, I could see now it was her turn to be scared. We ran to Mother and told her there had been an accident. She cleaned the wound and put a bandage there. The wound healed, but I had a scar. No matter, I had one on her now, could tell on her if I wanted to, something to use as blackmail, at least for a few days.

Evie, who favored our father, had short brown hair like a boy's. This made me wonder whether that is what they wished for. I had mother's looks, blond and blue-eyed. Later in life, people said Evie and I were pretty, but we never competed with each other. I always looked up to her and felt special when she would play with me. Because of our age difference, this seldom occurred. At times, I thought our parents always considered Evie to be the smart one, and I ended up being the one to hand tools to Father when he worked on his hobbies. I also cleaned up when he was done.

Father and Mother told people that Ulli (their nickname for me) was a good worker and would become a good *hausmuetterchen* (a name of endearment for a housekeeper). This did not make me feel like my parents thought I was dumb or anything like that. After all, Mother was a hausmuetterchen. But when Evie was sent to a special school to prepare her for a university, I accepted that being a housewife like my mother was my life's goal.

As stationmaster, Father was addressed by the men that worked for him as Mr. Inspector. He wore a navy blue jacket with a high, red-velvet collar with gold stars on it, and lovely gold epaulets on the shoulders. As he was promoted from year to year, the number of epaulets grew. I always thought he looked handsome in his uniform, and sometimes he joked that Mother only married him because of it.

More than anything, Father was our family's authority figure, even though Mother mostly sort of ran the show. She made the small decisions where we kids were concerned, and Father was more the silent observer. I do not remember that Mother punished us physically when we disobeyed, but she would not talk to us until we said we were sorry for something she thought we did that was wrong. For me, this often meant that I wasn't sorry, but I said so since I could not stand the silence.

Much later on in life, Evie told me that she resented it when Mother gave our father the same silent treatment at times during their otherwise happy marriage. I remember Mother giving us messages for Father while she was pouting. She also had a whole repertoire of threats, but many times, she said "You just wait until your father gets home!" when we did something wrong. But he did not punish us much although I recall one time when he did. This occurred before I was five years old. Evie ran into our room and threw herself on the bed crying. I was so shocked and afraid that I started crying too. Minutes later, Mother walked in and tried to calm my sister.

Once Evie stopped crying, Mother asked her to turn around and show where she had been spanked. I looked too, and my sister had a swollen, red handprint on her bottom. Mother left without saying a word. We put our ears to the door and heard Mother tell Father that he had overdone it while explaining what Evie's welt looked like. Years later, Mother told me that Father had not realized his strength and regretted very much what he had done. This is the only time Father ever laid a hand on either Evie or me.

Even though I felt sorry for my sister, it was not such a big deal. Many of our friends were spanked, and even the teachers took a wooden ruler and hit us hard on the inside of our hands if we didn't sit up straight or something like that. We had to hold them out for him when he did not like what we had done. I tried not to cry when he hit me, but sometimes I couldn't help it. The boys were hit more than the girls, but I had my share.

Father was a very calm man and always appeared to be in control. He seemed to know the answers to everything. Sometimes he would enter our living room in his nightshirt and start quoting Shakespeare verses, and I loved to listen to him do that. He also had a saying for everything, some little bit of words to describe what was happening. He knew Latin and Greek, and those words sounded funny to me. He wore reading glasses and had a small mustache right under his nose.

Dinner was my favorite meal because I had time to ask him all sorts of questions. To me, he was the smartest man in the world.

At that time there were two types of secondary schools once a child had completed grammar school: realschule, a four-year school like high school preparing a student for technical work by teaching science and modern languages, and gymnasium. It was like a junior college, and the teachers taught courses such as Latin, Greek, art, philosophy, and history. It prepared the student for university. Father graduated from gymnasium, but my grandparents could not afford to send Father to a university. Later, I learned that Adolf Hitler graduated from realschule.

Mother worked around the house sewing, cleaning, and cooking until Father arrived from his downstairs office. She dusted every day, and I can still hear him say, "You're going to dust yourself to death." Before Father walked upstairs from work, Mother would always wash up and change out of her housedress since it was important to her to look her best for him.

While Mother was sewing, knitting, or doing other handwork, Father spent time on a variety of hobbies when he did not have to be on the job downstairs. He was quite clever, always tinkering with things. We had the first radio in town when he built a crystal set. At one time, he re-bound classic books in leather until he cut himself with the extrasharp knife. I was scared when he fainted and fell to the floor after he held his bleeding hand under running water to stop the bleeding. I thought he was dead until Mother revived him by putting a wet cloth on his forehead.

Father also worked on beautiful woodcarvings and built all kinds of toys for us. Once he built dollhouses with electricity in them so that the lamps in the windows shone through. But he never played with us. German fathers did not do this.

Living in Karow brought us much closer to my beloved grandparents on my mother's side. It took only minutes by train to reach Malchow. We saw them quite often. Even though Tante was my favorite person overall, Grandmother became the most loving person at that time. I remember her snow-white hair tied in a bun, her smiling eyes. I can imagine her holding me in her warm embrace. And the smell of her clothing; I still remember it fondly. She smelled of cooking, of milk freshly pulled from the cows, of hay and straw, and yes, even cow dung from the stable or meadows where Evie and I ran barefoot, squealing in delight as we squished through the often warm dung of cows. This might seem repulsive to some, but we loved it.

Amidst this secure life, there were things that scared us as kids. First, as far back as I can recall, grownups warned us that the *schwarze mann* was going to get us. It meant the black man, and hearing about him invoked the same fear that I learned later the bogeyman did with American children. I had never seen a black man in person at that time, so to me, it never actually meant a Negro (as we used to say in German) but just someone scary. Whether this affected my thinking when I finally met black men later is something I am not clear about.

Even scarier than the schwarze mann was when Mother said, "The loving god will punish you," a threat she used a lot. I could never understand how a god that was supposed to be loving could also get angry enough to punish me. Maybe this is why I had trouble with religion or any type of spirituality as the years passed. God was all around, but I couldn't understand why He was important since I looked at Him as an angry, punishing type if I did anything wrong.

Another scary thought occurred when we were told about Rosenfeld, a man suspected of molesting and murdering children. When dusk set in, my girlfriend's mother would tell us, "Hurry home or Rosenfeld might get you," and I would run home as fast as I could. I never asked my mother about him because I sensed that it had something to do with sex, and that subject was taboo in my family. Because of his

Jewish name, I later wondered if he was real or made up by the Nazi propaganda.

Another fear I had as a child was Communism. Mother talked more about it than Father. She said that it was a noble idea but not working in reality. It was not that she had any firsthand experiences; it was just something bad that was left over from the depression times. I heard the family talk of Mother's brother being a Communist but not, of course, to his face. Later, when I became involved in the Nazi movement, we had to learn all about the meaning of Communism.

A young person named Horst Wessell was killed by reactionaries, meaning the Communists. We were shown a picture of him, lying dying in a stairwell of a Berlin tenement building with his blood smeared on the wall where he had fallen. He was portrayed as a martyr, and each year, there were celebrations to honor his memory and to remind us of the evils of the Communists. I remember the Wessell song very well. It was an anthem for young people called "Die Fahne hoch" ("Raise High the Flag"). It later became the Nazi Party anthem.

One cold and snowy day in late January 1933, when I was almost four, a big event occurred in Karow that would change my life forever even though I certainly did not realize it at the time. Before this happened, Evie and I noticed that people in the town gathered together in small groups and whispered to each other. We heard words we really did not understand such as *Communist*, *Fascist*, *Socialist*, and then *Nazi*. We were afraid to ask the men what the words meant, but we heard *Nazi* all the time.

The big event occurred when more strangers than usual gathered around the train station, talking in small groups. They were obviously not there to catch any train. We always felt safe and comfortable at "our" station, so Evie and I moved among them. We could feel the excitement in the air since nothing like that had ever occurred in villages where everyone knew everyone. As we passed through the crowd, we kept hearing the word *Nazi* again. We had never heard this word before at home. Evie asked Mother what it meant. She replied simply and with little expression, "Communists are bad people, and Nazis are good people."

The noise below increased, and Evie and I walked out on our balcony to gain a closer look at the people milling around. We saw a group of men marching to the station, dressed in brown shirts, black ties, riding pants, and shiny black boots. It looked like they were all involved in something together, and I got even more excited when some of the men actually entered our home and came upstairs onto the balcony. Working together, they hung a large picture from the balcony rail, and on either side unfurled two huge banners that almost touched the ground. Evie and I ran downstairs and found ourselves looking back up at the face of a man with dark hair and a small moustache. Large lamps were switched on, and torches were burning, creating a spectacular effect and exciting the crowd. Little lamps with orange lampshades from the nightstands in our house were used to help with the light to shine on the image of the man.

Mother called us back inside because of the approaching darkness, and moments later, Father walked into our living room wearing the same uniform as the men outside. He also wore a red armband with a symbol on it, which I later learned was a swastika. Although I didn't understand what it meant, I realized that my father was now a part of something and that meant we all were and I felt proud and happy.

As if they heard my thoughts, my parents took me by the hand, and with Evie by their side, we walked into the crowd. Everyone seemed happy, calling out and congratulating each other as if they'd just won a prize. We walked along, and I noticed more decorations on other buildings and men holding torches up into the night. I looked back at the picture hanging from our balcony, and I recall that a breeze stirred it in the torchlight, making the man with the moustache look alive. For our small community, this was not a usual event; something big was brewing.

"Come, let's hurry back to the station. We don't want to miss the beginning," Father said as he glanced at his watch. As we turned back, it sounded like every house had a radio blasting, and I wondered how this could be since at that time it was not so common for everyone to have one. But then I realized it was not radio voices I heard but voices from large loudspeakers set up outside the station for the crowd.

Within seconds after we stood in front of the railway station, I heard one voice that boomed with a sound that it gave me the shivers. It was so clear and distinct and the man was telling us things that made everyone more excited. Somehow I felt that that voice had real power, and I noticed others, including my parents, felt the same way. When he wanted to make an important point, his voice was so dramatic, falling and rising so that everyone nodded and clapped and shouted. This man was promising that Germany would rise again, talking about how Germans needed to be proud of their country. He said if we were, then Germany would rise to power again.

Later, I could nearly repeat verbatim what this man had said. His voice was so distinctive, and I listened closely to every word. Some might say I was too young, only four, to remember, but a child never forgets something like that. His words stuck to me and never let go.

Some of the people were cheering like at a sporting event especially when the man, a man whom I would learn was Adolf Hitler, finished his speech. Others were crying, sobbing really; they were so happy. This man was going to save everyone. That was what people wanted to hear. When I was a bit older, I considered how ironic this was that Hitler, Austrian-born, was talking to Germans about being proud of their heritage when he wasn't even German.

I didn't know it at the time, but Hitler had become chancellor, which, as I understood it, was sort of like a president. Years later, Evie found her old diary in which she had made an entry to the effect that in the district of Karow, there had been only one no vote against him during a subsequent election.

When I looked at the banner again and Mr. Hitler's face, I could not take my eyes off his eyes. It seemed they were looking right through me.

That night, Evie and I thought it was fun helping Father pull off his riding boots. I did not know at the time, but the uniform he wore and his having the boots even though he did not ride horses meant he was in the Sturmabteilung, or SA. They were called Hitler's Brown Coats, and the original members were like his gang before he became powerful. I had never seen signs that Father was a part of this group, and this was the only time I saw him in those boots and this uniform. Later the gang was disbanded, but from that night on, I became aware that he always wore his Nazi Party insignia in the lapel of his work uniform or when wearing a suit.

Father being in the uniform made me proud since he looked so nice and everyone was so excited. Over and over during later visits to Germany, people my father's age would tell me that, for the first time

URSULA MARTENS AND MARK SHAW

since the First World War, somebody was giving them hope, that the first members were the idealists, the ones that were hoping for a better Fatherland.

One day, Father brought home a book called *Hitler Like Nobody Knows Him*. It was packed with photographs by Heinrich Hoffmann, his official photographer. Mr. Hitler was shown with kids, older people, and his dog Blondie, always smiling and having a good time. One photo showed two pretty women gazing up at Mr. Hitler as if they were in love with him, somehow worshipping him. Some photos showed him in military uniform, and he looked quite handsome really, impressive. But no matter what he wore, he had a smile on his face, and he looked like he could never hurt anyone. Somehow he looked like the common man, one everyone could relate to. Father certainly thought so, and if Father believed that, I believed that.

Soon I would learn that Germany had lost the First World War, and the penalties the Germans were forced to pay by the Allies resulted in a weakened economy. The depression that hit in America and spread throughout the world during the year I was born hit us even harder. Hitler said he would lead people to regain their property and hold their heads high again. He promised there would be more jobs and enough to eat, and for a long time, he would deliver on his promises. I remember only one girl in my class whose father was unemployed, and as cruel as kids can be, we looked down on her with suspicion as if something had to be wrong with the family.

My seeing the image of Hitler that January night, and hearing his voice, marked a change in our lives like I never could have imagined. Father was part of something big, I was sure of that, and I couldn't wait to hear Hitler again and perhaps even see him in person. He seemed like sort of a god to me, and being impressionable, I was fascinated by him like everyone else. How handsome he was. Very handsome, and the best-looking man I had ever seen. Later, some girls said Hitler was sexy. I guess in some ways they were right.

CHAPTER TWO

Station: Karow, Germany (1935–1937)

In 1935, school began for me in Karow at age six. On the first day, each child received a beautifully decorated large cardboard cone filled with candy. When Mother arrived for me after school, she found me smiling and gripping a cone almost as big as me.

Indulging my sweet tooth normally occurred at the little store not far from our station. It was owned and run by the mother of my best friend Siegrid. Siegi, as she was called, was the same age as me, somewhat frail-looking, with fire-red hair and green eyes. She had the cutest freckles. Siegi's sister was much older than we were, and when she wasn't studying, she helped her mother. Since there was no man in the family, the mother never could take time to play with us kids. I felt sorry that she had to work so hard. Their mother was older than mine was. She was a simple, kind woman and always extra nice to me. I don't remember Siegi ever talking about her father. I never felt free to ask about personal things. It was just not done, at least not in my family.

The small store was located on the only main street of the village, and people passing through, as well as farmers from outside the village, stopped to buy something. On one wall was the large counter with jars filled with candies and other goodies. Sometimes we were allowed to eat the leftover candies that stuck to the bottom of the jars before they were washed and refilled. The other walls were lined with shelves that were stocked with groceries to be sold. Barrels filled with sauerkraut, pickles, and dried items, like beans, were standing on the floor.

Siegi and I dearly loved animals, and in a tiny village like Karow, there were many around. Her aunt owned a large farm, and we helped take care of all the livestock. The baby animals were our favorites. We made sure to know whenever new calves, rabbits, or puppies were born and, if necessary, even stayed overnight to be there for the new arrivals. My mother used to worry when I came home with bites and scratches all over me, but it did not stop me from visiting farms whenever I could.

We played games as kids do. One that was fun was where we put a chain around the neck of one kid and then he or she would be led around like a dog. We called it playing dog.

Soon after first grade began in 1935, some three years after we moved to Karow, I appeared in the school talent show. My part was to run onto the stage as if I were in a hurry, out of breath, and recite a verse from a song titled "Whirlwind." Mother always said this fitted my personality perfectly since I was always on the move. The lyrics of the song were as follows:

> Got no time to take it slow,
> Got a lot of leaves to blow
> Ocean waves to role ashore,
> I'm busy evermore.
> Trees are dancing at my sight,
> Birds in flight are my delight,
> Here's to give you just one hint,
> I'm a little whirlwind.

Being in the talent show was lots of fun. Mother said I did real well. And yes, I guess I was a whirlwind because I liked to do so many things. Especially with Siegi. We often played with Heine Witkatitz, a bony, little boy whom Mother told me was mentally retarded, a term I did not really understand. He was about as tall as I was, and I remember his hair flashing in all directions except during the first part of school when it was patted down with water or when his mother spit on her hands and then patted it down.

Heine was definitely different, and little did I know that one day I would think people like him were not worth anything and shouldn't be alive. He walked so slowly and heavily that it looked like he was always stomping his feet. His nose was runny most of the time, but he never had a handkerchief, so he wiped it on his coat. On cold winter days, a layer of ice built up on his right sleeve. Siegi thought it was horrible, but to me it made him seem tough. It was such a carefree act that I often wished I could do it without getting in trouble.

After school, Heine followed us around wherever we went. At first we felt sorry for him, but after a while, we adopted him as a friend, and he began sitting with us during lunch. Siegi always had the biggest sandwiches because her mother had the store, but I remember liking Heine's sandwiches the most. His family was very poor, and for lunch, all his mother gave him was a piece of bread with margarine spread on top. Each slice of bread was wrapped open-faced in newspaper, and all the print from the newspaper was on the bread after he pulled off the paper. To us it seemed like magic.

Once, in school, Heine peed in his pants, and everybody made fun and teased him about it. I wanted to put my arms around him, but that was unthinkable for me to do. From that day on, Siegi and I sort of protected him from the other kids. We simply made it known that we would deal with whoever was bothering or teasing him. We also threatened to tell the teacher when people were mean to him.

Heine lived at the outskirts of Karow. One day, out of curiosity, Siegi and I went to look for him. The house he lived in was small and seemed more like a cabin. It was clean in spite of dirt floors. Heine's mother was a tiny, neat-looking woman compared to her big, rather old, and rough-looking husband. She was dressed in a colored housedress with an apron around her, and I could sense that she felt uncomfortable around us. Once I had overheard my mother tell a friend that Heine's father was what one might call the town drunk, but at the time, I did not know what it meant. I watched Heine's mom scoop ashes from her woodstove and rub them on to the table and chairs. As she wiped this dirty mixture on to the wood and afterward polished it, a clean bright shine suddenly came alive from each piece. It seemed like more magic, another one of the strange things about Heine that made me want to be his friend.

As winter gave way to spring in 1936, our threesome found new ways to indulge our love of animals. Many people raised rabbits, and during the cold winter months, the owners just kept adding straw to the bottom of the cage until the rabbits barely had room to move without hitting the top. Once the weather was warmer, it was easy for

URSULA MARTENS AND MARK SHAW

us to convince people to let us clean their rabbit hutches for a bit of candy or money. We took turns holding the rabbits as the other two pulled out the old straw. You can imagine the smell by the time we got to the urine-saturated straw at the very bottom. But Heine cleaned the bottoms while Siegi and I played with the rabbits.

One day after cleaning rabbit hutches, Heine and I went to the nearby pigsty to see the newborn piglets. We leaned our chins against the shack and watched the piglets for a while. Then, all of a sudden, Heine kissed me. It happened so fast that if it hadn't been such a wet kiss, I would have thought it was an accident. It was exciting because I felt like I had done something forbidden, and yet it made me feel loved in a way and special. I knew it meant that he cared for me in a different way than Siegi did. I told Evie about it, wondering if I had done something wrong, and she told my mother right away. She and Father asked me how I could have let someone "like that" kiss me. They really made me feel like something was wrong with me. I remember thinking, *Now both of us are retarded*. In later months and years, friends and relatives heard about the incident; they teased me about it and did not let me forget the incident for a long time. It caused me a lot of embarrassment, and I didn't really understand why what had happened was so bad.

Even though Siegi and I played with him so much, we were always aware that Heine was slow and, therefore, somehow what we called inferior to us. Not just inferior physically. From overhearing people talk, I knew Germans looked at disability and other differences as making people less human somehow. Some may think this occurred only when Hitler came to power, but this is not true. This belief came long before Hitler. I'm not sure why it did, but it did.

Mother always warned us kids to stay close to home. She was fearful something might happen to me. She would say things like, "Gypsies are stealing kids, and if the gypsies don't steal you, the Jews will." I did not know what to make of this talk, but it made me believe that gypsies and Jews must be bad people. In fact, hanging around Heine wasn't favored. I bet my parents thought I was playing with other kids since Mother always said, "Don't play with him, he's not acceptable." This was true of other kids too, or people, especially the ones who did not speak High German. I knew I was supposed to stay away from them.

One day, Siegi and I were walking home after we had all played together. Heine tagged along, hoping that this time my parents would allow him in the house. We knew it could never happen, so we fooled him into a game of hide-and-seek, then sneaked inside when he was not looking.

After a while, we had forgotten about Heine and thought he had gone home. I looked through a picture book while hearing the usual sound of metal crashing against metal as train cars bumped together loudly before being hooked together on the tracks outside. Suddenly, Evie yelled my name loud, and at the same moment, she came running into the room. "Mama, she's here! She's here!" she yelled to Mother as she rushed downstairs with me following her.

A group of railroad workers, with lines cut deeply into their dirty faces, spoke loudly with my parents. Their glances told me it had something to do with me. I made out the words "accident . . . a boy . . . between the boxcars." I started shaking all over and crying when I realized that they were talking about Heine. Mother told Evie to take me upstairs, but we stayed and put our ear to the door and listened. By now a small crowd had gathered and eagerly waited for a doctor to arrive from a nearby city. My idea was, if I waited on the other side of the street, I could see his car coming and get to tell everyone he had arrived. I flew out of the house and down toward the corner when I heard Mother behind me as I ran into the street. There was a loud squeal of brakes, and I looked up to see the doctor's car skidding toward me. In the open cab, he was wearing a brown leather cap, and he was standing straight on the brakes, with his glasses dangling under his chin. His eyes had a funny look to them, like he was seeing a ghost.

My legs were frozen, and I couldn't move, but then something grabbed my braids and jerked me backward to safety. By the time my senses were restored, I saw that the doctor was running toward the tracks, black leather case in hand. Mother, my savior, shook me by the shoulders and screamed, "Why did you do that?" I did not understand why she was so angry with me and started crying even harder.

"You could have been killed!" she shouted. "Don't ever do that again!" She stopped shaking me and threw her arms around me, hugging me so hard I couldn't breathe. Then she looked angry again and pushed me away from her, shooing me into the house. It felt good to have Mother hold me close. I needed it very much, and this was not Mother's usual way of being with me. I wanted so much to be assured that everything was going to be all right with Heine. As she pushed me

URSULA MARTENS AND MARK SHAW

away, I knew it was not. When I found out Heine was dead, I felt like running away from all that was happening, guilty for my part in it. *Why could it not be a dream?* I was thinking.

There was a funeral a few days later, but my parents would not let me go. As the days went on, I could tell that although the adults were sad, the fact that Heine was slow and retarded made it easier for them. I overheard them talk about how unfortunate it had been that it happened at our station. It was as if they believed that because he was a lesser child, he was less of a loss. Slowly, I think I began to believe it also and felt less guilt. Still, I wanted to be alone more often after school. Being with Siegi was too painful a reminder of what had happened. Our carefree days were over, and even after we resumed our friendship, I somehow felt much older. But I didn't feel the right emotions about Heine's death. We were taught to think that his life was not that important.

I wanted to talk to Mother or to Evie about what had happened, but I could not. Evie was still my sister, but she was interested in new things. This included being part of a new group, the Hitler Youth. I didn't understand much about it, but since Evie and her friends were excited, I was excited too.

CHAPTER THREE

Station: Teterow, Germany (1937–1938)

Soon after Heine's death, my father was transferred to the beautiful town of Teterow, the city by the lakes as it was called, in the district of Güstrow in Mecklenburg-Western Pomerania. It had a population of nearly ten thousand.

Since this was a big city, it also had a much larger train station. Railroad employees' families traveled free, and I often returned to Karow and visited Siegi on weekends and school holidays. Sometimes she took the train to visit me. This made missing her a little easier. A small what was called a city-farm was close to the station where we lived, and I met the owners. They did not mind it when I brought Siegi along with me. Who would mind since we helped with the dirty work of cleaning the stables? While I was there, a small baby goat followed me around, maybe thinking I was his mother because I was allowed to feed him. I enjoyed that a lot, but it just was not the same as living in Karow where everyone knew me as the Inspector's Daughter. That made me feel important, and I liked that feeling.

After a while, I felt lonely in Teterow since there were no animals around, and to me, animals were like family. I became very quiet and shy as I celebrated my eighth birthday. I was a country girl lost in a big city. Evie was always busy with school and other activities, and she did not want to be bothered with the little sister.

Evie's friends were more worldly, and she didn't care about someone that only had animals on her mind. But sometimes I would ask Evie to fix my dolls, and she would dress them and comb their hair. Other times when my parents were not around, we played cats by pouring milk in saucers, adding lots of sugar, and licking it up like cats. To me, those were fun times we had as sisters even though we were not close and didn't have the same interests. I remember her always reading in her free time. That was her passion throughout life. Her wish was to become a librarian. Although we lived in Teterow for a year, I don't remember too much that happened, not even the name of a girlfriend I had for a while. Her parents owned a general store in town, and they would give us the candies that were old and stuck together in boxes. Teterow was also my first school that wasn't coed. All my classmates were girls, but that was okay with me.

One afternoon, Mother sent me to the bakery to get some pastries. It was a beautiful day, and I was excited about the sweets. I felt better than I had since moving to Teterow, and on my way back home, I actually started skipping while swinging the bag back and forth. When I arrived at the station, I saw Mother standing at the balcony. She yelled something at me, but I couldn't hear her, so I answered by swinging the bag over my head. I thought to myself, *How pretty Mother looks, like a queen waving to her people.* When I got closer though, I realized she was angry, and I did not know what I had done wrong.

As I climbed the stairs to our apartment, I could hear Mother saying something to Father in an angry voice. I put my ear against the door and heard "Willie, do something with her! For months she walks around like a ghost, and today when I send her to the bakery, she comes back swinging the pastry all over. I yell at her to stop, and she just waves the bag over her head. Now all we'll have is crumbs for dessert!"

I didn't know what to do. I waited at the door for a second, and then slowly walked in. Mother looked my way, then threw her hands in the air and walked away. Father called me to him. He took the bag from me, looked inside, then looked back up at me, frowning. "Ulli, you're not a baby anymore. You need to pay attention to what you're doing. If you want to destroy pastry, you wait until you're grown up and on your own."

I was so ashamed that all I could do was say I was sorry and run to my room. This incident was symbolic of how I felt while living in Teterow. It felt like I couldn't get anything right. I even remember being told many times, "Do not put so much butter or jam on your bread. Wait till you're old enough to buy your own." Wasting food was a big thing in my family. Maybe it was left over from the depression days.

One day I realized I was not the only one in the family struggling to live in the new city. This happened when I started to notice that Father seemed rather dazed when he came home from evening work meetings. He joked a lot and seemed a lot funnier to me. Sometimes he came home late, and after we had all gone to bed, I could hear him dropping things and stumbling around. No one talked about it, so it took me a while to make the connection between these things, and even when I understood he had been drinking too much, it didn't seem like such a bad thing to me.

One night, though, a huge crash in the kitchen woke me up. I sat up in bed, frightened, and heard something thumping against the wall. I got up and opened my door just enough to peek out into the hall, and I saw Father staggering in the doorway between the living room and the kitchen. Our big porcelain washbasin had been knocked off its stand and was lying on the kitchen floor, broken in many pieces. I knew that was the noise that woke me up, and as Father kept trying to bend down and pick up the pieces, he lost his balance and stumbled against the wall.

Mother came running out of their bedroom and tried to hold him up by his arm. He slurred "I'm fine!" and jerked his arm away from her, throwing her against the wall. Reaching again for the broken washbasin, he slammed into the kitchen table. Mother tried to help him up, and as he struggled to pull away from her, they both crashed to the floor. I screamed, and she looked up, surprised to see me standing there. She told me to get back in bed. I quickly shut my door and flew back under the covers. It was frightening, seeing my parents like that. Mother never said anything to me about what occurred, and I never asked.

Many years later, after Father had died, Mother explained to Evie and me why she took both of us to her parents in Malchow. At the time, we thought it was just a vacation. Mother said Father came a few days later and begged her to come home. She did, and he stopped drinking heavily from then on. This all made sense since I recall people, whether train passengers that he knew and had stopped to talk to or coworkers and friends, always inviting my father to have a drink. Sometimes he attended evening meetings where I heard him say they always had a round or two. Father was certainly not an alcoholic but what they might call a social drinker. Otherwise he could not have been so successful in the job he had, one where he had to be so responsible.

Meanwhile, Evie and I were falling into another kind of intoxication as the year turned to 1937. Because Evie was older, she was the first to join the Jungmädel, or young girls of the Hitler Youth. She wore the uniform and after a while got a rank. I watched her put on the white blouse, the blue skirt, and a brown short jacket with leather buttons, thinking how it beautiful it was. I envied the fact that she was so involved in something, and I couldn't wait until I was old enough to join and become part of the excitement of what was happening in Germany.

Evie was very proud of that Hitler Youth uniform, and although we did not go to church, she had a confirmation ceremony. All the girls in town had one, and their parents bought them a new black dress. But Evie decided she did not want a new dress, and instead she and some of her closest friends wore their Hitler Youth uniforms. During the ceremony, she looked so good, and I wanted more than ever to be part of the Hitler Youth. I was so proud of her; she was right, I thought, and everyone else was wrong.

Toward the end of 1935, when I was six, I had heard Mother and Father talking about a law that had been passed in Nuremberg. Somehow I understood that these laws put the Jews where they belonged, at the bottom of society because they were bad people who snatched away kids and stole money. They were dangerous and dirty, and the new law made this official. Now they could not run for office, be involved in newspapers, or radio or farming or teaching or even theater. My understanding was that the Jews were not real Germans anymore, not citizens, and that they could not marry real Germans, Aryans. All this meant to me was that these people were inferior and not to be trusted. That was okay with me because apparently Hitler said it was so. When we did not like a kid at school or wanted to make fun of them, we called them a Jew.

Also in March of 1936, Hitler had begun reclaiming the pieces west of Germany that had been torn away after World War I. After he won back the Rhineland, the boys at school began playing a game called Rhineland. All of us girls joined in. Hitler and Germany always won. We always won.

Then Hitler combined Austria and Germany, and we began using the term Anschluss, which meant the linking of two great things. This I could understand because passengers at the station were looking for an Anschluss, a connecting train, all the time.

Through what was taught in school and from others, I knew Hitler also made us believe that we needed Lebensraum, more room to live. This had been one of his first and most important goals, and afterward people sang "Deutschland Über Alles," or "Germany above everything." Through the schools, radio, and news, we were made to believe that we had to conquer these countries because our fellow Germans were being treated like Jews, deprived of their rights, unable to sing German songs or wear white stockings. If they did, they were beaten and tortured. We were told it was our duty to take over these countries and bring our compatriots home. I loved the excitement after each victory and felt like I was coming out of a shell and had found my vision. How proud I was when Father hung a large photo of Hitler in our living room. Now my god was right there with me.

In September 1937, the excitement increased when a man named Mussolini from Italy came to Germany to sign what Father called the Pact of Steel with Hitler. We lived in Teterow, but Father was familiar with the old place we lived, nearby Kröpelin, and was ordered to report there to give the final signal for the train to leave that carried the two men. He had never done this kind of job because it was below his position, but this was quite an honor. He looked so handsome in his new uniform, a blue suit and the customary red hat of a signal man. When he came home, he told us that as the train slowly moved away from the station, both Hitler and Mussolini, leaning out of the open window, saluted him. After a while, he received a picture with both of them. The caption read "In honor of fulfilling his duty" and was signed by the two dictators. How proud Mother, Evie, and I were of Father. Imagine, him having his picture taken with Adolf Hitler. My friends were all envious. This was really the start of my being under the spell of Mr. Hitler.

URSULA MARTENS AND MARK SHAW

BOOK II

CHAPTER FOUR

Station: Schwerin, Germany (1938–1939)

In late 1938 or early 1939, when I was about nine years old, Father was promoted to the district's head office in Schwerin. This was the first time in my life that we did not live over the train station; my parents had rented the second floor of a duplex building. It was almost too quiet compared to the constant noise of the trains coming and going at our former homes. For Father, it meant that from now on he wore a suit to work and that we were no longer at the center of activity.

The first floor was occupied by an older widower who lived there with his grown son and a housekeeper. The building was a sturdy *fachhaus*, meaning it was built of bricks set into large wooden boulders. In the lovely garden-type backyard was another similar structure. It housed a print shop that our landlord, his son, and some workers operated. There, in the attic, was a large hand-operated pressing machine that I considered a toy. I used to run pieces of paper through the large wooden rollers. Every time Mother caught me doing it, she would say, "Ulli, that's not a toy. You're going to hurt yourself one day." Of course, she was right, and one day my finger caught in the press. I have a scar where my finger popped open.

The scar, my friendship with Heine, my attraction to Hitler's movement, these are warm memories compared to so many things about my family that feel cold. I was still a little whirlwind, always getting into some kind of mischief. Things occurred like tearing my dresses while jumping over fences, not showing up for dinner (which was always served at twelve noon punctual), or bringing home dogs that had followed me. I suppose the word *mischievous* described me. One time, some kids and I were supposed to observe a moment of silence when President Hindenberg died. This meant that we were to stop whatever we were doing and just stand there. But this wasn't good enough for us; we had to do something dangerous. We decided to climb a fence at the end of the railway station that had pieces of glass imbedded in it to keep people off even though we could have cut our hands and knees on the glass. We didn't care; we climbed the fence anyway, and then we had the moment of silence while we snickered at what he had done.

There was a cold room in our house. This was a formal living room, only used on holidays or for parties, probably because it was too expensive or too much trouble to heat in wintertime. At the time, most houses were still heated by large furnaces built from tile. They needed a constant supply of wood or coal. A few weeks before Christmas, the cold room magically became the Christmas room. It was kept locked then, and it seemed like all kinds of things went on inside. The Christmas tree disappeared behind its door, secret packages were carried inside, and Father spent hours there. Later, I realized that he was assembling toys that he had built in the attic.

Then came Christmas Eve, and finally our patience was rewarded. Just after dark, we were allowed to enter the magical room. A huge Christmas tree reached to the ceiling, decorated with beautiful shining bulbs and tinsel. The burning candles on the tree were the only light in the room, and sometimes a candle would touch a twig, so fresh and green that it could not start a fire, just release an exquisite aroma. This added to the smell of oranges and apples coming from the tables of presents. As was the custom, presents were not wrapped but were displayed on tables around the tree, and in the center of each one was a cardboard Christmas plate with nuts, sweets, apples, and an orange. Later, the smell of oranges always reminded me of Christmas in Schwerin. The aroma would slowly fade once the holidays were over, and the room was not heated again until my mother's birthday in February when the candles were burned down to their ends. At this time, we also got to "plunder" the tree. It was a chance to find all the candy ornaments that were either too high to reach or were missed earlier.

Schwerin was much larger than the villages and towns we had lived in before. It was the state capital of Mecklenburg where there were more than 650 lakes. Schwerin became a city around eleven hundred built along a lake that also surrounds the beautiful castle. It was the residence of royalty. In the center of the city was a large pond that froze over in winter. It was our favorite place for ice skating.

Our apartment was near a park with a large hill. In the evenings, older children dumped pails of water on the hill that turned to ice during the night. It became the Death Track, and kids flew down it on sleds. One time, lying on my belly, as I pushed off my sled, several friends jumped on top of me. I remember my head being pushed between the opening on the front of the sled and the ice as I headed downhill. The next day, I had a scrape on my forehead.

That year, we heard about the huge Hitler Youth rally in Nuremberg. It was located near the northern edge of the Bavarian Alps. Later we learned that more than seven hundred thousand members of the Nazi Party gathered including eighty thousand from the Hitler Youth. That rally lasted a week as everyone paid tribute to our führer. At one point, I was told that the crowd in the stands used flash cards to spell out first a capital *A* and then a capital *H* like they did at sporting events.

Mother and Father went, and Mother told me how the women there were so in awe of Hitler. She said women were crying because they were so overcome with emotion and love for our leader and what he was doing for us. He even promised every German family a new Volkswagen after the war, paid for by a tax that had been imposed.

They also told us black and brown uniforms filled the streets and flags with the swastika were everyone. It was a true celebration with athletic events, and the army showed the German might by riding in tanks and using artillery. Some of the Hitler Youth got to participate in pretend battles. Germany always won. Hitler spoke, telling the youth they were the future, the leaders who were going to be strong for Germany. Later, I learned he said, "You, my youth, never forget that one day you will rule the world." Hearing this gave me goose bumps. I was so proud to be a German even though I was only nine years old.

I had just turned ten in 1939 when one summer day on my way home, I noticed a dark-skinned man walking a little brown and white dog. He was holding a stick, and as they walked, the little dog jumped over it again and again. I could not stop watching them, and eventually the man noticed me. He sat down on a park bench, and we began talking. He said, "This is Wanda the Wonder Dog. She can even count."

I told him I did not believe him, but then he asked me to hold up four fingers. When I did, little Wanda barked four times. When I held up eight fingers on both hands, Wanda barked eight times. My face lit up. I could not believe what I was seeing.

To further excite me, the man had Wanda jump from one of his hands to the other, and one time she did a somersault. Then Wanda jumped on my lap and licked my cheek. The man told me his name was Jacob and that he and Wanda performed at circuses around the area.

Jacob's accent was definitely different from mine, but I didn't care. He told me his dog knew many tricks but would not perform around so many people. He said if I met him in the afternoon after dinner we could go down to the lake and the dog would retrieve sticks out of the water. I knew that area to be deserted of people, but he gave me a dime to buy an ice cream cone, and he also said it would be better if I came alone. I was so excited that I ran the rest of the way home. Mother was sitting in the backyard, drying her hair in the sun, when I came running up to her. I was out of breath as I told her what had happened. She kept interrupting me to ask me questions. I never did repeat that Jacob had also asked me to come alone.

When I finished telling her about the man and dog, the dime, and our meeting later, she went inside and made a call from the landlord's phone. It was too early for lunch, and when Father came home minutes later, I knew something was wrong. Mother made me repeat the story to him, and this time I told it with less excitement and made it sound like I took the dime and told Jacob I would meet him just to humor him.

Father asked me to sit down so he could talk to me. He said, "Those stories you heard about gypsies and Jews stealing children weren't just stories, they were true."

"But Jacob and the dog were so nice," I told him.

And he said, "Just because that man loves animals doesn't mean he likes children. I'm going to call some friends, and they will decide if he is okay or not. If he's not a gypsy or a Jew, then okay. If not, my friends will know what to do." Hearing Father say this about gypsies and Jews sounded strange, but if Father said it, it must be true. He was always right.

A little while later, two middle-aged, serious-looking men in civilian clothing pulled up in a car. Cars were rare at that time, and I knew these men must be important. They said that they were going to go with

URSULA MARTENS AND MARK SHAW

me and wanted me to show them where the man was. They made me believe that I was still going to go and meet the man and his dog. At the agreed hour, we drove to the bench where we had met in the morning. The man was sitting with the dog and throwing sticks to him. The men asked me if this was the one, and I said yes. I never said a word to Jacob because at that moment, they got out of the car, walked up to him, and pulled out badges. From the car, I could see that he wasn't nervous or acting like he was trying to talk his way out of anything. I didn't know what to do because I felt I had somehow deceived him. Another car pulled up, and they put Jacob and the dog in it and drove away.

Days later, a young woman came to our house. When my mother answered the door, she said, "Why did you do this? He was my fiancé. Why did you do this?" She had an accent like the man, and since people were told to be wary about foreigners, Mother did not let her in. She stood crying at the top of the stairs, asking why we did this and saying that her fiancé had never done anything. Finally Mother closed the door. In my heart, I did not think of Jacob as bad. I never asked but assumed that the man was sent to one of the internment camps where we had heard that asocial elements were sent. My parents never explained the incident. I did not understand what I had done wrong. I even felt guiltier when the young woman came to the house, but in my mind, I could not have dared to question the authorities plus Father had spoken and that was that.

Later, I asked myself why I did not tell at least Mother that the man had asked me to come alone, and I wondered why he wanted that. In those days, I did not know about kidnappings or child molestations, but maybe Jacob just did not want the authorities to know about him and his dog. No matter, I think I should have known not to go with strangers. I suspect it was the excitement about the dog that made me forget what I had been taught by my parents. We were told to beware of asocial people, but I did not really understand that term. What I did understand was that it was a "them against us" mentality and that hating others was part of that mind-set. This was the right thing to do for our country. I was convinced of that.

During this time, we learned that a law had been passed requiring children to join Hitler Youth organizations at age ten. I had waited impatiently so long, and I couldn't believe anyone would need a law to want to join. I may have taken an oath of some sort, but maybe I have blocked all this out. I know I had my picture taken and got a pass from the police after registering since one couldn't move anywhere without one. At the first meeting, I was congratulated by all the other kids. I smiled all the way home.

When I finally got my own uniform, I tucked the blouse into the top of my skirt, pulled the slipknot on the scarf, and then stood back and looked in the mirror. I loved the uniform even though I envied the boys because their uniform came with a dagger. Even adults couldn't wear daggers unless they were in special units, but my girlfriends and I wanted one. Boys also got to go to all the larger rallies out of town like at Nuremberg, and so whenever the girls were invited to attend a rally, we made sure we outsang the boys.

Until age fourteen to sixteen, girls were included in the Bund Deutscher Mädel, the German Girls League. From seventeen to twenty-one, the girls advanced to the Glaube und Schönheit (Faith and Beauty). The latter was equal in rank to the Reich Labor Service for young men. My dream was thus to be accepted into the German Girls League while Evie focused on the Faith and Beauty.

Most of the older girls in our district got excited when we went to meetings or rallies with boys, including Evie and her friends. After the war, I learned that out of the thousands of girls, between the ages of fifteen and eighteen that attended that 1936 party rally in Nuremberg, nearly a thousand of the girls came home pregnant. This made me realize that other girls in Germany were not as ignorant about sex as I was. Just like Mother did not tell me about the fear she had when the man wanted to meet me, that he could have hurt or even killed me, she never educated me on how babies were made. I had my sex education from friends and always felt that Mother thought sex was a taboo subject.

Every city had centers where members of the Hitler Youth met maybe two or three times a week. On Sundays, we had camps all day where there were lots of things to do.

When the weather allowed, we marched to the park while practicing singing, or we participated in sports. It was so much fun, and I laughed with my friends. The Nazis had taken over almost all the theaters, so we got to go to operas, concerts, and stage plays as a group, and admission was free. Some of us constructed toys for children, planted gardens, collected herbs, dried them, and helped farmers bring in their harvest.

We went camping and learned survival skills and how to make packs of our equipment. Sometimes older members gave lectures on important dates of Nazi Party holidays and celebrations. This was all like a dream to me, and I felt really important since I was helping Germany recapture its pride and keep it strong against all the enemies that wanted to destroy it. I was so excited since I was somewhat of a tomboy. I loved all that, the training; I was truly a happy child.

Even though Schwerin was further away from Malchow, where my grandparents lived, we still visited them some Sundays or on special holidays because the train was free for us. Sometimes I accompanied them to their church. It seemed to me like the pastor was always mad, threatening the congregation with the wrath of God. My grandparents talked of the pastor with great respect, but I had my doubts about his religion. In the Hitler Youth, we studied the *Niebelungen*. These were books of German mythology. We learned about Odin and Thor and the god Wodan that would ride through the sky and conquer all. Instead of my grandparents' god, I believed in Hitler, a conquering god like in the old German sagas. I also wondered what good a god was who didn't answer your prayers. Our prayers were being answered by Hitler, so Hitler was all we needed. He was willing to do anything for Germany. Also, he was the creator of the thousand years Reich and would never die. To us, all other teachings were fairy stories, and I thought of churchgoing as outdated and only for old people. We, the young generation, the future of our country, had no use for religion. Hitler himself had said in one of his speeches, "We will be the people's religion." This confused me some since in his speeches on the radio we always heard him say "Heer Gott," meaning the Lord God, and "God bless me." Maybe he did this to make the older generation people feel better, but all of us said "God bless Hitler" all the time. This just seemed right and connected to grandmother saying that while Hitler did not go to church, he believed in God. I tried to make sense of all this, but I could not.

At Hitler Youth meetings, speakers included political and historical notables who preached the Nazi doctrine. Singing was a popular evening event with songs being sung, passionate ones about the greatness of the Third Reich. This included verses from "Deutschland" and the "Horst Wessel" songs. How I loved to sing and to march. I was no longer an outsider but a part of a group, an important group.

Also at the meetings, we memorized information about the führer and the struggle we were going through to regain some sense of pride in Germany. We learned why Nazi Party holidays were times of celebration. Speakers also explained why the Treaty of Versailles was so unfair in punishing Germany for its acts during World War I.

Learning and then practicing the Nazi salute was also very important. Leaders got upset if we got it wrong. The form had to be perfect with the arm extended in the air at just the right angle. Sometimes our arms tired when we had to hold them high during two songs or more. I smiled when a youth leader told me I was good at the salute. I practiced all the time.

By far, the most important lecture at Hitler Youth meetings dealt with what was called the race education issue. Before the older member of our group spoke, he had one of us join him to act as a teaching aid and as an example of the perfect Aryan that Hitler believed to be the future of Germany. When I was chosen, I was so excited especially when the lecturer used calipers to measure the size of my skull. This was a means of knowing what the lecturer called the cranial index of the ideal Aryan. How proud I was when my head size was perfect. And, of course, I was blond-haired and blue-eyed—perfect too. I smiled all the way home.

In the news and mostly in our youth meetings, we were told that Germany had no use for Jews. We were taught that the Jews wanted to destroy our country, that they were like maggots, eating us from the inside out. They were the enemy, and I was told to hate them. Parents did not dare interfere for fear of being reported by their own children. I knew then, without a doubt, that if my parents had said anything or done anything derogatory, I would have turned them in. I did not like to think that I would have done so, but I believe I would have. The racial education classes further warned me and my young friends against the Jews. We were told that the Aryan race stood above all others. And that it was our duty to keep it that way. We were taught that only the strong survive and lesser people, meaning those sick in mind and body, should not live. Just like a law of nature.

There was also a film I heard about but was too young to see, but one I heard people whisper about since it was part of what they called at the time propaganda. It was about the Jew problem and called *Jud Süss* (Jew Sweet) by a filmmaker named Veit Harlan, a Swedish producer who later married my favorite film star of all time, Kristina Söderbaum. I went to see her in a film called Immensee about fifteen times when I visited my parents in Berlin during the war.

At the time, thinking that people were different meant they were not normal. And I wanted to be normal. I remember Mother showing me a popular children's book called *Strewwelpeter*. It was about a boy who did not like hair combed and his look. The book had different stories in it that were meant to give kids something to think about. One story featured a picture of a huge man. He was holding several children in his arms, and he was in the process of dunking them into a large pot of black ink. The verse under the picture said, "So you will be black as ink, like the little Negro boy that was walking by and that you made fun of." Later, Mother sent me that book when I was older, but at the time I thought the story was old and outdated.

Physical fitness requirements were a big part of the Hitler Youth. We had to run sixty meters in twelve seconds. That was not hard for me because I was a fast runner. But we also had to long jump two and a half meters, throw a ball more than twenty meters, perform somersaults, walk tightropes without falling, and be a part of two-hour exercises or swim one hundred meters. At the Youth Hostel weekend retreats, we learned how to make beds and how to pack the right way for marches or hikes. When some of my friends were not as interested as I was, I didn't have much to do with them. They just weren't as enthusiastic as I wanted them to be since for me, this was my whole life.

Best of all, we were able to hear repeats of Hitler's radio speeches. One time we heard the speech where he said, "There can only be one yardstick for our conduct. Our great unshakable love for peace." He was always talking about peace. I liked that. Later, when they said he was a mass murderer, I could not believe this was true because he always seemed to be interested in peace.

Huge photos of Hitler were all around. There was a wonderful portrait of him that somebody made into a poster, and it was everywhere. They used some dramatic lighting to give the feeling that he was walking right out of the darkness to save us. With his right hand positioned at his waist just above his hip and his left arm across his body, he looked quite formidable. I could look at the poster and imagine him raising his right hand with the Nazi salute as people cheered and shouted, "Heil Hitler!" In bold letters across the bottom of the poster were the words "Ein Volk, ein Reich, ein Fuhrer!" This meant "One People, One Reich, One Leader!" One slogan we had was "Today Germany Will Listen to Us, but Tomorrow the World Will Listen." Then the lyrics were changed to "Today We Own Germany, Tomorrow We Will Own the World."

Above all, the Hitler Youth leaders made us realize the whole world was our enemy. When Hitler spoke, and we listened intently to every word, he always talked about protecting the German people. He had told world leaders that if he was permitted to take over the Sudetenland, that would be it. But then Hitler said all the countries were against us when all he wanted was justice and peace. When he proclaimed that Czechoslovakia was like a loaded gun against us, just waiting to invade our country, everyone, including me, believed him. But the real culprit, we kept being told, was the Jews. They were plotting against us on a daily basis.

This was proven, Hitler said, when a Polish Jew named Grynszpan had killed a young secretary named vom Rath at the German Embassy in Paris in November 1938. He was a youngster like me, and when I heard this, I hated the Jews and how they were troublemakers all around. Reminders of this were everywhere since signs were posted everywhere that showed a funny-looking little person and words that meant something like "Don't Talk: The Enemy Is Listening," a warning to not talk around the Jews, the enemy. They were the ones, I knew, with the big noses and the crooked legs, the ones whose names sounded Jewish.

The next day after the killing, I was on my way to school. All at once, I saw more people than usual standing around in the streets. One large group stood around a crystal and porcelain store I passed by every day. It was a favorite. The shop had been roped off by the police, and there was shattered glass everywhere. Mother owned crystal, and we all thought of it as precious. I would have never dared to walk in and buy anything there because it was a Jewish store, but whenever I passed it, I looked out of the corner of my eye at all the beautiful figurines. That morning I could still make out the former beautiful pieces, but now they were lying all over, broken in pieces. It was eight o'clock, but the sun was already out, and the pieces were shining in the sun. Everything was destroyed! All at once, I felt short of breath, like someone had kicked me in the stomach. Why had this happened? I wondered.

I felt sorry for all the beautiful crystals. It seemed like such a waste to me. I knew that because the owners were Jewish, they weren't supposed to have a store, and so I didn't question what had been done to it. But I questioned why someone would break a piece of art because he or she didn't like the owner of it. I thought it should be taken away from him, or the store closed, but I didn't think anger should be taken out on the beautiful crystals. But this made me feel nauseous, and I dismissed these thoughts almost immediately.

When I arrived at school, everybody was revved up about what "we" did. I found out that all Jewish-owned crystal, porcelain, and china stores in Germany had met the same fate. At the time nobody admitted to knowing who exactly had done it, but everybody was calling it *Kristall Nacht*, or Crystal Night. It had happened all over Germany while everyone was asleep. I knew that my thinking was not in tune with what I had been taught in the meetings, but it did not stop me from feeling angry over all that waste. I did not dare tell anyone what I thought.

I did wonder too why no Germans did anything to stop the destruction. Maybe the German soldiers and the Hitler Youth who had been involved were just too strong, but ordinary people just stood and stared like me. I guessed the Jews had gotten what they deserved since, as Father and Mother said, they were bad people. Later, I wondered whether things would have been different for the Jews if they had fought back on that day when the shops were destroyed. But they must not have fought back; at least I never heard that they did so.

Later, I would learn that the Hitler Youth did things I never knew about. When I was just little, they had broken into some offices and stole files. They also harassed Catholic priests and nuns who spoke against Hitler when ordered to do so. Other times they attacked Jewish businesses along with the storm troopers and SS people. Some destroyed synagogues. No one told us about this, but maybe we knew some young people from Hitler Youth who were involved. All I heard was that Jews were called bloodsuckers and parasites, and that they were the reason Germany was bad off since they took all the money. There were signs, "Don't Buy from Jews" and "Jewish Filth," above the doors. The first time I saw some of them wearing yellow stars, I wondered what that meant, but I didn't dare ask anyone.

That weekend, we visited my grandparents. I think that in order to convince myself that Crystal Night was right, I started an argument with my grandfather during our visit. We were having an evening meal, and everyone was talking about what had happened. Mother asked if a store she knew in Malchow had been hit, and my grandfather said yes. "What a waste of all that beautiful china," Mother said, and my grandfather agreed. I butted in, saying, "Wasn't it good what we did? We showed them!" Everyone looked at me in surprise, but no one responded at first. People, even family members, had become cautious, because they knew they could be reported for any comments criticizing the Nazi Party. Later I realized there was tension between my grandfather and me because he did not believe in all the Nazi stuff and I was always boasting about it. He got red in his face when he was really mad, and he was the one who finally said, "You little snot nose. What do you know?" This made me angry in turn, and I answered, "We're going to get every one of them. We are going to get them all. They're making it bad for us, and we're going to kill our enemies."

Grandmother, trying to smooth it out, said, "Ulli, don't you see that what they did wasn't right? You cannot do that, those are good, hard-working people. There were other Jewish-owned stores in Malchow, and I enjoyed shopping there, and you could get the best prices there." I refused to be calmed down, muttering, "We're going to deal with them, you'll see." As a child, I wasn't supposed to do all this talking. I was supposed to be seen but not heard, and Mother made me shut up by saying, "Nun wol'n wir 'mal essen"—"Now let's get back to eating." Since Mother said this, that was the end of the discussion. All I could do was say to myself, "Yeah, well, I can still think what I want to think!"

Certainly there was much to think about during this time. I saw huge flames during a book burning in the same park my friends and I used to play in. I may have been wearing the uniform of the Nazi Youth, or just following Father to the park. When I arrived, there was a crowd of people, mostly men and boys in Nazi uniforms. A column of smoke snaked up into the sky, and we were told to stand back. But I snuck through to get as close as possible. I could hardly stand the heat as I watched boxes of books being emptied and thrown into the fire. No one needed to tell me what kind of books they were. I had heard people talk about the list of authors that weren't suitable for Germans to read. I knew they were Jews, Communists, and other writers that

URSULA MARTENS AND MARK SHAW

wrote anything against the Nazis. Books did not mean as much to me as the beautiful crystal and porcelain broken into millions of pieces that Crystal Night.

In bed later that night, I thought of all the work and energy that went into writing and printing those books. I had been taught to respect books. I found solace in a saying of Mother's, "Sometimes it hurts to remove a splinter, but it has to be done nevertheless. A foreign object can infect the whole body and that would be even more serious."

As the calendar turned to 1939, all of the Hitler Youth were so excited since we were going to celebrate Hitler's fiftieth birthday. On April 20, the largest military parade in the history of the Third Reich was held in Berlin. We always celebrated his birthday with celebrations and singing, but this was going to be even more special.

All of us dedicated ourselves to being smarter, more physically fit, and more intent on helping the führer bring Germany back to its rightful status in the world. Lectures focused on how important it was to keep the purity of the Aryan master race; no Jews or minorities allowed. The people we were supposed to hate now included the Bolsheviks, most of whom were Jews.

Despite threat of war all around, it was also a time for lots of fun for me. I had crawled out of my shell and made friends. Like me, I think my parents also enjoyed the years in Schwerin. Most of the couples they knew had sailboats, and in no time, my parents bought their first boat, named Undine. It was a heavy-duty boat that had sailed the Baltic Sea with the former owner. My parents learned to sail, and it became one of their greatest passions. Mother grew up near lakes. She felt at home on water, but Father never learned to swim. Many weekends we took several recovering wounded soldiers sailing. Evie especially found this enjoyable. I am sure the young men did not mind the young, pretty girl being on board. Seeing the soldiers made my mouth dry. I made fists when I was nervous, and I was nervous around them. Sometimes I looked at their faces or their arms in bandages, but I couldn't look too long since it made me sad. It was like when I saw animals hurt. I hurt too.

For vacations or just long weekends, several families sailed to special spots along the large lake. We always had a marvelous time especially since the rivers and lakes were all connected in this area of Mecklenburg. Because of the times, gasoline was rationed, so we could use the engine only for emergencies. When the wind blew from the wrong direction and there was no room to cruise the boats, the men went on land and pulled boats along the edge of the river.

Once, when we were entering the inlet to a harbor, our motor did not start, and we were drifting. Father pulled and pulled the cord over and over, but nothing worked. He was working furiously with perspiration running down his face. Suddenly, a very large warship headed toward us. It came closer and closer, and I was sure we were going to be hit and killed. Father tried harder and harder to start the motor but just could not make it turn over. I bit my fingernails since I was scared. To stay within the buoys, the ship finally had to curve around us very carefully. They blew the horn as they passed, and the navy men saluted. Father saluted back; Mother, Evie, and I waved; and we were all very thankful that an accident had been avoided.

By the next vacation, my parents had purchased a sportier boat named Stina with a more reliable motor. They sailed in races, and the yacht did well. Visiting my grandparents by boat one summer was the most fun. I got to see them, my uncle, and his family, and I had time to be with my beloved animals, especially their dog Lux.

While I loved this time with my family, I was too caught up in the excitement of how Germany was going to rise from the dead and become a world power. Day after day, I dreamed about how that would be, how our beloved führer was going to defeat our enemies so that Germans like me could be proud of their country once again.

URSULA MARTENS AND MARK SHAW

CHAPTER FIVE

Station: Schwerin, Germany (1939–1942)

Most kids my age knew that people who challenged the government were taken to camps, but we didn't know what that really meant.

I saw a movie about the war of the Boers' Dutch Colony in Africa and how prisoners were kept in barracks, behind tall picket fences. I figured that everybody that was against the government, or asocial, would have to be put in places like that, but I always thought they would be released after the war or sooner.

One of my girlfriends had a neighbor with a dachshund that we liked to play with. One day when I asked her if we could go next door to see the dachshund, she said, "Mr. Schulz isn't there." I asked, "Well, where is he?"

"He listened to the shortwave radio, and so they picked him up," she answered. I didn't ask her any more about it because I knew that he had done wrong and that he had been taken away. To me, this meant that he had been put away in some internment camp. Later, at home that evening, I told Evie what I had heard. She just shook her head. It seemed to me more and more that she did not share my enthusiasm for Hitler or she was afraid to say anything one way or the other. We were just not close enough that we could talk about anything. It seemed to her other activities like dance classes, going to parties, or talking about boys were more important. After the war, and in later years, when I went home on visits, the Nazi subject was not talked about. Later, I called it the ostrich symptom.

In 1939, we had learned German troops invaded Czechoslovakia to liberate our German compatriots. Warnings had been heard that England might come to their rescue, but we did not worry about that occurring. We, the Hitler Youth, knew the German Army was invincible, and true to this belief, there was little resistance. When we heard that our vaunted Luftwaffe never even had to fly during the battle for Czechoslovakia, we rejoiced, singing and clapping and marching around.

Perhaps more important was Hitler's demand that the government in Memel in Lithuania near the border of East Prussia surrender this territory to Germany. We were told this was where the legendary Teutonic Knights had defended foes behind a great fortress. When we learned the demand had been agreed to without a shot being fired, more celebrations occurred at the Hitler Youth meetings since everyone knew we were direct descendents of these Teutonic Knights, a German Roman Catholic Religious order. I had seen pictures of them. They wore white robes with a black cross.

Warnings from America scared me when an older Hitler Youth read a newspaper that quoted President Roosevelt as demanding that Hitler guarantee he would not invade a long list of countries. But my fear went away when Eric, the leader, told the packed house, "Americans are not fighters. They have no idea how. They have not uniforms, only coonskin hats. And they run around the woods since the only battles they ever had where they were victorious were against a band of Indians." A burst of applause and shouts of "Heil Hitler" greeted these words, but Eric was not through. He added, "If these silly troops ever fought against our panzer divisions, or the Luftwaffe, they would run back to the woods. Also, only scum of the earth are in America, beggars, criminals, and especially Jews everywhere. The black sheep of every country ends up there. They know nothing of Aryan blood. They are just a mix of the mongrel race." We all cheered Eric, who was handsome and even though he was blonde, looked a lot like the führer.

When Hitler replied to Roosevelt, it was carried on the radio. He spoke about peace and who was being threatened, us, Germany, by outside aggression. This was the real danger, Hitler said, and everyone cheered his every word.

In late 1939, we had looked with horror at the photos of dead Polish soldiers who had attacked a radio station and transmitter in the tiny

URSULA MARTENS AND MARK SHAW

frontier town of Gleiwitz. Hitler spoke the next morning and told us he would lead the fight against Poland, and we would either win or he would die. How brave this man was, I thought, how brave to risk his own life for Germany. I believed this even though I was confused to learn that Hitler had signed some agreement with Russia, who was supposed to be our enemy. But if our führer decided that was the right thing to do, then I agreed.

True to his word, Hitler fought back and conquered Poland. All the major cities fell like dominoes, and with each victory, we in the Hitler Youth cheered our brave soldiers.

News reports said Poland had been defeated in less than two weeks, and we were excited at the good news. Our troops had marched on and could not be stopped, but soon we began feeling the effects closer to home. Rationing made things harder and harder to come by. When butter became hard to get, I took a small patty and divided it up into six or seven pieces, one for each day of the week.

More and more wounded soldiers were coming home, and some school buildings were converted to hospitals. Girls went to school in the mornings, boys attended in the afternoon, and from time to time, we switched. The girls were trained in giving first aid and began volunteer work in the hospitals. On our visits to wounded soldiers, we helped them write letters to their loved ones. Sometimes, because of their injuries, they were unable to write themselves. Oftentimes, their sad faces made me cry. How brave they were.

We also read to the soldiers and sang for them, and sometimes we brought homemade cookies. Other days we rolled clean bandages or peeled potatoes in the kitchen. Evenings, at home we knitted gloves and sweaters for the soldiers at the front. I most enjoyed visiting the hospitals because I felt needed, and I was doing something to help bring the war to a victorious end. It also meant time away from my parents' strict supervision. Evie was already at the flirting age and was always very attentive to the young soldiers.

Every day, the newspapers heralded another victory, and at every Hitler Youth meeting, speakers gave us reports about the Nazi invincibility. We were told that our tank divisions swept through Holland in five days; that was the introduction of a new word *blitzkrieg*, or lightning war. Reports said that our armies were going to overtake everybody so fast that they wouldn't even know what was happening to them. At some point, when the English began their air raids, their route to Berlin passed right over Schwerin, and we wondered if we were okay. No matter, we were told, Hitler was going to save us; I was sure of that. This would occur despite the shocking news that someone had actually tried to kill Hitler. Some carpenter was arrested, but I could not believe this had occurred. When we met at the Hitler Youth, all of us agreed that we would give up our lives for our führer.

When victory had been declared over Poland, I was so excited and when I saw Evie on the street, she smiled as she saw me coming toward her. We were both wearing our Hitler Youth uniforms. I stopped, threw my right arm in the air, saluted her, and said in a very loud voice, "Heil Hitler." She seemed surprised, but then did the same thing to me. "Isn't this exciting?" I said, and she agreed. Later, I sang that special song but changed the words to "Today, Poland, Tomorrow, the World."

Running with a big smile on my face, I neared the kiosk across the street from Father's office. This had to be an important building since soldiers were all around with attack dogs. When he took me with him to the kiosk, the soldiers let me pet the dogs. That was really fun, and I never considered what they did to humans who might get them mad.

To my delight, there was Father with two of his friends. Without hesitation, I stopped, thrust my right arm in the air, and said loudly, "Heil Hitler." Father seemed a bit shocked, but then he did the same thing. And then his two friends did that as well. I smiled and then moved on past them. They were back to talking, but I was so proud to show Father and his friends that I was a true German, a true disciple of the Reich even though I was only eleven or twelve at the time. This made me feel like a big girl and important. I was a soldier even though I did not have to fight at what people called the front, wherever that was.

About this time, we learned a law was passed that if you belonged to a church, a church tax would be deducted from paychecks. If you said you didn't like the church, you didn't have to pay that tax. This way, the government knew who was a member of the church and to which denomination they belonged. Later, I understood that the Nazis feared that most people's loyalty would belong to the church. We were no longer members of any church after the law was passed. Father thus did not have to pay any tax.

One day as I completed my homework in another room, I heard my mother ask, "Well, what did they make him do?" My father answered,

URSULA MARTENS AND MARK SHAW

"He had to fill out a form, and he didn't want to. Everybody in the office was telling him he was a fool if he didn't fill it out because they were going to find out and get him anyway." Father continued by telling Mother that Hanns, one of his coworkers was still a member of the church, though everybody at the office had told him that he'd better resign. But he was living with his mother, a religious woman, and he was afraid of hurting her feelings. Mother just sat listening and sucking her tongue. Father said Hanns had forgotten to answer the question on page six of the form denouncing the church. The gestapo visited him and said that he had to answer it. Hanns said he had just forgotten, and they told him he "better comply," as Father put it. This meant that he'd better not be a member of the church, otherwise, as Father told the story, "He can forget about promotions or any other government job." Frightened, Father said, Hanns signed. I knew that my parents were both agreeing that he had to comply; otherwise, the man would be unemployed or even worse, arrested. I didn't see why signing was such a big deal. Why did this man care about church anyway? We didn't need them with the Nazis taking care of things.

My parents had already left the church and took me out of it with them, but after the age of sixteen, one could decide on their own whether to leave. Evie, being sixteen, decided to stay to participate in that confirmation ceremony with her friends that she met while attending dancing school. I couldn't understand how she didn't see Hitler as her god. I wondered what was wrong with her.

Despite the reported successes on the front, there were signs all over showing where the nearest shelters were in houses and public buildings. We were told that wherever we were when the sirens sounded to look for those places. Older adults were assigned to each shelter, to give assistance. Father always told me not to run home if I heard the sirens while I was in the street. He would say to me, "Sei man nicht tapfer"— "Don't be brave," meaning I should take cover in one of the shelters.

As the war progressed, many nights we were awakened by sirens, grabbed our blanket and pillow, and hurried down into the basement. It served as our bomb shelter. When the airplanes had passed, a different siren sounded, and all of us could go back upstairs. I didn't really mind the air raids too much because if we were awakened in the night, we could go to school later in the morning. That was great.

Word reached us that Norway and Denmark were in German hands. The German Empire was spreading swiftly across Europe, and we heard that the assault continued as our forces attacked Belgium, France, and then England. *Blitzkrieg* was still the favorite word at the Hitler Youth meetings. We were told the army was trouncing the enemy at every turn. The Luftwaffe were dropping bombs daily, and we all laughed when we heard that British and French soldiers at a town named Dunkirk dove for cover in the water during the assault. What weaklings they were, I knew, against our strong forces.

One beautiful weekend when the sun was shining bright during 1942, we sailed the boat to an island in the lake with two other families. The men caught fish, and we fried and ate them with potato salad that someone had brought. Usually we took a walk on the island, but it was dark because of the air defense blackout, so everyone felt it was time to go to sleep. Suddenly, in the middle of the night, I was awakened by loud noises. My father got everyone up, and we gathered on the pier, watching sparks of artillery fire shooting at the planes overhead. We heard explosions and saw fire in our city across the lake. It was hard to judge because of the distance and the water, but we all hoped that it was not as bad as it looked like as it was practically in our backyard. My hands were shaking since I knew we were in danger. When we sailed back the next day, everyone was in shock, and nobody wanted to say much, but at least the damage wasn't anywhere close to our district. Factories in the outskirts of the city had been hit by bombs though, and I wondered how Hitler was letting this happen since our army was supposed to be so strong.

My mother belonged to a Nazi women's organization and proudly wore her Nazi swastika pin on her lapel. More and more soldiers were coming home with missing limbs and other serious injuries. The women helped out in the hospitals and wherever else they were needed. Mother's best friend, Frau Lorenz, was a district leader for the women's organization. Her husband wasn't accepted in the party, Mother said, because he had been a Freemason, a religious organization of some sort. They were on the list of undesirables. Coworkers were a little worried whether it was safe to be associated with him. Even though he should have been higher in rank than Father, he had not been promoted for years. I think that is why Frau Lorenz worked so hard in the women's organization, to kind of even things out for their family. It also helped that her youngest son was a member of the SS. He and his older brother were missing in action and never came home.

Helga was my very best friend in Schwerin. We met in school and didn't live far from each other. She was a tall, city girl, a pretty, long-haired brunette with blue eyes and the cutest turned-up nose. Helga seemed very sophisticated, older somehow, to me. We could talk about anything, even the most intimate stories that I couldn't share with Evie. Helga's parents owned a delicatessen store where both her mother and father worked. Often, while Helga was talking to her father in the office adjoining the store, I helped myself to a handful of candies from jars on the counter, and we would both share them later.

Helga's mother was beautiful and had been an actress some years before. Her father was quite a bit older than his wife was, and I always thought they were a mismatched couple. Mother really didn't like my association with Helga, especially when it was later rumored that her mother had left her father for a younger man. But I still kept the friendship even though she was not very active in the Hitler Youth. Helga stayed with her father after the divorce since her mother had been labeled as an adulterer. The courts believed she was an unfit mother for that reason. Sometime later, her father married a much older, matronly woman. She had two children by a former marriage. They were older than Helga, and we did not like them. We thought they were "taking over" type of people, ones who tried to tell others what to do. During those days, I did not like anyone to tell me anything. I wanted to believe for myself and do what I wanted to do, and that belief was centered on the führer, the one who would lead us to victory.

Helga and I stayed friends until the end of the war, and when she got older and went to stay with her mother and stepfather, I enjoyed visiting her sometimes. The three of them had a very loving relationship, and unlike my family, they were very open and talked about feelings. Helga and her stepfather got along well, and I wondered about all the stories I had heard about mean stepparents. We lost contact in the turmoil of the war's end.

Years later, after the war, I mentioned to my mother that I wondered what had happened to Helga and was surprised by her reply. She told me, "Helga sent many letters to you at our address, but I did not think they were appropriate for you to read." My eyes flashed at this news, and I asked her, "But what right did you have to open her letters?" She looked at me with her mouth open and said, "The letters came to our address, and you did not have to know about the descriptive details of her affair with a Russian officer." For my mother, *Russian* translated to *Communist*. And they were hated enemies of our beloved Germany. But I was really interested in learning the details of Helga's love affair with the Russian. That sounded quite fascinating to me.

Secrecy was always the byword as I was growing up. One evening my parents left for a party meeting. It was summer, and the days were very long. I knew I wasn't supposed to leave the house, but I walked across the street where I had made friends with the Landers, a couple that had a hauling business done by horses. They also had cats, dogs, and rabbits. As I entered the yard, I saw a couple of the workers sitting around outside, relaxing and cooling off with some cold beer.

A cat had birthed a litter of kittens in the hayloft in the barn in the back, so I climbed up the ladder and enjoyed watching them for a while. I missed so much not having any pets of my own. Suddenly, I heard someone climbing up the ladder to the hayloft. I looked down and panicked when I saw that it was one of the men, a typical German with blond hair, big and strong, that I had seen drinking. Quickly I crawled toward the ladder. He was all the way up in the hayloft by then, and he grabbed my arm with one hand and my breast with the other. I could smell the liquor on his breath and thought my heart was going to stop beating. I was trembling but used all my strength to pull away and hurry down the ladder and across the street to my house. All the way home, I kept looking back to see if the man was following me. I ran the fastest I ever ran.

When I arrived home out of breath, I had another surprise waiting for me. My parents' meeting had been canceled, and they wondered where I had been. They were furious by now, and I'm sure my flushed face didn't help matters. Sent to my bed in my room, I lay awake for hours wondering what could have happened if I hadn't gotten away. Part of me felt excited in a way I never had before. Helga was the only friend I could confide in, and later all we could do was speculate on how *it*, sex, might feel.

At the beginning of June 1940, I raced home once again after a Hitler Youth meeting. Father was drinking coffee, and I was all lit up since it had just been announced that Paris had fallen and France was ours. Father asked where I had been, and I said, "We sang songs after school. Didn't you know—we won France. And now Hitler can go to Paris and bring back the Eiffel Tower." Mother just shook her head and said, "No, I don't think he will do that."

"But he could if he wanted to," I replied. Father looked at me and said, "Listen, you need to be in the shelters when the warnings come, right?" I said, "Yes, but with France falling, the war will be over soon." Father's face became a bit stern, and he said, "Yes, I hope you are right, but those planes are flying over now and dropping bombs, and you need to be careful."

Father was right. Two nights later, after our Hitler Youth group had held a meeting and sing-along in a bomb shelter, we emerged to hear the loudest explosions I had ever heard in my life. The ground shook, and the sky lit up with flames all around us. Smoke bellowed across the tree lines against a dark sky that looked like fireworks were being set off every minute. I hovered near the ground as my legs trembled. Finally the bombing stopped, and I breathed a sigh of relief.

Once in a while, my friend Siegi visited us. She was a proud member of the Hitler Youth, and we spent time dreaming about what we might do when Germany had conquered the world. We talked about swimming in the English Channel or heading to Africa so we could work with the animals there in the name of the Fatherland. Another person from the past, Tante, the old woman who had been so kind and loving to me, sent a Christmas card every year, and I fondly recalled how she had held me in her arms and showed me so much affection. But then I thought about her and that dumb Bible of hers and wondered what she thought she might learn from Jesus the Jew. This made me confused, and so I did not think about her anymore.

At Christmas, we sang about Jesus the Christ child, but we didn't really think much about the meanings. That was just the way it was in our family.

———————————

More people I knew simply disappeared from where we lived, and I guessed that they were bad people who deserved to disappear. A neighbor whom Mother liked got caught listening to a shortwave radio, and one day she was gone. Then the mother of a Russian girl I liked disappeared as well. I didn't think much about that because I did not know what to think. People who were sent away were just sent away. In fact, when people made me mad or even angry, I thought they should be sent away so they would not bother me anymore. And those who were bothering the führer by not devoting their lives to him, well, they should be sent away as well.

A neighbor named Mrs. Kruger worshipped Hitler like I did. Her son was in the SS, and she had a photograph of him in uniform in her living room. He was quite handsome, and I dreamed of seeing him one day. He was like a movie star to me, so brave. Mrs. Kruger talked a lot, and soon I began hearing her say things to Mother that were disturbing and completely counter to what I was hearing at the Hitler Youth meetings. She talked about things getting worse, said someone tried to kill Hitler again, and said that some guards were killed. At night, I sat on my bed and wondered about these things. I felt edgy and anxious, and that made me scratch my head or rub my hands together. Many days my hands were sweaty even though it was cold outside.

On the weekends, Father took some of the soldiers he liked on his boat. Evie liked one of them and began to date him. One evening, there was a lot of noise in the house that woke me up. When I peeked out the open door, Father was scolding Evie for kissing the soldier before she came in. The word he used, *whore*, was new to me, and he kept repeating, "Whore, whore, whore." He was so angry, but when Evie came to bed, she covered her head with a pillow, and when she took it off, she was laughing instead of crying. She said she didn't really like the soldier anyway but decided it would be fun to kiss him. Now Father's anger made it possible for her to never see the soldier again.

During May 1941, I was shocked even at twelve years old when we learned that a Nazi official named Hess tried to make peace with Germany's enemies. Why a deputy führer did such a thing was a topic at our Hitler Youth meetings. Nobody could understand his actions, and he was branded a traitor by some.

Late one afternoon a short while later, I arrived home to find the house empty. I went into the kitchen to look for my mother and saw the coffeepot still warm on the stove. Down the hall, the door to my father's study was cracked open, and I could see the room was empty. I called out, and when no one answered, I stepped inside with an idea forming in my mind. There were two books in my father's bookshelf that I had always wanted to see. One was titled *The Most Beautiful*

Women in the World and the other was something like *Sex in Primitive Cultures*. We were forbidden to see them, and they were always locked in the bookcase, but when I checked, my father's main desk drawer was unlocked. I thought maybe I would find the key for the bookcase in it.

Pulling the top drawer open, I saw only one key, but I tried it on another drawer and it opened other drawers in the desk. I started snooping through them. I played with papers, hole punchers, and other things I found that held a little bit of my curiosity. Then, I opened the middle drawer and noticed a big, brown manila envelope.

My heart was racing for fear Father or Mother would come home and catch me in the forbidden room, but I looked inside the envelope anyway and saw a pamphlet. When I pulled it out, I was staring at an SS soldier with a pistol in his hand. People were lying on the ground, apparently shot. The pamphlet had a bloodred border and black print that said, "The Parasites of the Aryan Race." I stared at the pamphlet for a minute knowing this was something I was not supposed to see. Part of me wanted to see more of what was inside, and part of me didn't.

The part that did won, and I quickly flipped through the material and saw pictures of rows of bony and shot prisoners. They had the yellow Jewish star on their striped uniforms. There was also writing, but I didn't take the time to read the content since I was frightened of what I saw, really frightened. I rubbed my cheek and just sat there staring at the picture kind of in a daze.

Finally, after a couple of minutes or so, I put the pamphlet and pictures back in the envelope and shoved it way back in the drawer where I found it. My hand moved something, and I grabbed it and pulled it out. It was a big, black gun. For my father to have a big gun, and for none of us to know about it, was even more surprising to me than the pictures. I held the gun for a minute, placed it back in the drawer, put everything back the way it was, closed the drawer, laid the key in the top drawer where I found it, and ran out of the house half-scared and half-amazed at what I had seen.

I kept on running until I got to the Landers, telling myself silently, "Ignore this. You didn't see it. It wasn't there. Everything is okay." I had heard horrible bits and pieces of what happened in internment camps, but I always told myself that the people saying these things were no good and against the war and Hitler. I never thought about my own father knowing about such things and being involved. I loved him as a daughter should, and I hated the fact that he might have been involved in bad things. I decided to put what I had seen out of my mind, but I don't think I ever did since later I realized that those trains that Father helped move about were ones that had people on them going to the camps. Seeing the photos confirmed this fact. This made me frown and feel sad to think that he must have known about the mass killings. But when I was so young I really didn't think about that; I just blocked it out.

One time I decided the photographs must have been altered by our enemies using trick photography. That had to be the reason, I told myself, that Father would have such disturbing pictures. But I could not ask Father about the photos since kids, and I was still a kid at thirteen, simply did not ask questions in those days. We did what we were told and shut up. But the experience of seeing the bad photos and the gun made me wonder a bit. I kept attacking anyone who questioned Hitler and what he was doing at Hitler Youth meetings, but maybe my spirit had been broken just a bit. The man who was to all of us a combination of Alexander the Great and Napoleon would still save us, still win the war. I was sure of that but perhaps not quite as sure as I had been before. Our leader had conquered ten countries by now, and when he decided to attack those awful Communists in Russia, we celebrated the decision. Then the best thing happened; the Japanese bombed the Americans at Pearl Harbor, and Hitler declared war on them too.

Father had told me the German railroad was always government-owned. Promotions came automatically. With so many young men drafted, Father had gained power when we moved to Schwerin. He was now in charge of all the train shipments from France, with access to all types of French things. Rationing was beginning to wear on people, but because of Father's position, we always had more than enough. He brought home all sorts of things, from household goods and hard-to-get food items to beautiful art objects. One of the first things my father brought home was a large block of French jam. I think it was some kind of berry preserve, and it was two feet long and several inches wide. It must have been dehydrated because I remember my mother chipping pieces off and adding boiling water to it before we spread it on our bread.

Tablecloths, napkins, and silverware with beautiful embroidery and engravings showed up every day. My eyes were big as Father explained the different crests on the tableware. There were crowns, and he said that the number of points a crown had told whether the owner was a king, a prince, or a count and so on. I couldn't understand why these things were in our hands when they weren't ours. I knew they had belonged to someone wealthy and using them made me feel like a thief. But Father explained to me about the spoils of war, and I accepted that explanation without thinking about what had happened to the people who used to own the goods we now had in our home.

After graduation, Evie and the other girls her age had to leave home for a year to help with the war before they could continue their education. She was assigned for six months to a farm, where she had to assist the farmer's wife while her husband was fighting in the war. Other girls were assigned to ammunition factories or wherever else they could help the war effort. One day, when Evie was home for a visit, Father brought home a box that was larger than usual. Mother and Evie were unpacking it when I came home. I looked over Evie's shoulder as she undid the packing paper and saw that it was a lovely oil painting of a man sitting and being shaved in a barber shop. The man didn't look German, and it seemed obvious that the painting had come from Italy or France. Evie fell in love with it immediately, and my parents gave it to her. We never talked about the picture's original home, just accepted that it was another example of the spoils of war.

During the same time that valuable pieces were being delivered to our house, Father arrived with what he believed to be very exciting news. I overheard him telling my mother that there was a list of who was going to foreign countries after they were taken over by Germany. He said that he was on the list to be in charge of the freight train station in London. "How would you feel about living in London?" he asked with a big smile on his face. She answered that she should have learned English in school instead of French. I couldn't question them about this because I wasn't supposed to listen in on their conversations. Father thinking like this was symbolic of how we all felt about the war; that Germany would prevail and be the most powerful nation in the world. Hitler would make sure that occurred. This was certain.

CHAPTER SIX

Station: Schwerin, Berlin, and Malchow, Germany (1942–1944)

During the war, I had heroes like everyone else, but they weren't music stars or athletes. Instead, I hung pictures of flying aces on the walls. I would look at them as my parents played classical music. I liked this very much especially ones by Wagner, Beethoven, and Mozart.

One favorite hero was Hans-Joachim Marseille. He flew for the Luftwaffe and shot down over 150 enemy planes in Africa alone. He was very handsome, like a movie star, and was called the Star of Africa. I saved newspaper clippings and other accounts of my hero. I thought nothing could stop him. One time he shot down seventeen English fighters during three missions. He was the ace of aces, and I was in love with him as my hero. He was twenty-two.

One night in September 1942, we were all sitting and listening to the radio when the regular broadcast was interrupted for the announcement that Marseille, the Star of Africa, had been shot down and killed somewhere over Africa. My parents were obviously upset, but they weren't crying. I was horrified. I thought this man couldn't die; he was a hero, and heroes lived forever and ever. It had already been my bedtime when the broadcast came over the air, so I ran to my bedroom and threw myself on the bed. While lying there and crying, I tried hard to come to terms with my feelings. I wanted so much to believe that heroes lived forever. I had no one to talk to, no one to share my innermost thoughts with about what had happened. Certainly, I was collecting these kinds of thoughts, and they were building up, but I just kept denying that Hitler and Germany and my flying ace hero might be the bad people. That is something I could not do.

I had fallen in love with my African Star when he first flew into the newspaper and the radio broadcasts. Then I mourned my hero, a man I'd never met, when he was shot down and killed. He was an idol to me, like Hitler, and everyone needs idols. Some look at God that way, but I didn't because these were my gods. So I did what I was taught; I buried my feelings and passion deep inside my mind and heart where it could never hurt me. Had someone told us about the necessity of sharing feelings and fears with others, we would have laughed at them. Instead, I kept the repressed emotions hidden. That was the way a good German thought, and I was a good German, loyal to Hitler and the Nazis.

Later on, I believed that my parents had been reluctant to explain anything to me that might shake my faith in the Third Reich. I wish they would have, for it would have explained a lot of things that needed explaining. Certainly during this time, as I learned later, some people were speaking up including Hans and Sophie Scholl, who became part of what was called the White Rose. Disillusioned with Hitler and the Nazis, they passed out leaflets and pamphlets against Hitler in cities such as Stuttgart, Mannheim, Frankfurt, and even Vienna. They were very brave, I would be told later, but the Nazis learned about what they were up to and arrested them and several others. All were executed. Just before he was decapitated, I was told Hans yelled, "Long live freedom." If I had known about what they were up to, I would have turned them in. Many children turned in their parents or neighbors or friends. This was our duty.

In 1943, when I was fourteen, we received word that Father was being transferred to Berlin. The move was his most important promotion because Berlin was the headquarters of the railroad department.

Evie was ready to begin her studies at the University of Berlin, and Father looked for a house for all of us to live in. I stayed behind with Mother to finish the school year and help her pack all our belongings. I dreaded moving to Berlin. We had lived in Schwerin longer than any other city, and I did not want to leave all the friends I had. I hoped it would take my father a long time to find a place for us, but to my disappointment, he soon found a nice house in Hermsdorf, a suburb that would eventually become part of the French occupation sector after the war. The house was located in a lovely neighborhood with tree-lined streets. The bedrooms were on the second floor, and there was a huge basement large enough for a family room and a room for my father to pursue his hobbies. In the front, the house had a closed-in porch. A lovely garden surrounded the whole house.

Since the British had entered the war, bombings were a daily occurrence, and there was much talk about bomb shelters. Newspaper headlines told us that Churchill had ordered his pilots to kill civilians, including women and children. But the writers said that only minimal damage was being experienced. Hitler used the word *cowards* in his speeches to denounce the English pilots and said German pilots would never do such a thing. Still, the English made sneak attacks on the cities and villages, and when we arrived in Berlin, the raids continued.

There was not always time to find a public shelter in an air raid, and often the cellars in houses did not prove to be safe enough. We lived in a residential area, and the more secure larger buildings were too far away from us, so Father decided to build a shelter. It was exciting for me because it was like helping him with his hobbies when I was younger. He designed it and then had some workers come and dig the hole. Railroad ties were delivered for the walls and ceiling.

The shelter had a trap door and stairs that reached down about ten feet deep so a person could stand up straight. A row of level seats, also made from railroad ties, on each side of the shelter could be used to sleep on. We stored blankets to keep warm. The shelter was big enough that two people could lie down and two people could sit. Father had rigged electricity to go into the shelter, so we had light, and we kept books there to read in the event of a lengthy air attack. Luckily, we never had to use the shelter, and I don't know if my parents ever did. It was quite sturdy because of the railroad ties, and I am sure it would have held, but I felt claustrophobic in it, and it reminded me too much of a grave. I thought, *What if a bomb buries us and we all die down there?*

After signing up with my neighborhood Hitler Youth group, I heard about the Spanish youth leaders' visit to Berlin and the huge meeting that was to be held at the Olympic Stadium in 1943. We knew from Youth meeting leaders that the Spanish fascist government of Franco was Nazi friendly, so it was acceptable to swoon over the good-looking Spaniards. At least among girlfriends it was. My parents were a bit worried about my going since the city was new to me, but a neighbor's daughter promised to stay close. Dressed in our uniforms, we left together.

From early childhood, I had seen the stadium in pictures and movies, but when we arrived, it was much bigger than expected. The stadium was made famous during the 1936 Olympics. It was there that American Jesse Owens had won several gold medals, and Hitler refused to shake his hand because he was black. But we didn't care since we were told that because Germany won so many more medals than any other country, this showed how Germans were truly superior people.

I was amazed when I entered the stadium with its huge walls, arches, and great columns because it was filled to capacity. Everywhere flags were blowing in the wind. The white blouses and dark blue skirts of the girls mixed with the brown shirts and black pants of the boys. Torches were burning all around the top of the arena, and young people were holding banners. How I envied them! I would have loved to hold a banner too. Then the fanfare began, the drums rolled, and we all began singing patriotic songs as a Nazi leader walked into the stadium and through the crowd. He went to the podium and announced the Spanish youth leader, and again we sang as the Spanish leader walked in with his escorts and took his place at the podium. We then sat down for his speech.

I believe the new leader of the Hitler Youth named Axmann was also there. How handsome he and the Spanish leader looked in their uniforms. All of them and all of us yelled "Sieg Heil" (Hail Victory) over and over and sang songs while we saluted like the Romans did with Caesar. As I looked around, I felt like I belonged to something big, and when the trumpets blared, wow, that was really powerful.

When the ceremony was finally over, it was nearly dark. It took a long time for the stadium to empty, and in the confusion, the girl I had come with was suddenly gone. I didn't want to be scared, but I didn't know what to do. I looked and looked, but there was no way I could have found her. Everybody was dressed the same. I asked some people for directions to Hermsdorf, and they showed me the way to the subway. When I got there, I felt comfortable asking the conductor for help and learned what train to change to and where to get off. It got later and later, and even though the train ran every few minutes, I missed a few of them. By the time I got home, the streets were deserted except for my parents standing outside of our house. Their faces were full of worry, and I had never seen them so upset. I explained what had happened and could tell how glad they were to see me safe even though they did not show me with a warm embrace and some loving words.

Before I could enroll in school, there was an order that all schools were going to be evacuated to an area of Poland where there had not been bomb attacks. I wanted to go with my school, but children could also be sent to relatives in the German countryside as long as they lived in an area not thought of as dangerous. My parents decided that I would stay in the country with my grandparents in Malchow. When my parents told me in the evening that I was going to stay with them, I cried so hard that night that I had scabs on my eyelids the next day from rubbing them dry. Since it was the end of the school year, it never dawned on me that we were being sent away for safety because we were not doing so well in the war. That never entered my mind. That was simply not the mentality.

My grandparents lived on a street that ran along a lake in Malchow, a town surrounded by the lakes of the Mecklenburgische Seenplatte and woods of the Müritz National Park. Historically the town had been a center for Slavic paganism during the Middle Ages. During the war, the dark side of the area would include a concentration camp, but I did not know that when I moved to be with my grandparents.

It was a lovely area, and some well-known Mecklenburg writers and artists had settled there. It had several unique villas with straw roofs like ones by the waterways I had seen of pictures from Holland. The style of my grandparents' house fit that description, but they also did farm work, unusual for that kind of residential area. Neighbors did not mind because they could visit in the mornings and evenings to pick up delicious fresh milk, eggs, and vegetables.

When someone visited, the first thing they noticed was a huge barn that had separate stables for six cows, four horses, pigs, chickens, ducks, and several cats. The barn also held all the farm equipment, and there was room for milling. Higher up was the storage for straw and hay. Between the barn and the house was a huge pit that took up a large part of the yard. In the pit, the waste from the stables was kept until it was used as fertilizer. You can imagine the smell on hot days, but it was a necessity so no one complained and just got used to it.

The main entry to the house was from the back. The front faced the lake, and above the second floor balcony was written the name of the place, Villa Marie, named after my grandmother. A spacious garden in the front of the house stretched all the way down to the lake. The garden was divided to grow vegetables, fruits, and flowers. Next to the lakeshore was a huge lawn where the wash was hung to dry. When Mother was young, my grandparents used to rent out rooms to couples vacationing in Malchow for the summer. The same families, some of whom also stayed at a luxurious summer resort near the lake, returned year after year to enjoy the country, the hospitality, and my grandmother's cooking. Her favorite dish was chicken with gravy made with sour cream.

My grandparents moved to the upstairs of the house after their semiretirement, and Uncle Bernhard, my mother's brother, took over the farm. Grandmother still got up very early in the morning to milk the cows. Uncle Bernhard, Aunt Mieken, his wife, and their son, Rolf, lived downstairs, and my aunt took over the evening milking shift. Grandfather gave up working the fields, but he fed the animals and did other lighter chores. That left my uncle in charge of the fields, plowing, planting, and harvesting.

I slept in my grandparents' bedroom. I did not like sharing a room with them, but I was not consulted and reminded instead that they had sacrificed themselves by taking me in. Every room in the house had a large ceramic oven. All the bedrooms had to be heated daily during the winter months. One bedroom stayed cold so that they could hang big smoked hams from hooks on the oven. The cold kept them from spoiling until they were used, and it was one of the few places the cats couldn't get to. I loved the smoky fragrance in that room. Sometimes I just sat in there and smelled it for a while.

On winter nights, it got so cold that the water for the washbasin was frozen by the time we got up in the mornings. Omi (Grandmother) got up long before anyone else; she made sure there was hot water, a warm kitchen, and breakfast waiting for us. At night, in bed, I was never cold. The feather beds, one to lie on and one to cover up with, kept me warm, and before going to sleep, Omi warmed a cloth bag full of chestnuts in the oven and put it under my covers to keep my feet warm all night.

Indoor plumbing was not installed until after the war, and we had to deal with the inconvenience of an outhouse. At night we used a pee pot, and you heard it filling up by the sound. You did not want to be the last one to use it toward morning.

At dinnertime, my aunt walked up the street and called my cousin, Rolf. She would call in a loud voice, "Rolfieeeee," and the whole neighborhood could hear her. By then, he was eight years old, and we knew he hated being called Rolfie, especially when she yelled it loud like that. During one of Evie's visits, she and I jokingly followed my aunt out, and when she started calling Rolf, we joined in and made the "Rolfieeee" sound a lot louder. When he finally came in, his hair was all messed up, and he was all out of breath from running. We could see how furious he was by his red face, but he didn't say anything because his mother was already annoyed that he wasn't home at dinnertime. We all walked into the dining room together, Evie and I still singing "Rolfieee!" He was more and more embarrassed, and his face became redder by the second.

My uncle Bernhard was the unusual one in my family. It seemed like he was always working, and I think I saw him in a suit only once—at my grandparents' fiftieth wedding anniversary after the war. He had a rough temper, and sometimes he beat the horses when they nibbled at each other. It hurt me a lot to hear them neigh. Nobody dared stand up to him, not even my grandparents. He could be violent one moment and then, in the next moment, be funny and sweet. His son, Rolf, felt his temper most of all. When Rolf didn't comprehend his homework, my uncle yelled at him and slapped him on the back of his head. This of course confused Rolf even more, and he tried hard not to cry. This infuriated my uncle. To me though, he was always kind, and I did not mind his gruff way. I tried to please him however I could, by fetching his pipe and stuffing it with tobacco or rolling his cigarettes, and I was always willing to help him with his work.

Bernhard had a habit of sometimes grabbing my aunt when she was passing him, halfway lifting her skirt or patting her on the behind. My grandmother hated it and thought my aunt was provoking him. My grandparents hadn't approved of my uncle's marriage to my aunt. They felt that my mother and her sister had married well but that my uncle had married beneath him. My aunt was pretty and a very good housekeeper, but she wasn't very educated or from a good family.

One morning I woke up and went downstairs because I knew that my aunt was fixing breakfast for my uncle early. When I walked in the kitchen, I thought they were fighting since they were wrestling with each other. I stood there for a while, and then I saw her face, and she was smiling as she struggled to get away from him. I was stunned because this was something I had never seen anywhere, especially not in my family. When she saw me, she got very red in the face, but my uncle just laughed in his rough way. It was nice to see that people could be so playful with each other. I had never seen my parents showing that kind of affection. They were always so proper and formal, but I was always sure that they were very much in love with each other.

During my stay with the grandparents, I rescued many a stray dog, and we found them homes. But, as a child, I kind of had the sense that some animals were more important than others. That some you could easily kill and some were of a higher class. No matter, my mother told me over and over, "Quaele nie ein Tier zum Scherz, denn es fuelt wie Du den Schmerz"—"Don't ever torment an animal for the fun of it because it feels pain as much as you do."

This wasn't the type of message we were taught in the Hitler Youth. We were told that some humans were not meant to live, if for example the person was retarded or had an incurable disease. We were taught that only the strong race survives. That's how nature wanted it. Just like in the animal kingdom.

As the war raged on, more and more people were being displaced, more sick and wounded soldiers were returning from the front, more homes were being destroyed by the continuing bombing raids, and more and more refugees were arriving in Malchow. They were mostly Germans that had settled outside of Germany. Some came from as far as Russia. The refugees were mostly women and children, and if a man was with them, he was usually old or crippled. They spoke different dialects and had different customs. Because they were on the run, they couldn't change their clothes or keep themselves clean like they might have back home. Most pulled wagons with their belongings tied on them, and some were lucky enough to have a horse or a cow to pull it. I remember sadly how our attitude in the Hitler Youth changed toward these people as more and more of them arrived. At first we were looking forward to being of help, but then they got to be a burden and a nuisance. At least those were the words the Hitler Youth leaders used, and I could not object to what was being said since I had to be loyal.

When I moved to Malchow, I was still in middle school, and for the first time I had coed classes. Then we were moved to smaller facilities so that more housing was available for refugees. Housing assignments were also given to people who had extra room in their homes, but first they were allowed to take in family members or friends to satisfy this requirement.

Summer and Easter vacations were enjoyed the most since I was able to join my uncle out in the fields. I learned everything there was to know about plowing, planting, and harvesting the crop. He often hired refugees to help him with the work. Due to the war, only women were available. The prettiest women always had to work up on top of the wagon to be loaded, and whenever he threw hay up with a pitchfork, he would try to look up their skirts. My job was to gather the leftover hay with a rake, and he would look over at me and wink, as if it was our little joke. I blushed and felt uncomfortable.

When all the hay was loaded on the wagon and securely tied down, we rode home way up on top. I remember how good it felt to lie on top of a full wagon of soft, wonderful-smelling hay, to look into the blue sky while the warm wind was gently blowing on to my face. The only sound was the horse's shoes clonking on the cobblestones and an occasional crack of the whip. I really felt at one with all of nature. It was there that I learned to always be at peace when I took the time to tune in to the wonders that surrounded us.

While I was in Malchow, Evie met and fell in love with a teacher named Heinz Zielinski. They met at the balcony of a movie theater, sitting next to each other. Since there were many empty seats at the orchestra level they were asked to move down, and when they did, they found each other in adjoining seats again. They started talking and this led to them dating.

Heinz had been a public schoolteacher and was drafted to teach at a Nationalpolitische Erziehungsanstalten (national political education establishment), or Napolas for short. It was one of two boarding-school systems created to prepare young men to be part of the Nazi elite. The other was the Adolf Hitler Schule (Adolf Hitler Schools). The Napolas trained government and army personnel, while the Adolf Hitler Schools were supposed to turn out future political leaders.

URSULA MARTENS AND MARK SHAW

To show his love, Heinz gave Evie the cutest little schnauzer puppy. His name was Hajo. All our family loved animals, and when I visited them in Berlin, I spent all my time with Hajo. During one of my visits, he was very sick. He had distemper and wasn't getting better. Since everyone was at work, I had to take him to the vet. He was too weak to walk, so I carried him. The doctor couldn't do any more for him and had to put him to sleep. The walk home from the vet was a very sad one for me. I had to carry my dead friend all the way home in a box. I cried all day and in the evening. When Evie came home, we buried him.

One time when I met Heinz, his hand was all bandaged. I asked him what happened, and he said that he got hurt during war-game maneuvers. "To toughen up the platoons," he said, "I make them wrestle with our Alsatian hounds. If they can survive that, then they can certainly destroy the enemy." When I asked how he got hurt, he said he pulled one of the dogs off a soldier. I was amazed at his bravery. Was I in love with Heinz too? When I asked him if he trained with weapons, he said that yes, they did. Then I asked him what weapon was the best, and he said the machine gun. I told him I wanted to learn how to shoot one. He said that was great.

Evie loved Heinz and Heinz loved Evie, but then I found someone to love as well. This occurred in 1943. But I had already at least met someone I liked before that. His name was Karl, and I knew him in Schwerin. He and I became boyfriend and girlfriend for a while, and we used to sit under a lovely tree and talk about many things, including the Hitler Youth (he was a member too), school, and our mothers and fathers. One day he put his hand out in front of me, but I did not understand what he wanted. Then he said, "Ulli, don't think I am being forward, but would you hold hands with me?" I looked into his eyes and smiled, and then I put my hand on his. It was sweaty, but I didn't care. From then on, we held hands a lot, but we never did anything else. As the years passed, I would recall Karl with affection since our touching that first time was so special to me.

One day during the time I was friends with Karl, I came home and my mother was waiting for me. Usually she greeted me at the door, but this time she was sitting at our table with a funny look on her face. She wasn't sewing or drinking coffee or doing anything, and I immediately knew something was wrong. Then she said, "Ulli, I want to talk to you about some things."

When I sat down, she got up and started pacing while talking fast. "I have been wanting to talk to you for a while. You're becoming a young woman, and I wondered if you have ever . . ." Before she ended the sentence, she looked away. I asked her if everything was okay, and then she looked away again before saying, "Ulli, I don't want you to think I have been spying on you, and I haven't said anything to your father, but I've noticed you with the boy, your friend." I asked, "You mean Karl?" and her saying that made me blush since I never knew she saw us together. I said, "Mother, please don't." But she said in a stern voice, "Sit down. I am not finished."

I looked at Mother and then she said, "I didn't see you do anything wrong, but being with boys can get you into trouble." I said "Mother, please" again, but she continued on while looking out the window. "I saw you two holding hands, and I have a question, did you kiss him?" I did not know what to say, and then she repeated the question. I finally said no, and her face relaxed, and she sat down again apparently relieved. Mother then said, "Good, because good girls like you can get pregnant like that." I didn't know what *that* meant, but then she said, "You must be a good girl. You don't want to be pregnant . . . no kissing. That is what kissing can get you."

I did not know what to say to that either. I never knew that kissing could get a girl pregnant, but from that day on, I knew I would be careful. Mother had scared me and later, when Karl tried to pull me close to him in a barn, I jerked away while elbowing him in the ribs. No kissing, no pregnancy; that was what I had learned.

When I met Wilhelm, I had been in the Bund Deutscher Mädel, the girl's branch of the Hitler Youth, for more than four years. He was in a group of kids that took the train every day to a nearby town to attend the Gymnasium there. He did not look like what you might think of as typical German. He reminded me of the dark Spanish boys I had seen at the Hitler rally at Olympic Stadium since he had dark-brown eyes and brown hair and a strong-built body. After seeing him at Hitler Youth meetings, I asked my aunt about him. She said that he was the oldest son of the town miller, and in confidence, she also told me that she thought my mother had dated his father when they were both unmarried. He was the only boy in the family and had four sisters. He looked so handsome in his uniform.

Little by little, Wilhelm and I sought each other out and tried to engage in the same activities. We were together with the same group that was going swimming or to the movies where we went separately and then sat together. During the movie, we sat together, and after I knew him for a while, I let him hold my hand. I knew that dating was out of the question for me without even asking my grandparents. I was only fourteen in 1943, and he was sixteen. But puppy love doesn't pick an age; it just happens. And then the whole world changes. At least it did for me since even though I still was dedicated to Hitler and Germany winning the war, I now had someone to care for, to love. My head was spinning, and I sometimes just sat around and smiled. When the war was over, and I was sure it would be soon, everything would be grand, and Wilhelm and I could be together forever.

One warning did occur when I first met Wilhelm. He said his mother told him he should go with our family and flee with us to the west. She must have had some feeling that trouble was on the way. I never told my parents about the warning since I did not want to get into trouble. I simply did as I was supposed to and kept quiet like a good Nazi should.

Ursula's grandfather and grandmother

Ursula's mother and father—he is wearing
his railroad inspector's uniform

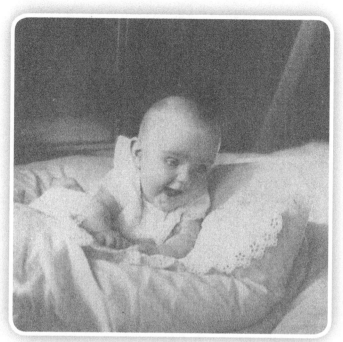

Before Ursula ever dreamed of being a Nazi

Friend Siegi, Ursula's mother, and Ursula (June 1935)

Ursula, her mother, and friend Tante

Ursula and sister Eve at Schwerin Castle

Ursula on her parents' boat

Malchow in Mecklenburg, Germany, where
Ursula lived in mid-1940s

Ursula in her first Nazi Youth uniform

Out of uniform, Nazi Youth gather herbs

Hitler Youth marching in uniform

Eve's Henrik in his SS uniform

Ursula and her nephew Wolfgang

Ursula at the end of WWII looking to the future

Ursula's daughters, Janet and Maria, at an early age

Ursula visiting Germany after ten years in America

BOOK III

CHAPTER SEVEN

Station: Malchow, Germany (1944–1945)

The war may have been raging on all fronts, but other things were on my mind during the time when I was fifteen going on sixteen. I'll never forget my first real kiss. It happened during a siren warning of a possible air raid. Wilhelm was walking me home when we had to look for shelter. I was wearing a short-sleeved embroidered sweater over my white uniform blouse. Wilhelm wasn't in uniform because he had come straight from school and the train station to the meeting. We had talked before about liking each other, but this time was different. We were all alone and the shelter was dimly lit. I knew I couldn't get in trouble for not being home on time since we weren't allowed on the street during air raids.

At first, we sat very close to each other, expecting more people to join us, but no one came. Then Wilhelm put his arms around me in a way he had never done before, and I felt thrilled. He told me, "I do like you very much, you are not like any of the other girls I know. You are the most beautiful girl at the meetings." My heart was racing and not because of the danger of an air attack. I answered, "I do like you too, very much. I hope I will always stay in Malchow." Then he kissed me, and I felt good and warm all over. We did not talk after that, and I did not stop him from slipping his hand between my sweater and my blouse. I did not mind him doing that at all. Too soon the air-raid alarm was over, and when we walked out of the shelter, I was at least on cloud nine.

After that day, Wilhelm and I were inseparable. I felt as if suddenly I had grown from a girl into a young woman. I was in love, whatever I considered love to be, and there could be nothing wrong with the way I felt. I had discovered something very precious and was overwhelmed with a happiness that I had never experienced before. It felt as if I possessed something sacred because it was pure love. Yes, I did worry a bit that I might become pregnant by the kissing, but when we kissed, really kissed the next time I saw Wilhelm, I decided kissing was worth the risk of being pregnant. It was just too wonderful, and I was not going to give up kissing.

My grandfather warned me once, after I walked with Wilhelm to bring the cows back home, not to get serious with him. He said his father had been a ladies' man and that the apple didn't fall far from the tree, whatever that meant. I didn't like what he said, didn't completely understand it, but in a way, I was flattered that he even considered we were maybe going to get married eventually. Grandmother and I had more woman talk. She knew I loved Wilhelm, and she did not ridicule me. One summer evening, while sitting on the veranda, with the full moon shining bright, she recited a poem for me, "Moon, tonight you are happier than I, You can see him while he is not with me. Once I was luckier than you, he kissed me while you were looking on." I hugged Omi after she said that; I loved her so much.

When I was with Wilhelm, I felt like I was dreaming. To have someone care about me, to even perhaps love me, that was what I always had wanted in my life. When he touched me, there was a tingle, and I felt so close to him.

My feelings for Wilhelm were real, but I did have a dream about Africa just after I had become a Jungmädel, the first step to a leader. Many people at that time talked politics with the focus on our colonies. The main points had to do with how they were taken from us after the First World War and how now we would reclaim them by force if necessary. We thus needed young, strong people of good character that could teach the Nazi ideologue. When I thought about this, I knew I was perfect since I could combine my love for animals and my duty to the Reich. To do this, I knew that I would have to graduate from a colonial school that was located not too far from Mecklenburg. It was the only one of its kind. They taught everything you might ever need to know about living in Africa, from repairing shoes to building houses and anything in between.

URSULA MARTENS AND MARK SHAW

In the dream, it was the animals and the wide-open spaces in Africa that attracted me. A place for adventure and new beginnings. There I would continue to promote the pride in German nationalism. Father didn't think it was a good idea. He said that kind of undertaking wasn't for women, and he used the expression *Schnapps Idée*, meaning an idea conceived under the influence of alcohol. I kept that dream like others to myself until I met Wilhelm. Only in him could I confide, but he knew that being the only son, someday he would have to take over his father's farm and mill, and he didn't want to think of me going away so far. I never lost this yearning for Africa, even though feelings about Hitler and the Reich changed over time.

While living with my grandparents in Malchow, we learned that Father's office was moved to a suburb of Berlin because of the air raids. It had become too dangerous to use public transportation to and from work. Barracks had been built for the employees, with a complete kitchen and an excellent chef that did all the cooking for them. Mother was lucky to become Father's secretary when every able person had to work in order to receive a ration card. They were able to stay together while most of his coworkers were separated from their wives. They had been evacuated to the country with their children.

Suddenly, we received word that Evie was coming to live with us in Malchow. The Napola where her boyfriend Heinz taught was being closed, and he was being transferred to one of the occupied territories. Only wives were permitted to accompany the men. It was getting crowded at my grandparents' place, and Evie decided to rent the maid's quarters in the house next door. I didn't say anything, but I was a little hurt that she didn't try harder to be closer to me. A few weeks later, Heinz came to visit Evie for the weekend, and I felt much better when I realized that she had moved into the house next door so they could have privacy when he visited. Now that I was in love myself, I was more understanding. Evie also visited Heinz at the relocated Napola, just outside the Polish border.

It was Sunday night when she came back from one of these trips. All of us were eating dinner together. My uncle and aunt had come up from downstairs with my cousin, and my mother's sister and her daughter were also visiting. When we were almost finished with dinner, Evie stood up and tapped her glass with a spoon. She said she had an announcement to make. She was excited and looked radiant. "Since you all know that Heinz and I've gotten very close," she said, "I want you to know that we got engaged on our last visit, and we are going to get married." Everybody was happy for her, but I was probably the most excited because I liked Heinz a lot. Even though I was only fifteen in 1944, I was hoping to make the same kind of announcement in a few years.

One day, at a Hitler Youth meeting, two young soldiers arrived holding what they called a Panzerfaust. It was something like what I learned was as an American bazooka, an antitank weapon of some sort. I was so excited since I had always wanted to fire a weapon, and I hoped I would get to do so to help Hitler and the Fatherland win the war.

The leader told us that with the increased bombings, real Germans were going to have to do more to help our soldiers. "Today, more than ever," he said, "the führer needs us." With that, he asked the two soldiers to demonstrate how the Panzerfaust worked. They had set up a small wrecked truck in the distance, and while saying to the soldiers, "We will show you what happens when the enemy walks on sacred German soil," he pointed to the truck as the one soldier, no older than me, stooped down and picked up the weapon. He told us that the shell protruding out the end of the five-foot or so barrel was a rocket made for the Panzerfaust. Then the other soldier, a bit older, hoisted the weapon on his shoulder and pointed it straight at the truck. When he squeezed the trigger, it was only an instant before there was kind of a booming sound, and then the wrecked truck exploded with fire and pieces flying everywhere.

The leader looked at us, most of whom were kind of shocked at the explosion, and then told us again that we needed to do more for Germany. "If one of you ever see an enemy parachuting to the ground or see a plane that has been shot down with the pilot there, find any weapon you can, a pitchfork, a shovel, a gun, anything, and attack the enemy." Then I was startled to see he and the other two soldiers began swinging bayonets they grabbed from somewhere and shovels and pitchforks and every such thing at each other. The leader said, "And when I tell you to attack, I am not saying capture the enemy, but attack and kill." He said this and then the two soldiers held knives to each other's throats like they were going to kill each other. "This is what our führer and the Reich expect you to do. This is what is required of

URSULA MARTENS AND MARK SHAW

all of us. Heil Hitler." All this was said to kids my age and those much younger, some perhaps only ten or so. They all had baby faces.

When Wilhelm joined us, I couldn't wait to tell him what happened. But then the leader said we should sing a few patriotic songs. He also talked to us about the success of the war and how we were going to be victorious. Then he said that there were going to be some new assignments, and since there were more and more young men being drafted, some of the girls were going to take on more duties. He said the outlying districts, mostly farms and very small villages, were going to be consolidated when the need came for HY to work there. Girls were also going to be working closer with the boys and would meet together to strengthen our units. Then they divided us up into groups and explained the districts.

Before making the assignments, he pointed to Wilhelm and said, "Just look at this specimen. He is handsome, tall, smart, bright, and dedicated to our führer and to the Fatherland. If he had not been needed to help with the farm work, he would have been on the front fighting. He is what we need, a natural leader. This is the kind of person we need to control the outer regions around Malchow." All the kids cheered this, and I was clapping the loudest.

With that, the leader stood in front of Wilhelm and said, "Are you ready to be a leader, to help control smaller groups?" When Wilhelm hesitated, the leader said, "What do you say? Will you work for the führer? Speak up." Wilhelm paused again, looked down as if thinking, and then raised his right hand while shouting "Heil Hitler." I was relieved since while I loved Wilhelm so much, I had a feeling that he wasn't as strong in his feelings about Hitler and our cause as I was. Once I had talked about it with him, and he said that while he would give up his life for his family and loved ones, he wasn't that sure about fighting for Germany and for the Reich. But now he had agreed to be a leader in the surrounding areas, and so I felt he loved Germany as much as I did.

After this, Wilhelm made me very proud by asking whether I could help him. He said, "After all Ursula did in Berlin, I think she could be an inspiration to the younger members." I couldn't believe he said this, and I was so happy that I wanted to scream. I wasn't sure why he said these nice things, but perhaps he thought because I was from the big city, Berlin, that I was a star of some sort, that I would bring a lot of energy to the new job.

After a couple of seconds, the leader said, "Yes, this is excellent. She can have one or two villages to work with when you cannot be there. And on the weekends you two can work side by side." This caused me to yell "Heil Hitler" as loud as I could while lifting my right hand to the sky.

I took my new job very seriously. Once or twice a week, I put on my Hitler Youth uniform and pedaled my bicycle to surrounding villages. The meetings in rural areas were a little different than the ones I had experienced in Schwerin. Mostly we met in schoolrooms and taught what was sent to me as orders from headquarters. Certain songs had to be learned, important political dates remembered, news digested, and plans made for future events and so on. Much of the time was taken up training for sport events and making toys for underprivileged children. In the rural areas, many young people had to help their families with work on the farms, especially at harvesttime.

Often only a few boys and girls showed up, and we had a joint meeting that pleased everyone. Sometimes we accomplished very little in those meetings, and when it wasn't worth having a gathering at all because of low attendance, Wilhelm canceled them, and we had the time for ourselves. Some days we went swimming or found a nice spot and had a picnic with whatever we brought to eat and drink. Wilhelm talked about his plans to attend agriculture school, and I said I had dreams about living in Africa. What a special summer it was, and I was convinced he and I might really spend the rest of our lives together. That all this occurred as the war escalated didn't bother me much. We were doing our part, and what else were we supposed to do?

My parents gave quite a few parties when I was young, five or six couples, colleagues of Father's at work and friends. I had to go to bed early, but the next morning, I got up before anyone else and raided the kitchen and living room, drinking leftover drinks and looking for change in the sofa and club chair seats. Mother and Father never found out.

Evie's wedding was quite a time. It was a small ceremony in Berlin with just the immediate family of both sides. It was the last time we all laughed together, and the food and drinks were delicious despite the times. Everyone was very happy for Evie and Heinz, and she was excited because she planned to join him at the school he taught. We were hoping that the war would be over soon, and no one doubted that our army would be victorious. One real highlight at the wedding party happened when Heinz asked me to dance before anyone except Evie. I am sure my face was bright red since I was embarrassed. Heinz looked so handsome in his uniform. He asked me how many villages I was in charge of, and I told him three. He said, "You are the kind of person Germany needs," and I felt like kissing him. But of course I couldn't do that.

After Evie's wedding, Mother decided to return with my grandparents and me to Malchow for a short visit. With transportation deteriorating, there was no telling whether there might be many more opportunities for her to join us.

Mother's sister Grete and my cousin Christa, who lived in Berlin and had attended the wedding, also decided to travel with us to Malchow and to stay with my grandparents. My aunt was married to an engineer of the Siemens company. He was older than my father but was drafted because of his skills.

The morning after we arrived in Malchow, I walked downstairs, where everyone was sitting, talking. At the door, I heard someone ask my mother about Tante Loteisen, the woman who had been so special to me during my first years. Over the years, Tante had visited us on holidays or other special occasions or sent us cards. And as I got more involved in my own life, I did not think of her as much as when I was little, but my memories of her were always fond ones.

Mother saw me, and I could tell she was embarrassed about something. My grandmother asked again, "Is Frau Loteisen all right?" Mother answered in a hushed voice, "I'm sure she's all right, she's still making fishnets." She then turned to me with a big smile and welcomed me into the room, but the conversation ended, and I had a strange feeling that something wasn't right. I knew that making fishnets wasn't something Tante would do on her own. And besides, I had heard that fishnets were made in jails or prisons or that poor people made them.

Later, I saw my mother sitting on the porch. I sat with her, and for a little while we talked about what I was doing in the Hitler Youth and how school was going. Then I asked her how Tante was doing. She tried to be very nice, but she was not being herself when she started fussing with my hair braids, something she did not usually do. She tried to explain to me that Tante belonged to a group that studied the Bible and that it was against the law. She then told me that Tante was picked up and put away. She didn't use the words *concentration camp*, a term I still did not know, but made it seem more like Tante was put away for security reasons. I believed that people that were against the government had to be put away, but I certainly didn't feel that old Tante had ever done anything bad in her life. I felt awful for her, but part of me was also angry with her for doing what she did when she should have known better. "Why did she want to read a stupid Bible anyway?" I wondered. Why did she need to study about this Jew, Jesus by name, when the Nazis and my god, Hitler, offered anything she would ever need?

Just before we quit talking about Tante, Mother said something very strange, "One thing I know, Hitler would never do anything like this to Tante. It is those men around him that must have done it. He would never allow something like this." Her words were surprising since this was the first time I ever heard her defend Hitler.

While in Malchow, my loving feelings were reserved for Wilhelm. My cousin Christa and I got along all right, but we weren't very close. She attended Hitler Youth meetings but hated it. It was partly because she wasn't very athletic, and to be a good Hitler Youth, everyone needed to be good in sports.

Christa did not share my love for animals, so we had little in common. Her brother, Klaus, my cousin, was serving in the army but had been reported missing in action. We were all upset about it and hoped to hear news from him, but he was never found. He was the first war casualty for all of us. I could see my aunt was suffering, but I could not really understand what she was going through.

All this happened during the summer or fall of 1944. My grandmother, mother, and aunt had started canning bushels of fruit and vegetables that they had harvested from the garden. They would leave the delicious sugared strawberries sitting around the kitchen in big tubs while they did other cooking and canning. There were also bowls of cream left out to sour, and bowls of sugar. Once, my grandfather walked into the room with cream and strawberry pasted all over his moustache, and Grandmother teased him. "Oh, Bernard, you've been in the sour cream," she said. It embarrassed him, and he got angry and denied it, but we all had seen the evidence all over his beard.

Later that day, Christa and I also snuck into the kitchen. We grabbed as many strawberries as we could hold, dunked them in cream and sugar, and then ran outside to eat. When we went in to get some more, my grandfather walked in and caught us. He yelled "Shame on you, there's barely enough food for everybody, and here you girls steal sweets!" before stomping out of the room. I hated him for this outburst, especially since I knew he had done the same thing. He was like a little general that was used to giving orders and people minding him. Nobody dared talk back to him because he was the final authority.

One hot day during the fall of 1944, Wilhelm and I stood, with our bikes leaning against the fence. We were saying good-bye, which always took a long time since we kissed several times before parting. We didn't notice my grandfather coming up the walk from the barn. When he saw our kissing, he was furious, his face as red as a nearby barn. He started ranting, asking me how much longer I was going to stand there, and what the neighbors were going to think. Then he said I was acting like a *strassen maedchen*, a street girl. I felt like I had done something really dirty and didn't know what to say. Wilhelm tried to apologize to him. He explained that he had walked me home, and we were just saying good-bye. My grandfather told him that he was disappointed in him and was going to let his mother and father know, then sent him home. He grabbed my bike, shoved it at me, and told me to go ahead into the house.

When we got inside, he was still angry. My grandmother felt sorry for me and tried to smooth things over. Here I was, almost sixteen years old, and being scolded for kissing. All the women in my family had gotten married early, meaning they must have done some kissing of their own at my age. That thought made me feel a little bit better. At any rate, my grandfather sure didn't stop me from kissing. We were just a little more careful after that. Deep down though, I also remembered what my mother had said once: a girl could get pregnant from kissing too much. That still worried me a bit, but I didn't care. I was in love, and I was a leader in the Hitler Youth, and my life was wonderful. What I didn't want to admit at the time was that Germany was losing the war. Signs were everywhere that this was occurring, but I still believed my god Hitler would come through for us.

CHAPTER EIGHT

Station: Malchow and Schwerin, Germany (1944–1945)

During fall 1944, the war hit home on all fronts. Soon we heard that every able man sixteen and older had to report for what was called the Volkssturm.

This meant the last reserves were being gathered. News reports said the English, French, Americans, and Russians were closing in and suffocating our beloved Germany. People who had never said anything negative now said negative things. Everyone was scared and wondering if we would all be killed. Sort of a nervous tone hit the population, with each person aware of the danger on a daily basis. This atmosphere caused me to be on edge, to worry more, to never feel at ease like I had before. Seeing the suffering of people firsthand, especially those who wondered whether their loved ones were dead or alive, increased the pressure, increased the inability to cope with the danger at every turn. Those who had lost loved ones had it the worst as casualty lists increased and families were torn apart when a son or daughter was reported missing or dead. Screams were heard constantly as fathers and mothers learned tragic news. And the bombings, the awful sound of the bombings, and the artillery were a constant reminder that war had no winners, only losers.

All around Berlin and other cities, buildings were devastated, beautiful buildings reduced to rubble. No street was safe from being torn apart, and even the parks were ripped up where the green grass once welcomed kids like me to play. When bombs are dropped, they play no favorites, and so many civilians were being killed, innocent people, women and children, swept into the hate despite their having no say in Hitler's plan to save Germany.

Many times I simply sat on my bed, or stood outside, and could not make sense of what had occurred. It seemed my eyes were always moist, always on the verge of tears, always frightened even though I tried to block out such things as a tough German. Loving Wilhelm was my only saving grace, but when I looked closely at his face and that of Mother and even Father, there was defeat there, worry lines that had been absent before the war began. I heard the line "War does something to people," and while I was not sure what it meant, it had done something to me and to everyone around me. It seemed like I had to grow up too quickly; one day I was just a child happy and carefree, and the next a young woman who wanted to fire a Panzerfaust and kill people who were my enemies even though I didn't even know who they were. My hate had escalated, and for a child, this is tragic in itself, for no child should hate like I did or like millions of others in the Hitler Youth did. I wasn't even sure why I hated, except that I was told to hate, trained to hate, and so I hated. This included the Jews despite my not even really knowing who they were and what was wrong with them. I was told to hate them, trained to hate them, and so I hated them. End of story.

Still, despite these feelings, all of us in the Hitler Youth clung to the hope that Hitler's secret weapons of revenge would help us win the war. We had learned that the V-1s and V-2s were unbelievable advances in war technology. They were bombs that didn't need a plane or pilot but found and destroyed targets on their own. The radio was filled with reports of the destruction in London caused by these rockets. There was no doubt in our minds that the war was going to be turned around in our favor, even though we were beginning to hear more bad than good news.

After the Hitler Youth meeting where the Panzerfaust was demonstrated, permission papers were passed around that parents or guardians had to fill out and sign so that we could use the weapons. When I arrived home that day with mine, I thought, *Oh, this is just going to be a matter of a signature, no big deal.* At supper, I told Grandmother and Grandfather about wanting to join the ones that could shoot the Panzerfaust. My grandfather stopped eating and said, "That's out of the question. I'm not going to let you go there. I'm responsible for you." My grandmother agreed but didn't say much. He kept on, "That's definitely not going to happen, and I know that your parents would say the same thing. Even if they agreed, I wouldn't be responsible for sending you."

Despite my somehow realizing he might have been right, that I was going too far, I was furious based on one thing: I was being told what to do. My independent streak had reached a new level; here I was a member, a leader really, of the Hitler Youth and someone lowly like my grandfather was telling me what to do. Didn't he realize how important I was to the cause? That I was becoming a grown woman and could think for myself? Mostly though, I thought, *There he goes again. He's not willing to fight for this country or to win the war.* I was upset, and I pouted all day, but that was the end of it even though I was so upset that I thought about running away from home.

Since so much of our family was in Malchow, it was decided that my parents would somehow manage to join us for the Christmas holidays. Heinz had a leave from duty and would be able to reach us also. But before this occurred, everyone was talking about the state of the war. Nightly news bulletins said that women were being raped by advancing Russian soldiers. Families and lovers, the reports said, were being made to watch the rape of their loved ones, often by several soldiers. Everyone was afraid for the women in our family. It scared me, even though I didn't know what it meant to be raped. I knew that it involved pain and probably blood, but no one in my family talked about sex to me, so I couldn't picture in my mind exactly what rape meant.

Even though things were getting worse, by the end of the holidays, my parents decided to return to the barracks in Berlin. Heinz returned to his duties. One day I felt the ground kind of shake, and I wondered what that was. When I told Wilhelm, he said that he had felt the same thing and that it was artillery fire close by. I was so surprised, and I asked him who was doing the firing. When he said the Russians, my whole body shivered since I was so scared of them and what they might do to me and other girls and women. Soon the *boom boom* of the guns was more of a daily noise, and sometimes I covered my ears to block out the ugly sound.

After one of my Hitler Youth meetings, I took a shortcut home. It had been a nice day even though the ground was covered with snow and the temperature was subzero. But now it was dark, and the wind had picked up. I was late because we had been trying to finish a project and the meeting had dragged on. Some of us were working on a replica of a

URSULA MARTENS AND MARK SHAW

farm, with all the little animals, barns, and everything else one might find there. It was cut out of plywood, carefully glued together, and painted. We were very proud of what we had made and were going to give it as a present to some refugee children for Christmas. Doing this made me feel good and brought a smile to my face. I truly loved helping people, and refugees needed help. Those who said the Hitler Youth were bad did not understand the good. They only thought about the bad.

The railroad station in Malchow wasn't a busy one, especially at this time of the evening. I knew that the next passenger train wouldn't come through until about eight o'clock. Then I noticed some activity near a train at the far end of the station and some freight wagons on the track next to it. Barking dogs captured my attention, and I went to check it out.

It was foggy and bitterly cold, but there were some lights. As I got closer, I saw men in SS uniforms with pistols drawn. The people they were herding out of the train wore black-and-white-striped uniforms, and there was a yellow star sewed on them. Jews! I couldn't even make out if they were women or men. All of them were very skinny and their heads were shaved. They looked cold in their thin suits. I had a strange feeling watching them being loaded into the freight wagons. I had heard talk about camps, but I didn't really know what to think. Then I saw the worst thing—the dogs the soldiers had on the leashes barked and growled and then were let go and jumped at the prisoners. They could not fight back and fell to the ground with the dogs biting them. The sound of this, of the dogs tearing into the helpless Jews was like a nightmare, the worst nightmare sounds I had ever heard.

The others were herded along like cattle toward an open boxcar as the soldiers used clubs and whips and rifle butts to beat them mercilessly. I could actually hear the gun butts hitting the flesh; it was another terrible sound. And the dogs were so vicious, the same kind I had petted when I visited the kiosks near Father's office in Berlin. Suddenly, my mind flashed to the ugly photographs I had seen in his office drawer. There had been no trick photography; this was real and awful. Did Father know about this and turn his back? He must have, I thought.

I watched for several minutes as tears began to well up in my eyes and my legs were wobbly. I then turned and ran home as fast as I could. All the way, I tried to forget what I saw, tried not to remember it, but I couldn't. I ate my supper and went to bed without talking to anyone.

It was painful, and I tried very hard to make myself believe that those people were just criminals from prison. In some ways, I treated what I had seen as yes, a nightmare, because that is what it was. Those people were defenseless, and I had stood by and done nothing to help them. Yes, I was only a young girl, but for weeks I felt guilty that I had not done something to save those poor, suffering people. I never talked to anyone about it and put what I had seen inside me buried along with other awful emotions that were scarring my soul. Sometimes I would wake up in the middle of the night and the scene, that awful scene, was in my mind—especially the part about the dogs attacking or the rifle butts hitting the people in the head. Would I ever be able to wash away what I had seen?

Only after the war did I learn that there was an underground factory in Malchow, where some parts of the V-1 and V-2 rockets were manufactured. What I had seen were probably workers from there that were being returned to a concentration camp, the one I didn't know about at the time. But I never talked to anyone, not even Wilhelm, about what I saw that night. I felt that it was better not to tell anyone because it was sort of like believing in something without questioning whether it was right or wrong, and then you discover that what you believe is maybe not all what it seemed to be. But you are in it too deep already and you fear that if you voice what you saw, then you might be put away just like Tante. Later, I would be told that what I was experiencing was denial, but that wasn't a word I understood at the time.

Before the war, Malchow had been a quiet town. Once in a while a plane flew overhead or you'd hear a ship's horn, but even that was rare. As the war came closer, more rumblings occurred. At first it was intermittent, like the small earthquakes or something like that. I didn't pay much attention to it, until I heard it again and again. My friends talked about it, but no one knew what it could be. Rumors continued that the Russians were coming closer and that we were hearing their heavy artillery. I didn't know whether that was true, and I did not want to believe what they said, but it was scary nonetheless. All kinds of rumors were going around, but at least we, younger kids, tried to convince each other that something would happen in our favor and that maybe it was our own artillery we were hearing. As the days passed, as I found myself constantly watching more for any sign of a Russian soldier who would rape me, I became more apprehensive. I didn't want to think that this was going to be the end, that we were losing the war. Nothing had prepared me for a possible loss on our side since I was sure Hitler and the Nazis would win.

Soon, radio reports about crimes being committed by the Russians became more frequent. You could listen to people being interviewed about young girls and eighty-year-old women who had been raped. The broadcasts even included the sounds of people screaming as they were attacked and tortured. I was told much later that the Russian soldiers knew that they wouldn't be held responsible for their crimes against Germans because of the atrocities German soldiers committed while fighting deep in Russia. All this was very confusing, and I did not know what to believe, but I had been taught to think of Germany first and be proud of our country fighting back against enemies that hated her. This made me forget any thoughts about Hitler doing anything wrong. We were just fighting to survive, and I was proud to be part of the fight.

The mail service from Berlin wasn't working well any longer, and we were thus surprised when my parents arrived from Berlin. To my disbelief, they explained that they had gotten out of the city on a truck that was driven over one of the few last intact bridges leaving Berlin. They said they saw it being blown up right after they crossed it. *What? I thought, The enemy is in Berlin?* This cannot be possible, but Father described the devastation for us, that everything was being blown up and people with it. Now it was a matter of survival, he said, and I tried to comprehend what he meant. At fifteen years old, there were still things that made no sense, and that was one of them. Did he mean our brave Hitler and the soldiers, the ones like me who considered the swastika the symbol of our fight, were going to surrender? That word wasn't even something I had ever considered, but with the bombs bursting all around every day and night, I finally uncluttered the fog that had infected my brain and began to wake up to the fact that Germany and its once mighty forces were in retreat with the Allies, especially the Russians, on the prowl. Was the master race about to be beaten? If we were superior, as Hitler said, then how could that be true? We had won all those medals at the Olympics. That made us superior, right?

By this time, Evie was around three months pregnant, and I certainly had become a young woman whose figure had blossomed out. We all talked it over and decided that because of the threat of rape, we couldn't stay. My aunt didn't want to leave. Both her son and her husband had been fighting on the eastern front, and when they returned, she knew they would come there to look for her if they were alive. She was always crying, always so sad, and fearful that the worst news would come any day.

Since Christa was staying with her, they prepared a hiding place in the barn for the women to hide if they needed to. My grandparents, my uncle, and his family decided to stay behind also to take care of the farm and the animals. It was rumored that the Americans would probably occupy Schwerin, and Father thought we would be safer there. The trains had run without schedule for several days, but finally, Father had confirmation of a freight train that would arrive the next day before dawn. He also learned that the stationmaster in Malchow was going to add some passenger compartments to it.

Everything was in total chaos as the dates turned to early April 1945. With my parents staying with us, it was quite crowded, and our nerves were on edge as everyone said biting things to each other that I knew they did not mean. The future was uncertain for all of us, and I felt lonelier than ever. Wilhelm couldn't be reached, and I didn't dare leave the house. I knew that Wilhelm couldn't leave his family either. I felt alone and scared and sensed that something terrible was going to happen. Were we all going to die? After we left, was I ever going to see my grandparents, Malchow, or my beloved Wilhelm again? There was still a flicker of hope though. Any day now another V weapon would be released, V standing for *vergeltung*, meaning revenge. At least the rumor gave us hope.

Grandmother and my aunt made some sandwiches for us to take along on the trip, while my grandfather and uncle tried to hide our valuables in a hole under the front porch of the house. They had to dig hunched over because there was no room to stand up straight. Later, I was told that the Russian soldiers who came did not have room to lift their bayonets high enough to stab them into the ground feeling for boxes or other obstacles. They looked in many other places in the garden and yard but found nothing, and that angered them.

One morning, Mother and I were going through our belongings, deciding what to take. My grandfather, who had a look of gloom on his face day and night, looked for anything that could be linked to the Nazi Party. I had just started packing my Hitler Youth things when my grandfather walked into the room with a grain sack and asked for my *dreck*, meaning crap. I could not believe he said that word. Hate welled up in me, as it had been trained to. How dare he call my sacred Hitler Youth belongings that? People like him had to be dealt with. I told him, "Don't you ever call it that. You are heartless, you're talking about Hitler, our führer." His face got red, and he yelled, "Just get rid of it. Throw it in the lake! You are all Nazi criminals." I started crying, and he started grabbing the rest of my stuff out of a little closet that I kept it in. All I could do was shout, "Don't take it! It's mine! It's mine!" I still had a little membership book in my hands, and he fought to snatch it away from me. I started screaming, and finally pulled it back out of his hand. Then I said, "I should have turned you in to the gestapo a long time ago. You are a traitor. Hitler will win the war. You will see. If you take anything from me, I will turn you in. Heil Hitler."

For some reason, I enjoyed the feeling of rage because he couldn't take that away. Mother and my aunt came running into the room and called him out, leaving me in tears. Mother returned, explaining that if those items were discovered on me, I would be shot, and if they were discovered after I was gone, the Russian soldiers would be harder on everybody that stayed behind. I didn't answer her, and finally she said that either way, I had to do it.

After I held the Nazi flag and cried some more, I gave in, and they must have buried everything or sunk it in the lake. I was upset that my grandfather could be so cruel, and I was hurt because I had lost my most precious belongings. It seemed like everybody was just anxious to get out of there, and nobody understood what I was going through. I was leaving everything, especially my beloved Wilhelm, behind. And I just wasn't ready to think of defeat. Hitler, our leader—*führer* meant leader—a man I also loved, would save us. No question or at least this is what I told myself.

Early the next day, my uncle took us in a horse-drawn wagon to the railroad station. It was a cold morning and not a word was spoken during the ten-minute ride. The only noise was the tramp of the horses' hooves. At the station, it seemed like hundreds, even thousands, of people were trying to get out of the city. Everyone looked so scared, darting here and darting there. I looked at people, but they did not look back. It was as if they were scared to look scared.

Years earlier, before he married my mother, Father had trained at the Malchow station, and he still knew some of the employees there.

After saying a quick good-bye to my uncle, we were ushered into the office to stay there until the train was ready. Through Father's good treatment, we even got tickets for seats. Finally the train pulled up to the platform, and with our heavy luggage in hand, we pushed forward. Passengers were everywhere: on top of the train, hanging off the sides, and on the platforms outside. After we boarded, every few minutes the train stopped in little towns and villages along the way, and often didn't get moving for half an hour or so. People were pushing and shoving each other for a spot on the train. How could this be happening? I wondered. How could Germany be on the run?

Communication had ceased to exist, signals were no longer working, and the trains were run on sight alone. At each stop, Father left the train to see what was going on and how far the Russians had advanced. On a stop near Schwerin, he came back and whispered to us that there was no way the train could outrun the advancing Russian army; there were just too many trains ahead. Ours couldn't move because people kept climbing on top and refused to get off. No one could make them stop doing that; they were scared like we were. We had to leave right there.

Without making a scene so as not to alert anyone to what he knew and the danger ahead, Father told us to drop our luggage out the window to him and then to meet him outside. As we were getting our luggage together, I stumbled on something and dropped a jar of egg whites my aunt had given me. She knew how much I liked them when beaten with some jam added for sweetness and flavor. I couldn't believe I had made such a mess, and Mother and Evie helped clean up, but I was still sticky all over. We held hands and tried to make it through the people who packed tight inside the train. While stepping out of the car, a tired-looking man said to us "God bless you and your family." Without thinking, I said, "God bless you too."

It was the first time anybody said that to me, and I did not shrink away or think he was crazy. And then I said, "God bless you too." I have no idea why, but I somehow felt touched by what the man had said. For me, someone who had forsaken any thought of God for my own god, Hitler, and had told a teacher to never mention Jesus the Jew, to feel this way was strange, and I wondered what had happened. Later, I thought maybe God was chasing me again, but right then I was so scared I didn't know what to think.

Mostly though, I wondered what I had done wrong. I had listened to Hitler Youth leaders tell me why I needed to serve Hitler as my god. Why did they lie to me? Why was I so stupid? Why was I so evil? I wasn't sure what my true sins were, but I was certain I would never be forgiven. Never ever.

The main road was just up ahead, but the heavy luggage made it seem far as we tried to carry it all. The highway was packed with row after row of people in horse-drawn wagons, soldiers in trucks, and some people on foot pulling their belongings behind them in carts. Many of them carried nothing with them except what they had on their bodies. Father said everyone was trying to get to areas occupied by the Americans rather than be captured by the Russian army. This was because, I was told, the Americans would not hurt us while the Russians were mean and angry and hated all Germans.

Since it was obvious that Evie was pregnant, one of the army trucks stopped and asked where we were headed. Father told them we were trying to get to Schwerin, and they offered us a ride. Mother and Evie sat on a bench in the truck bed while the soldiers, Father, and I sat on the floor. The large truck moved along slowly because of the crowded condition of the highway. Along the way, I looked at the faces of the young soldiers, some my age, and they looked tired, beaten, and scared. They had dirt on their faces too, and their uniforms were grungy and torn in places. None of them spoke to us, but I tried to smile to make them feel better.

The fields along one side of the road were barren at this time of year, and even though it was already April, it was still very cold. From where I sat, I could see dead horses and cows, and once in a while I could see that chunks of meat had been cut out of their bodies. At the sight of it, I felt sick to my stomach, ready to throw up.

After several miles, we heard what I thought was machine gun fire. The truck stopped, and everyone jumped out quickly. Soldiers helped my mother and Evie, and we ran into the woods on the other side of the road. Then I heard a plane and saw it fly low over the highway shooting at the army trucks, including the one we had been on. Somehow they missed our truck but hit several others causing them to burst in flames. I also saw solders hit with the fire and fall to the ground. This was the first time I had seen anyone killed. Before then, it seemed like a pretend war, like it was being fought other places and wasn't so bad. This was different, and I had to fight tears from coming down my cheeks since I was so scared we were all going to die. Like the image of what I had seen in the railway yard with the Jews, this one, seeing soldiers, many my age, fall to the ground, some dead, some crawling along screaming, would never leave my mind in future years. Death and suffering leave an imprint, one hard to ever extinguish.

My hands were trembling as I held tight to my mother. So many things had happened in the last few hours, and now the war in all its brutal reality was raging right on top of us. The sounds of the booming gunfire were everywhere, and Father told me several times to keep down, to stay low. He was not his usual calm self, but he was still calm. I was shaking from head to toe.

After the attack, we raced back into the truck and continued on the road for a while. Then we were shot at a second time, but we knew the routine and got out quickly. As I ran, I looked behind me to see if my parents and Evie were following. The next thing I knew, I was lying on the ground and looking up at worried faces. What I heard, "Are you okay, Ulli, are you okay?" in a loud tone, one I recognized as Mother's. Somehow, while running and looking back, I had run into a tree and knocked myself out. The following day, I had a big bruise on my forehead. Mother, who had scratches and blood on her forehead, held me tight and rubbed my forehead. Evie was there too, crying. She said, "I thought you were dead."

Finally, we saw Schwerin in the distance, and it wasn't long until we came to the park where I had attended many Hitler Youth assemblies. I looked up at the castle of Schwerin on one side of the park and the state theater where I had seen plays and heard concerts and operas. We got off the truck, the soldiers passed down our suitcases, and we thanked them. Father said that we should wait for him there while he went to see some friends for help with accommodations.

The park was packed with refugees, all running around looking for someone. Some had started makeshift fires to keep a little warm. No one knew how far away the Allied troops actually were. All kind of rumors went around. We waited a long time until Father finally came back and whispered to us that he knew of an unoccupied two-bedroom apartment. We followed him quietly as I looked at the faces that raced by. People had blank looks, each clutching some valuable they could not leave behind.

URSULA MARTENS AND MARK SHAW

Father said American and Russian armies were on each side of the city limits. But we were too tired to run further, even though we were not certain of who was going to occupy the city. Reports said Hitler was one place and then another, first in Berlin and then at Obersalzberg. I was certain at some point he would reemerge and lead our reserves to victory. Maybe I was the only one who believed this, but I still did. I had to, even though I knew in my heart we were probably all doomed.

After a short walk, we arrived at the address Father's friend had given him. The building looked nice, and we walked up the stairs to the second-floor apartment. It seemed like a family had just left moments before. Dishes were in the sink and the beds unmade. As we settled in, there was a commotion in the street below. We looked down from the balcony, and there were tanks driving through the streets. Father and Mother stood near a window without being seen below and tried to see whether they were the Russians. But then Father knew because people on the streets were actually cheering and I thought how strange this was that they were cheering for Hitler's enemy, my enemy. I felt funny about this, but Father and Mother and Evie were so happy that I was happy too.

Minutes later, we watched as soldiers began going from house to house. Mother talked more than she usually did and told Evie and me to fix our hair. When Mother thought the Russian soldiers were approaching, we were told to make ourselves look as ugly as possible. Now she wanted us to look presentable for the Americans. I did not understand this too much but did what I was told. My mind was all confused as I realized the dream of Germany winning the war was over, and now we were the losers. How could this have happened? I wondered again. And where was Hitler to save us? I had never imagined this, even in my wildest dreams that Americans could beat the Germans. I remembered that at Hitler Youth meetings we were told that its army was made up of people who were criminals, prisoners who didn't even have uniforms and used rifles that dead soldiers had used. Now they were the winners, and we were the losers.

Then we watched as the American soldiers came into our building. There was a hard knock, and Father opened the door. Two of them, dressed in brown army uniforms, walked in. They were wearing helmets and carried rifles over their shoulder. None of them had shaved and the bad smell meant they needed to take a bath. I was scared to death, certain they were going to rape me or shoot me because I was a Nazi. They were tall, and at that moment, I thought they were the biggest men I'd ever seen. As they walked in, one of them nodded to Father, smiled at Mother, then walked through each of the rooms. He looked in the closets, under the beds, and through the cabinets, then walked back into the kitchen where we were all still standing, nodded to my father again. I was shaking the whole time, grasping Mother's hand so hard it must have hurt hers. Then the two soldiers, without saying anything, both left. Father said they were looking for German soldiers in hiding and also for ammunition.

During the next few days, the most important thing was to look for food. It was very sparse, and it did not take long until the black market became active again. People were trading anything everywhere, our only way to survive. The American soldiers offered PX (post exchange) rations of cigarettes and candies. People took them and traded a pack of American cigarettes for a lot of food. One day, I saw a carton traded for a large diamond. The soldiers that didn't smoke were lucky because they were able to trade in all their cigarettes. Nylon stockings were also worth a lot in trade. Sometimes soldiers brought leftover meat from the mess hall. It was for the dogs, but often people were the dogs. It was the first time I tasted what were called doughnuts. They tasted more delicious than any cake I had ever eaten in my life.

My parents were lucky to have jewelry and watches to trade. It kept us alive until the numbers on ration cards we were given were called. The lines in front of the stores were long, but because Evie was pregnant, she could go ahead to the front. Old and sick people could do so as well. Those had been the rules during the war, and they just stayed the same.

One day I stood in line with Mother. An American army truck pulled up and pretty soon they pulled bundles out of the back of the truck and handed them down. I thought they might be food supplies, but wait, those weren't bundles, I realized, they were actually people in the white-and-black-striped camp uniforms like the ones I had seen in the railway yard, and by then we had gotten to know well. Most needed help to even take a step, to walk. Their eyes were huge in their bony faces. I couldn't help but cry at the sight, and Mother put her hand in mine. Tears flowed down my cheeks, and as they did, my eyes met those of a Jewish girl about my age ahead of me in line who had a yellow star stitched to her sweater. We just stared at each other, and I saw her muscles twitch in her face as tears popped out of her eyelids. She had the saddest look on her face, and I bet I did too. I started to reach out to her, but Mother took my arm and held me back saying, "Her mother will take care of her." Father walked up to us and put his handkerchief in my hand so I could wipe my tears. Seeing that girl made me feel like I was in a different world. I could never have imagined anything like that. But I didn't have anyone to talk to because no one wanted to talk about it. Everyone was in shock.

Although I probably wasn't supposed to hear, people started whispering about the atrocities that happened in the camps. I didn't want to believe it at first, and it seemed like no one really wanted to talk about it, as if it would go away by ignoring it. After seeing the survivors that day, I could no longer deny it. My heart sank at the sight of these people, and perhaps this was the very first time I began to understand that what I had done to help the Nazis might have been wrong. But I hated to think that, that somehow I had a part in this, that I had contributed to these people's suffering. But seeing these people up close was a true wake-up call, and I cried myself to sleep one night after seeing a group of them who looked like walking death. Someone had earlier mentioned a word I had not heard too much before, *propaganda*. That meant things were made up, and this was how I understood any information I heard about any camps. But after I saw what I saw in the railway yard with the Jews being beaten, and those people in trucks, I knew there was no propaganda involved in that. It was the truth.

Then the biggest shock of all occurred. During the first days of May 1945, news spread through the streets that not only was the war officially over but that the unthinkable had occurred; Hitler was dead! He had been killed, we were told, leading the troops in defense of the Fatherland at the Battle of Berlin.

If I hadn't been so busy and preoccupied with our day-to-day survival, I think I would have gone out of my mind. All I could think was, *This cannot be. It can't end like this.* Hitler couldn't die! He was more than human, and I believed in him with all my young heart and soul. I would have gladly given my life for him—a life that had been totally devoted to him. I had idolized him, and I had been willing to sacrifice anything for him. I was sixteen years old and still did not grasp the meaning of death. No one really close to me had ever died. And Hitler, my god, was now dead. Could it be true, or was this another lie?

Knowing he was dead finally told me the war was over. Before, I had resisted this feeling, but now I knew it was true.

Him dying was worse than Father or Mother dying, I decided. And sometimes it dawned on me that, yes, Hitler had really been my god—like an idol, like Thor or someone. How could this have been? I wondered. But I was too confused and did not know what to think. But the idea that I saw him as my god bothered me. How had this occurred?

Who could I talk to about my feelings? I wondered. Certainly not my parents, Evie, or other grown-ups. It seemed like everyone wanted to separate themselves from what had been their life for so many years. Suddenly no one was proud to be German, proud of what all of us had believed in. I swore then that I would never again follow someone blindly and believe in them with all my heart and soul. Everyone had let me down and misused the trust I had in them. Nothing was ever going to be the same.

Since there was no mail, we had no idea what had happened to my grandparents. I missed them, and I missed Wilhelm and didn't know what had happened to him. But I couldn't confide in my family because they thought that I was too young to be in love. So I just kept it all inside myself. But at night in bed before I went to sleep, I let myself dream about how everything was going to be all right at least between Wilhelm and me. The thought of our reuniting is what kept me going through the next weeks and months.

A few days after we arrived in Schwerin, I walked to the park to look for friends or other people I might know from Malchow. The park and surrounding area were still crowded with homeless people, the refugees. Many were living there in tents and other makeshift covers. Some carried large signs on their backs, with the name of a town or a surname on it. This was how people found their relatives, friends, and former neighbors. I met a few people from Malchow, but they had left at the same time we did and couldn't tell me anything new. Looking once again another day, I saw a young girl with red hair, and I thought of Siegi. I looked closer at the girl, and it was her. I ran over, and we hugged and cried and laughed. We were happy to see each other, but right away, I noticed a change in her. She was wearing lipstick and makeup, and I thought she was dressed kind of cheap.

I knew that some of the British army had arrived in Schwerin at the same time as the Americans, and they also were part of the occupation force. Siegi told me that she had a British boyfriend and that she was going to England with him. I was so disappointed in her. How could she be friendly with the enemy? It wasn't even allowed then to be seen with a soldier. She said he brought her a lot of food and stuff from the PX, and she offered me some chocolate that he had given her. My hunger was larger than my pride, so I took it.

Whenever I took a walk, soldiers whistled at me, and called out, "Hello, Fräulein!" but I would just blush and keep walking since to me that word meant "whore."

Once a soldier said that and then started to follow me. I ran as fast as I could toward our apartment. When I told Evie later that I thought I was going to be arrested, she said that the soldier probably just wanted to ask me out for a date. I laughed, but she said, "You have become a sexy young woman." I had never looked at myself that way, but it was nice of my sister to say that although I wasn't sure if being sexy was good.

At least the American soldiers didn't do anything as bad as the raping we knew Russian soldiers had done. In a large city like Schwerin, we heard of only one incident where a girl said a soldier in the park had raped her at night. Most people said, "What was she doing in the park at night anyway when there was a curfew?" On occasions, the soldiers got drunk, but mostly they were polite and well behaved. However, after several weeks, the American army released Schwerin to the Russian army for occupation. When they arrived, everything changed. We were scared once more, and food became scarce again.

Then one day, Father approached with the saddest face I had ever seen. He had perspiration on his face since he had been running, and he was out of breath. He said words I would never forget. "The war is officially over. They signed all the papers. Germany will be divided up among the enemies like a sack of potatoes, like a box of children's toys." Then he added, "Germany doesn't exist anymore. Schwerin and Malchow will be for the Russians, and Berlin will be like a jigsaw puzzle, cut into pieces." My heart nearly stopped hearing these words, but I felt so bad for Father. His hopes, his dreams, ones including going to London to be a stationmaster there, were over. Now he was a Nazi who might be arrested any moment. Would he be taken to prison or shot? I wondered. This kept me from sleeping at night. What would happen to all of us?

Within minutes after saying all this, Father decided we should leave and go back to Berlin. At least he would have a job there, and he hoped things would be more normal for all of us. Returning to Berlin was something I anticipated doing, but I had no idea what terrible shape that city was in. The war had been lost, Hitler was dead, and any chance that my beloved Wilhelm was still alive was very small.

URSULA MARTENS AND MARK SHAW

CHAPTER NINE

Station: Berlin and Malchow, Germany (1945–1947)

On a bright summer morning, in May 1945, our family left for Wilhelmshorst, a suburb of Berlin. Father told us this was a Russian-occupied zone, and here as everywhere else, nearly all the railroad tracks had been dismantled and shipped to Russia. Only a single track was left. This slowed traveling a great deal.

When we finally arrived, Father's colleagues greeted us warmly. The two rooms that my parents had occupied before they left were still waiting for them and now had to be sufficient for the four of us. We were relieved to find the canned food, porcelain, and other valuables my parents had buried before they left, intact.

Two weeks later, Father arrived home with another sad look on his face. Since he had been a member of the Nazi Party, he no longer had employment along with many others. I could tell he was upset, and Mother wondered how we were going to make it without his having a job. Since I was sixteen, I wanted to help out, but there was not much talk of that.

Father not having a job meant this was the end of our stay in the barracks. Whoever was in charge assigned new living quarters to us. It was a nice villa that had been vacated by the owner, a former Nazi official. We occupied the first floor of the large house, consisting of a living room, dining room, kitchen, bath, and bedroom. It seemed like the former occupants had left in a hurry, leaving dishes, silverware, and linens behind. The huge yard was surrounded by beautiful pine trees, and if the circumstances had not been so sad, it would have been a nice place to stay.

For many days, we worried about my grandparents and the rest of the family. I never really thought of praying, but perhaps it was in my mind since I wanted them to be safe. But I was still in a daze over all that had happened, and my mind wasn't thinking of any god to save them. Finally, word reached us that our relatives had survived the Allies onslaught. I jumped up and down at the news, and I had a smile on my face all day long. Everyone was so relieved. But my joy was short-lived since Grandmother wrote that Wilhelm had been picked up by the Russian KGB and that he had been sent to prison. I cried that night, worried about my true love.

German marks were plentiful, but the money was worthless. It did not buy much and really only paid for the rent and groceries that were assigned to us on our ration cards. Against Father's protest, Mother started working in the kitchen of an orchestra of the Russian army. He said they were killers and rapists, but she said it was only the music people, and they had been very nice to her. I think Father just felt bad that she had to work because he couldn't. He was a very prideful man. Every once in a while, though, I remembered the photos in his desk, and they made me think of him in a different way. How much had he helped with sending people to be tortured and killed? I did not know and could not ask him. I never asked him.

Every day, Mother brought home some scraps of food, but the musician's rations were almost as meager as ours. She got to know several of the officers who were around there, and once they stashed a large sack of brown sugar that was to be traded on the black market in our house. When they came for partials of it to be sold, they offered me spoonfuls to eat while they helped themselves. Being as hungry as I was, it was a delicacy for me, and I did not mind eating from the same spoon that they did. Being hungry is something I had not experienced before, and I felt very weak at times. This made me think back to the Jewish girl in the ration line and how sad she looked. Now I was sad too.

These Russian soldiers were friendly, and I learned to like them, a departure from the days when I was scared because of the rape stories. At sixteen, I was finally learning valuable lessons about who to trust and who not to trust. I still could not believe that Hitler was dead and that Germany had lost the war, but more and more I knew that what I had been told by the Nazis was not the truth. This sort of awakening was gradual, but it made me feel like a fool. Believing in something and then having it be false causes lack of any confidence. Grandfather was right; I was a war criminal, and I deserved to be punished.

The house we stayed in had a concert piano, and sometimes several soldiers would come and played for hours. My family and I enjoyed the classical music that these accomplished musicians knew even though some of the tunes were sad enough to make me cry while others made me happy and want to dance. They also sang sometimes while playing their instruments. Some spoke a bit of German and so we could talk to them. They wore regular soldiers' uniforms, boots, riding pants, and a blouse that closed along the shoulders and did not open down the front. Later we learned that most of them were members of the Moscow opera orchestra. I watched with my eyes wide at how good they were. At first I was edgy around them, apprehensive, but soon that went away, and I just enjoyed the music. I closed my eyes sometimes and listened to the beautiful sound. Imagine doing this with Russians around.

Sometimes the soldiers brought the ingredients for a cake and asked my mother to bake it for them. When it was done, there was always a generous sample for us. I learned then just as I had learned a little in Schwerin that these former enemies weren't the monsters that we had been told they were.

Once in a while though, we heard there were still sporadic rapes by drunken soldiers. Out of opened windows, women warned each other by banging two pot lids together. It meant, "Take cover! Hide yourselves!" I woke up when this happened and pulled the covers over my head. Sometimes I could not get back to sleep. I remembered how that German worker had attacked me in the hayloft and that gave me nightmares. I could never get the banging pots sound out of my mind since it meant evil was going on.

One month, a ration card number that was not valid in Wilhelmshorst was called in the neighboring city of Potsdam where beautiful castles existed before the war and where Hitler had spoken to thousands of Hitler Youth. Mother and I walked for miles through deep woods on the chance to buy some extra food. Evie stayed home because she was eight months pregnant by now. Mother and I both walked quickly and looked all around because we saw a lot of desperate, homeless people, many refugees, living in the woods despite the cold. I tried not to make eye contact because it made me sad to see them suffering so much. This was a change from when I thought they were a bother. If Mother had allowed me to, I would have helped them. On our way back, loaded down with our groceries, we made it back safely by finding other people that were going back to Wilhelmshorst. That made it safer too.

Despite our making a go of it, I could tell Father was heartbroken. There were no steady jobs available for him, and now only his wife was working. He was a heavy smoker, and cigarettes were hard to come by. He planted tobacco plants in the backyard, but when the huge leaves were just about ready to be harvested and dried, we had a hailstorm that left the leaves punctured with holes. He was silent, a sign he was sad again. Another time, we were all eating very small boiled potatoes still in the skin. Mother, Evie, and I were able to peel them much faster so we had more on our plates. Suddenly Father, so upset with his life, pushed his plate back so that potatoes were rolling all over the table and onto the floor. He stormed out of the room yelling, "I cannot peel as fast as all of you can, my hands are too large!" After that outburst, food was weighed on a little scale and divided equally. Seeing Father like that made me want to give him a hug, but this was not something a daughter could do in our family. No one wants to see his or her father like that. I could tell he felt like he was not a man, not head of the household anymore.

Almost daily, we made trips to the farms in outlying areas to trade pieces of crystal and porcelain for food. Some farmers were nice enough and allowed us to walk over empty stubble fields to pick up stems of grain that were left behind, just like birds do. I could never have imagined doing this, being like birds, but we had to eat and do anything to eat since we were so hungry.

American army trains came through Wilhelmshorst with provisions for their soldiers in the part of Berlin they controlled. Evie, some other young women, and I went to the railroad crossing to see them. This was because we knew the trains had to slow down and soldiers would shower us with K-rations and candy. All we had to do is wave to them. I did not like to take handouts from the soldiers, and it was not because they were Americans. I felt like I was prostituting myself, that I was flirting with the enemy, and after all, they were men. Evie did not want to show she was pregnant, so she hid a bit behind a pole. But my hunger was once again bigger than my pride, and so I took the good stuff. Our parents were happy to see us arrive home with our pockets loaded.

When it was time for Evie to deliver her baby, and there was no hospital in Wilhelmshorst, she made arrangements with a doctor in a nearby suburb who had converted his large house into a clinic to deliver babies. We were concerned about getting her there on time because the trains were still running very infrequently. For a few days, when she thought her time might come, we would walk her to the clinic so she could sleep there rather than risking having the baby come in the middle of the night. It was quite a long walk, but the doctor said it wouldn't hurt her since we were all used to a lot of walking. Several mornings she came back, saying, "Not yet." One morning, she didn't return, and we knew it was time.

With swift steps, my mother and I walked to the clinic. When we arrived, we heard bloodcurdling screams. I was scared to death for her and made up my mind that I would never have a baby if it meant this much pain. After a long time, which seemed forever to me, the screaming stopped, and the doctor appeared. I held my breath as he spoke but relaxed when he said Evie had delivered a healthy baby boy. She named him Wolfgang. By then it was starting to get dark, and we had to leave because it was dangerous to make the walk at night. They let us in to see Evie before they finished cleaning up. She was lying there, dripping with perspiration, holding her little baby, and there was blood all over the bed. But she had a happy smile on her face. I was surprised after what she had been through. She said, probably to calm me down, "I'm ready for another one!" On our way back, I tried to talk to Mother about what I had witnessed that day, but she was embarrassed as always and couldn't talk to me. She said that I was too young and would find out in time. I had so many questions on my mind, and I remembered that back in Schwerin, when I had my period for the first time, I had to get advice from girlfriends whom my parents probably considered "dirty" because they even knew those things. At sixteen, I felt left out that I did not know enough about girl things and never would for a long time.

As daily life began normalizing toward the end of 1945 despite the destruction all around, it was time for me to return to school. There was no high school in Wilhelmshorst, so I enrolled in another high school in Berlin. I found studying hard at first because most of the other students were much older than I was. They had been soldiers, returned from the war. They were preparing themselves for entry into the university.

Twice a day, I rode the train. Soon, I became friendly with a girl named Magda who took the same train as I did. One day, for some reason, our connecting train wasn't running, and we decided to hitch a ride together. Usually only guys did this, but we thought it would be fun.

We stood on the side of the road with our thumbs in the air. Several cars passed before an American army truck stopped alongside of us, and the young-looking soldier asked us where we were going. He seemed friendly. He couldn't have been much older than us girls. Magda said, "He's cute." He did not speak a word of German, but we were doing okay with our broken school English. I told him we were going to the school in Wannsee, and he said, "I go right by there. Want a ride?" I said, "No, but thank you," and we started to move away. But then he said, "What's wrong? My name's Billy. Are you afraid to ride with an American? I won't bite. Jump in." He seemed nice, but I still said, "No, we'll walk." He smiled and replied, "Hey, there are two of you, and if I tried anything you could beat me up." Magda looked at me and said, "He looks okay, not too strong. What do you think?" I still wasn't sure, but we got into the truck, and seconds later, he turned into the Grunewald, a huge park in the western part of Berlin. I assumed he did it so he wouldn't be seen giving us girls a ride.

The three of us were laughing and having a good time. He drove up and down the little hills in the park, and it felt like being on a roller coaster. I was sitting next to him, and as he was shifting the gears, he would rub along my thigh. There wasn't enough room for me to move over, and after a while, he suddenly stopped and said, "Who is going to pay for this?"

"The army," I answered laughing. He said, "That's not what I mean." Magda and I looked at each other, and suddenly we knew what he meant. She opened the door and slid down from the high truck. I started to follow, but he grabbed me. My blouse tore open as I struggled to free myself from his hold. But he was holding my arm, so I bit into his hand, and he let go. I dropped down from the truck, and we ran as fast as we could. Later Magda said that when I bit his hand, his glasses fell off his nose. We both learned our lesson and never hitched another ride. I never told my parents about this because I was too embarrassed and knew they would not understand. Anything to do with sex was dirty; that was their idea.

URSULA MARTENS AND MARK SHAW

The train rides into Berlin were often very dangerous. They were crowded and many passengers stood on the outside platforms, barely hanging on. In those days, the locomotives were heated with wood, and the pieces of burning ember flew out of the chimney and landed on us. There the embers extinguished themselves, often on our skin, because we couldn't let go to flick them off. I had many burn holes on my clothes and some on my skin. One day a girl had to "put me out" since my lovely orange parachute dress had caught on fire. Other times there were burn holes in white coats Evie and I wore. Made from curtains, they had been stitched together by a seamstress that Mother knew.

Father continued to look for work but, like many others, could only find occasional employment. The following spring and summer as the year turned to the middle of 1946, things stabilized a bit, and we were allowed to travel with the necessary permits. I was excited when my mother and I prepared to visit Malchow. Maybe I would find out something about Wilhelm's fate. At least I would be in the old familiar places where we had been so happy.

After a train ride that seemed to take forever, we finally arrived. Everything seemed different, almost as if sadness and dark clouds had overcome the former lovely city. It had been less than a year since we had left, but everything had changed. The town was crowded with strangers, mostly refugees that had been stranded there at the end of the war. These were the people that I had believed were worthless and had thus looked down upon. Now I felt sorry for them as I watched them trying to stay alive in makeshift tents with little food or water. Some guilt was spreading in my heart each day as I thought about being part of the Nazis who had treated people so cruelly. I still did not know the full extent of the terror, but I was learning more each day. This included learning that many lies had been told to us before and during the war. Fact had been mixed with fiction, especially regarding what had occurred to people who had been sent away. When I learned that many of the troops at the front were not even teenagers, I couldn't believe it. Many of those climbing into the cockpits of planes as Luftwaffe were very young too. We also heard about Hitler Youth who were supposedly part of a group called the Werewolves, a guerilla type of soldier who was going to hide in the mountains and then attack the enemy. That turned out to be only propaganda, a term that now meant *lie* to me.

The streets in Malchow were dirty; houses needed paint. It seemed like no one cared anymore. My family was glad to see us, but even the house was different. A Communist couple had been assigned to live with them, and we had to be careful of what we said.

Tears fell down my cheeks when I heard my aunt Grete had been raped. It was whispered about like it was shameful. I learned that it happened while she was looking for some food. She had to go quite a way through the woods to get to a farm where she knew the owner. The Russian soldier gave her a loaf of bread after he attacked her. When I heard this story, I felt bad again, for I felt that if I had not helped Hitler and the Nazis, the war would have never happened. And then the Russians would have not come, and my aunt would not have been raped. I was beginning to be ashamed of what I had done, but there was no one to talk about it with, so I tucked it into my heart and tried to cope like everyone else.

My aunt had no news from either her husband or son. Many months later, her husband was finally released from prison. He was a sick man, and he died a few years later. People were dying everywhere now, some from war wounds, some from being in prison, some from broken hearts. Germany had been brought to its knees, the so-called master race, the superior people, all beaten and destroyed. Some were trying to heal, but it would take a long time. I knew that about myself, and I sometimes looked into the bathroom mirror and wondered who I was as my eighteenth birthday happened without much happiness to celebrate it.

One day my heart almost stopped, and I had a hard time breathing for a while. While I was in Malchow, Father told me that I had been suspected of being a member of the Werewolves group. This occurred when I brought up the subject by saying, "I have no idea how the Russians could have believed any of my friends were part of the Werewolves." Seconds later, Grandfather leaped from the table, threw his napkin down, and left the room. I was shocked and started to leave the table before Father told me to sit back down. I did. "Don't be so tough on your grandfather," he said. "You know they, the Russians, came here looking for you."

My eyes darted forward, and I said, "What?" Father looked at me and answered, "Yes, remember when the Hitler Youth gave you something for that promotion where you were in charge of some of the villages?" I nodded, and then he said, "What was it?" I thought a minute and then replied, "A new braided cord, a green one to wear on the shoulder of my uniform."

"That's right," he said. "And the Russians decided that anyone with a green cord was one of the elite members of the Hitler Youth movement, a leader. They came here looking for you and tore the house apart. When grandfather swore you were not here, they roughed him up, beat him up, but he told them nothing. He saved you. Later, after they left, he said, "Thank God, Ulli is okay. Ulli is okay."

With tears in my eyes and a lump in my throat, I left the table and looked for Grandfather. He was sitting alone in another room just staring ahead. I went over and threw my arms around him and said, "Thank you, Grandfather. Thank you. Thank you." He looked at me with those sad eyes of his and said, "That's okay. It was good you were not here." To think of myself as a leader was a strange feeling. I never considered that. But I guess I was after Wilhelm asked me to help him in the villages. That was a responsibility, and I welcomed it, and the Hitler Youth gave me the braided cord. Ursula, a leader of the Hitler Youth; that was true. Now I felt more guilt for all that it had done since I was learning about the bad things the Hitler Youth had done like hurting people and blowing up synagogues and all that. I never meant to be a part of that, only to comfort wounded soldiers in the hospital and make things for the children. But yes, I told myself, at the end, I wanted to shoot a Panzerfaust, and maybe I could have even killed the enemy soldiers as the Hitler Youth leaders told us to. This made me wonder about myself. Could I really have killed someone?

I walked around in a daze for a day or so, but then a smile crossed my face a couple of days later when I saw Mrs. Schubert, Wilhelm's mother. But the smile disappeared when she said he was being held in a KGB jail in Waren, a larger city not far from Malchow. Several times she had tried to see him but wasn't allowed into the jail. All she could do was walk along the front of the building repeatedly. He saw her through the bars and would call out to her as she was passing. I promised to go with her the next time she went to visit him. She agreed that he would like that very much.

One very early morning shortly after I visited my grandparents, my aunt prepared a sack-lunch for me, and I went to meet Mrs. Schubert. She was a big woman, and when she had to sign a check, she had to put her bust on the table to steady herself. She was glad I was coming along.

Her husband, whom I had known before, barely even moved while I was in their home. And he never spoke while gazing out a window like he was in a daze. The blank look on his face was alarming. He barely looked alive. I had seen this look on many faces after the war. People were like zombies not knowing what to think or do. Their hearts were heavy and some just sat and cried all day over the loss of loved ones or their property. The word *Nazi* was not spoken now. Too many had been killed or imprisoned for being a part of Hitler and his Nazis. Where I once loved him, now hate entered my mind for not only my being used but many others as well. There are other kinds of blindness except for not being able to use one's eyes. I had been blind like a robot just doing what I was told without thinking. Now I had a lump in my stomach every day. Perhaps it was the guilt or just knowing I had been the fool. No matter, my love for Hitler as my god was no more. This feeling was heavy on my mind especially when we learned he had not been killed leading troops but had taken the coward's way out by committing suicide. He wasn't brave, just a bad man who had led his adopted country, my country, to destruction. And caused so many to be tortured, and die, especially the Jews, and millions of Germans. Yes, I believe I did hate him now, another part of my large amount of hate.

It would have been half an hour on the train to Waren where Wilhelm was incarcerated, but like in so many other areas, there were no train tracks left on this line. So along with other people, Mrs. Schubert and I walked and walked along the seemingly endless railroad ties that were still in place, and finally, after hours with just a few rest stops, we made it. The jail was an old three-story structure that looked like it had been an office building at one time. We weren't the only ones there. On the sidewalk across the street, there were several people, mostly women, who were walking by very slowly. We joined them, and soon there was shouting going back and forth. We heard, "Mother," "Olga," and "Sharon," and other names. The names were then repeated many times over.

Suddenly, Wilhelm's mother said she heard his voice and motioned to a barred basement window. I saw movement behind it but couldn't tell if it was him. We walked along the block and then took our sweaters off and put scarves on to change how we looked and to fool the guards into not recognizing us. We walked past again, and this time I could hear my name being called. "Ulli, how are you? Good to see you!" he was shouting. I wanted to run to him, but I knew it would endanger all of us. All I could do was shout back to him, "I am fine! I miss you!"

More and more people arrived, and the guards got restless. They started shouting at people in Russian to keep moving. Suddenly, an older lady ran across the street screaming, "I want my son. Give me back my son!" and then suddenly darted toward the prison. She raced along, and two of the younger guards seemed like they were playing a game to see who could reach her first. The youngest one then used a body block to knock the old woman down. Then the other one and some more soldiers started hitting and kicking her until she was just a bundle of rags. From inside the prison, we heard, "No, no, no, no!" Both Mrs. Schubert and I cried, and that walk home seemed like the longest walk of my life.

A few weeks later, I learned that Wilhelm was sentenced to fifteen years at hard labor for what he did in the Hitler Youth. My guess is that it was a way of keeping young men out of Germany where at the time a Communist government was being formed. Ex- members of the Hitler Youth might have been suspected of being potential troublemakers. Certainly Wilhelm and others I knew were totally innocent of that, but what did I know. What scared me is that if I had been caught before I left with my parents, I could have ended up in prison too. This made me cry one night, but then I was also crying for my beloved Wilhelm.

After fifteen years in Siberian slave camps, relatives later told me Wilhelm came home, a sick, broken man. Later I heard he married and had several children. He died in his fifties due to poor health following the trying times in prison. I never saw him again.

When Mother and I returned to Berlin, I ventured into the heart of the city. Everywhere, I saw women wearing shawls to keep them warm sitting in front of rows of bricks. With hammers, they knocked off the old mortar one by one. Their faces looked beaten, and their fingers were sore and swollen. They had the saddest faces, and their eyes had no shine. In order to get ration cards, you had to be willing to work, and for unskilled women, this was often the only work they could find. I saw women that were older than my grandmother and younger ones with their small children playing around them in the rubble. There were blocks and blocks of this, and it seemed like the whole city was one big pile of rubble. Everything was destroyed.

During and after the war, we learned to improvise. Women made clothing from all kinds of material—parachutes, velvet drapes, blankets, even rough sugar sacks from the American supplies. They were hard on the skin, but there was no choice. The kitchen was often the only room that was used because one could cook what little there was to eat and be warm at the same time. Full baths were a very rare luxury. Instead, we warmed a little water and washed in a basin.

We drank coffee that was called Muckefuck (pronounced Muckefoock). It was a mixture of barley and oats and was probably healthier than real coffee, but we still traded many precious pieces of porcelain or silver for the real thing. Farmers in the surrounding areas of Berlin and elsewhere wound up with whole sets of expensive Meissen porcelain, precious crystals, and sets of silver knives and forks for morsels of food, fruits and vegetables, or animals that they had raised.

Since survival was the most important thing, school was often missed. Parents overlooked this if the child came home with some kind of object that might be tradable on the black market. Stealing to survive wasn't looked upon as criminal. Because of their smaller size, children could often fit through small cracks in the rubble of bombed houses and find good things that were passed over by adults. Children were also sent to do the shopping at the black market because if they got caught, they were just sent home. A lot of Germans were living with what was called *restfamilien*. They were family members that had found each other through circumstances brought on by the war and the aftermath. The men were often still in prison, missing, killed during the war, or hadn't hooked up with their families because their homes were bombed, and the mother and children were staying with relatives.

Like everyone else, our family took the risk of trading on the black market when we could. Often, I brought briquettes at the other end of town and carried the heavy load back in a suitcase to make it look like I was traveling. One day, I was in the Russian-occupied section of Berlin trying to trade some beautiful silk skirts made out of an orange parachute. Besides the skirts, I had some razorblades, which were a rarity. Suddenly I felt a sharp pain in my side. When I turned and looked up, a Russian soldier was staring at me. He had jabbed me with the butt of his rifle. It was too late for me to run, and I was ordered onto a truck with others that were caught. They took us to a police station, but all the way I was shaking, afraid of what might happen. Surely I

URSULA MARTENS AND MARK SHAW

was going to be shot or sent to Siberia, I thought. I was interrogated by a German policewoman. She translated what I said to a man who was part of the Russian military police. They hadn't caught me actually selling anything, so I showed my ID and lied that I was on my way to meet some friends. I was asked to wait in the other room where two Russian soldiers went through my briefcase. They seemed to like the razorblades, and I motioned that they could have them. Their faces lit up, and a while later, I was told to leave. When I came home and told the story, Father said in his dry humor, "Now you're forever part of the Russian criminal element!" At the time, I wondered why my parents let me be the one to do the trading, but I soon realized that as a young girl, I had a much better chance of getting good deals.

For a long time, we didn't know what had happened to our house and belongings in Hermsdorf. One day, Father went there without us knowing. He came back with a beaten look on his face and told us the house was being used by officers of the French occupation army. He asked to talk to someone in charge and was told that he wouldn't be able to move back into the house at that time. While waiting, he noticed that the Persian rug he was standing on was ours. Except for a few pieces, most of the furniture was gone.

Hearing him tell about this made me think of the times when he brought home expensive articles like silverware and the painting Evie adored. Now the French were enjoying things that we had owned. Was this some sort of payback? I wondered.

After I graduated from school in late 1947, I worked for about a year as a nanny in West Berlin for a couple with two small children. I went home only for weekends. But being a nanny for the Schumacher family was not really what I wanted to do with my life. I was embarrassed by something I did while I worked for them. My feelings were the same as they were when I was about ten years old and had stolen coins out of Mother's apron pocket when I had the urge for an ice cream cone. It was small change that my Mother picked up here and there while cleaning. I got busted one day when the paperboy came to collect, and she knew for sure she had money in her apron pocket. After sending me to the attic to "Wait till your father gets home," I spent a fearful hour or so there, waiting to be punished by Father. I was lucky though since he just reprimanded me. But still, I thought later, stealing from Mother was really bad.

This time though, ten years later, I stole for my mother. Hunger was still very much with us, and for a surprise but without permission, I had mixed a concoction of oats, sugar, and cocoa to give to her. I had hidden the bag with the goodies in it under some diapers but forgot about it after my mother had called saying she could not make it. The next morning, I realized that I had been found out since Mrs. Schumacher had gotten up in the night to change the baby's diaper. The bag lay exposed, but she never said a word to me. Still, that did not make me feel any better.

Through his family in Berlin, Evie finally heard from Heinz. She learned that he was somewhere in the British zone of Germany, sentenced to prison for several years because of his activity as a teacher in a Nazi school. Since there was no way Evie and her son could get a permit to leave the Russian zone, she was eager to have her own home and was lucky to rent a small house from a friend that had fled to the west. It would be almost five years until Heinz was able to see little Wolfgang. Until then, Evie managed alone, and I was very proud of her for doing so.

Father still didn't get his old job back, even though some of his superiors that had been rehired in West Germany were trying hard to get him reinstated. My parents thus decided it would be best for them to go back to Malchow. In the meantime, my grandparents were successful in getting rid of the Communists that had been assigned to them.

During the same time that I was working as a nanny, Mother began working in the fields. It was hard on her since she was not used to that kind of work. Father was ordered to work underground, disassembling a rocket factory that the Nazis had built. He had to do very hard manual labor, and it took a toll on him. He was often sick. Everything at the underground factory was shipped to Russia where it ended up as junk. No assembly plans were shipped along with it.

When I saw Father after he had worked for a while, I gasped since I almost did not recognize him. Working underground, there was a lack of oxygen. The Germans had a good ventilation system when they were there, but the Russians had torn that apart and sent it to Russia. Father had suffered for that, and I first wondered who the haggard old man I was looking at was before recognizing him. He had aged terribly. He was very thin, and worse, the man who had always stood so straight and tall was now partially hunched over. But I never let him know I was so shocked. I just touched his arm and said, "Papa, it is so wonderful, so very wonderful to see you." But that night, I could not sleep thinking of Father and how he was suffering. He had lost his dignity and now his health. I loved him so, but I could do nothing to help him.

The land, equipment, and livestock my uncle owned were taken away from him, and he had to work the fields as a laborer. He told me later that under the Communist regime of Germany, no one cared. Farm equipment was run over stones and other debris so that broken down equipment was lying everywhere. Of course production went way down for these very reasons.

When I sat and thought about what had transpired over the early years of my life, I was so confused. I had believed in something that I thought was so right, and it turned out to be so wrong. Everywhere I looked there was destruction, death, and people who had been treated like they were animals, even worse than animals. Germany was once again occupied, and nobody spoke about the Fatherland with any sense of pride. Like me, so many were ashamed of what had occurred, but I could not really process all this yet. Had I been used? Yes, for sure. Had I been what people liked to call an enabler, someone who contributes to the wrong without knowing it or maybe by knowing it? Certainly there were signs along the way as there had been stations along the way where I should or could have realized that I was being indoctrinated like so many millions who believed Hitler was their god, their savior. Was I the fool, a word that came to me often? Yes, this is how I felt, like a fool, a stupid fool, one who should have, despite my being young, awakened much sooner to the Nazi propaganda. But I didn't, and thus knew I would have to live with guilt for the rest of my life over what I had done. No one would ever forgive me, and worst of all, I could never forgive myself.

Sometimes I remembered what that man on the train had said, "God bless you and your family," but I still did not see how God could help me. If there was a god, I wondered how He could have let so many die in the war, especially Jews that He must have hated. But more important, for what I had done, I knew that any god must hate me, and if I ever decided to turn to Him, I would be turned away on the spot.

BOOK IV

BOOK IV

CHAPTER TEN

Station: Berlin, Germany (1947–1951)

Wilhelm was never far from my thoughts during these days, but then a new man came into my life, one who would cause me to think about the world in a different way.

In early 1948, a girlfriend of mine introduced me to an American soldier from the San Francisco area named Jonas. He was a nice young man, but I was not especially attracted to him to begin with. What I liked though was his brown hair and brown eyes just like Wilhelm had. Jonas worked out and liked to have me grab his arm so I could feel the muscles. He was extremely polite, and I felt safe with him.

Jonas was kind of shy, didn't have much to say, but he was the first GI that I had met, and that was exciting to me. It offered me an opportunity to practice English. At first, while I was still living with my parents in Wilhelmshorst, he met me at the train station in West Berlin. We went to see movies on the American compound or went walking and sometimes stopped at a cafe. I enjoyed the movies more than anything because it helped me to learn more about the US.

One evening, holding hands turned to kissing and then more. It was kind of fun, but it was also somewhat scary for me. After all, I had always learned from my mother that sex was dirty and could get me in trouble. But things moved pretty quickly, and Jonas and I wanted to spend more time together. I asked my parents if I could rent a room closer in West Berlin. They agreed.

One night, when we were standing in the doorway, kissing each other goodnight, we got carried away. Within minutes, as Jonas held me tight, I had sex for the first time. I knew it was wrong to have sex before marriage, but I could not help myself. I was looking for love, perhaps in the wrong place, but it was love, something I felt was lacking from my parents even though I did know they loved me. I should have waited but couldn't do so.

Instead, I was excited, but I didn't really understand at that moment what had happened to me, what the sex was all about. Later in my room alone, I saw blood on my underwear. It made me feel both sad and scared. Sad because this special event in my life hadn't been at all what I had hoped it would be, and scared because I knew I had done something bad and would maybe be pregnant. I had also been told that no man would marry a woman that wasn't a virgin. Later, Jonas found a room for us in a house owned by Karl and Marguerite where he could stay longer at night until he had to go back to the barracks. How inexperienced both Jonas and I were, but our loving each other was quite special. He had quite a sexual appetite but had the negatives of a male who was more interested in his pleasure than mine.

After my parents moved to Malchow and while I was seeing Jonas, I visited them often. I brought back strawberries or other fruits to sell on the black market for good money. On my way back from one of my trips, I had to stay overnight at a hotel in a small town to wait for my train connection the following morning. In the middle of the night, there was a knock, and I got up and opened the door without turning on the lights or asking who was there. It was the police. They asked what my business was, and I told them about the strawberries and the visit to my parents. After checking my papers, they reprimanded me for opening the door without knowing who was there, and that was all. How relieved I was. I didn't realize until I turned the lights on that they could have seen the picture of Jonas in his uniform on the nightstand. What trouble I could have been in since German girls were still forbidden to see GIs. People were taken away for much lesser offenses than that, and often they were not seen for years, or they never came back.

Soon Jonas and I, probably more me, started talking about marriage. I thought it would be the natural thing to do, and in the back of my mind, I thought I better marry him since maybe it would turn out to be true that no man would marry me since I wasn't a virgin. I knew my parents didn't approve of my lifestyle with Jonas, and I was happy when he asked them for my hand in marriage. They had come to visit

URSULA MARTENS AND MARK SHAW

Evie and especially their little grandson. We had a small engagement party, and I remember how hesitant Jonas was when he put a ring on my finger. But I didn't care because my heart was fluttering the whole time. Other girls my age were getting married and now I was. And I would be going to America. This gave me goose bumps when I thought about it.

After we were engaged, Jonas and I visited Evie in Wilhelmshorst often. What a chance Jonas took to travel in his uniform into the Russian-occupied territory. Weeks later, he got his orders to be shipped home to California. I was sad, but I knew it was going to be just a little while until I would see him again. At that time, I knew of other German girls that were also going to marry American GIs.

After Jonas was gone, I started writing him daily letters telling him how very much I missed him and how I could hardly wait to see him again. Weeks passed and I didn't get any answers. I was getting worried, and then one day, I started getting my letters back in bundles. On the outside it was written "Address Unknown" or "Not at this address." I was devastated to think that my beloved Jonas was abandoning me, that I had been used for sex, used again by people who thought I was a fool. Evie still lived near me, but no one could really understand what I was going through. When I told my parents what had happened, they were not sorry it had occurred. But I cried and cried some more, wondering what I had done wrong. I felt like such a fool again. Then I buried the hurt inside where all the guilt I had over being a member of the Nazis was buried. That was in a dark part of my soul, one scarred in so many ways.

After my disappointing love affair with Jonas, it took a while for me, now eighteen years old in 1947, to even talk to a man. I was sure never going to fall in love again. Then one winter evening, as I was waiting for a bus, a GI walked by. He looked at me, and as I turned away, he said, "Gerda?" I turned back to him, slightly annoyed, and said with a stern face, "No, I'm not your Gerda!" There was something about him since I don't think I had ever seen a sharper looking soldier. He stood tall and proud, and his dark eyes looked at me in a special way. We stepped on the bus together, and he introduced himself as Frank.

We started talking, and hit it off right from the start. I found out that he was of Mexican descent and was a sergeant in the American army. He had been stationed in the south of Germany for a long time and hadn't been in Berlin for long. We started dating the following day, and it felt good to have someone in my life again. The sexual attraction between us was stronger than I had experienced with Jonas. At first I didn't know what he was talking about, but soon he said he liked my plainness. In Berlin at that time, most young girls wore makeup, at least lipstick. I was plain, very, very naive, and much too trusting. But Frank cared about me, and I needed someone to care about me after Jonas had left me cold. Even though Jonas had left me standing, I had sex with Frank. Had I learned my lesson? Hopefully Frank would marry me and then everything would be okay.

Through Frank, the young woman who had believed in the master race, the one who was certain only those of Aryan blood should be part of the future of Germany, the one who looked down on Jews, minorities, and sickly people as being worthless, heard about the same sort of bias and prejudice in the American army. Often, Frank complained about his superiors treating him unfairly. At the time, I thought one soldier was like the next and that all had fought the war side by side, but Frank explained to me that it wasn't the same, that even though he and his sisters had been born, raised, and educated in Arizona, they still had difficulties with racial prejudice.

More than anything, Frank was angry at what he called the system. Even using the name Frank instead of his birth name Manuel, he explained, didn't help much. He also said he was always defending his comrades who didn't speak or understand English as well as he did. He also said the white soldiers didn't like to be around the black soldiers. He said they didn't have any choice, but they resented the blacks being anything like equal.

Being involved with Frank made me think about something else for the first time. The war had been over now almost three years, and I had done some thinking. Because of my being in the Hitler Youth and supporting the Nazi cause, I felt that the rest of my life would be spent proving to myself and others that I was no longer a Nazi, no longer a racist or a bigot. Surely by falling in love with someone that was of a different race, a race that was thought of by some people in this world as inferior, I could show that world that my prejudicial days were over. Certainly I liked, maybe even loved, Frank, but I had to admit he was a symbol of what I wanted, a minority so that I could give myself the feeling that no more of the Nazi ways were in my blood. I know this may sound stupid, but this is how I felt. I guess I still had a lot of growing up to do, but loving Frank the Mexican American made me feel better about myself.

Just when I thought I might have found my true love, disappointment kept me up at night worrying. Soon after we started dating, I found out that there were other girls in Frank's life. I also found out that he had fathered a child while being stationed in the south of Germany. My illusion of having found true love crumbled. Then one night, he was angry with his superiors when he came to see me, and he didn't return to his company for two nights. I didn't understand the rules very well, but I knew Frank was in trouble.

Something had happened, but I wasn't sure what. Frank finally did go back to the barracks, but I didn't see him for a few weeks. I found out that he had been in a fight and had to serve time in the stockade. He was also stripped of his rank and demoted to private. When I saw him, he told me, "I am never going to go back. I will stay in Germany for the rest of my life." We talked about the dangers that the military might cause when the MPs caught up with him since he was AWOL. He knew he might go to jail, but he didn't care. This made me frightened for him, but also frightened of him since he was angry all the time. I said, "The MP is going to catch up with you." But I knew that he would not listen to me, and I was scared, very scared every time there was a knock at our door or I saw American soldiers anywhere. But I couldn't leave Frank and be a failure a second time with a man that I thought I loved.

Regardless, I had nothing of value left to trade on the black market in exchange for food, and Frank and I, as hard as it was later to believe, started to be like criminals. We had to move from one rented room to another as the landladies got suspicious. Mostly we rented from women that had lost husbands in the war, and to get by, they rented rooms to American GIs. I hated this, but Frank told me it was all right, and somehow I believed him.

At night, Frank left, and he didn't come back until hours later. He brought back food and things to sell on the black market. Mostly it was army stuff like blankets, boots, and fatigues. His buddies were helping him. During the day, he dressed in civilian clothes, and at night, he wore army fatigues. We had to eat in restaurants that served meals in secret back rooms for a lot of money.

A few months passed, and I didn't get my period. I finally went to the doctor and found out that I was over three months pregnant.

I thought the world was coming to an end. How could I ever tell my parents? It would break their hearts for sure. A few days after I found out, I started bleeding. The doctor admitted me to the hospital, and I had a miscarriage. Frank visited me there, and said, "You killed my baby." I felt so cheap, so used, and I hated Frank for what he said. Most of all, I wondered if I was being punished for being a Nazi or for having sex before marriage.

While all this occurred, my parents had visited and were staying with Evie. I will never forget the hurt look in their eyes when they found out I had a miscarriage. I caused them so much pain that it seemed like they were aging right in front of my eyes. But at least they did not find out that Frank was in trouble for going AWOL, and I was relieved when they returned to Malchow a few days later without learning that he was on the run from the army.

Our secret life continued a few more days until one day, two rough-looking MPs knocked at our front door. Apparently our landlady had turned Frank in. The two men took me instead to the company commander. I lied and said that I didn't know where Frank was. The commander made me promise to turn him in the moment I saw him, and he let me go.

I was so confused as to what to do, but that evening, Frank said he had an idea. He told me that all I had to do was involve one of the guys at the black market in a conversation, and he would do the rest. I didn't want to do it because I felt he was up to no good. Most of the men dealing at the black market were from displacement camps not far from us. They were people that had been freed and were waiting to be relocated. He said I had to do it for "us," and I finally agreed.

At the black market, I was approached by a short man, not much older than me. He asked if I wanted to see a watch he was selling. I said yes, and as he opened his bag, I saw Frank come up from behind him with a heavy stick in his hands. The shocked look in my eyes must have given me away, and the guy ducked just as Frank swung the club. The man ran in one direction, hollering, and we ran in the other. We got home, and I cried and cried. What an outcome this could have had! Frank could have killed the man. How much lower was I going to fall? I hated myself and what I had become. I was more ashamed of that than I had been even being a Nazi. At least I thought I was.

URSULA MARTENS AND MARK SHAW

Later that week, Frank was picked up in the streets. I was tired of running and just stayed in the room. The German police arrived and arrested me for hiding an AWOL soldier. They were tough on Frank because of his earlier trouble, and he was sentenced to seven years of hard labor. Later, he wrote a letter from Folsom Prison in California to me. By then he had lost whatever hold he had on me, and I wrote back and said that I wanted nothing to do with him any longer. But he sent one last letter threatening to come after me as soon as he could. He said he had learned from the Germans to "Cool it until you get strong again. Then strike back."

The moment I was taken into custody by the police, I realized that their treatment was not going to be the same than that of the military police. From the start, I was treated like a criminal who in their eyes was also a whore. I was locked up immediately with no opportunity to talk to anyone. I found myself in a four-by-eight cell, furnished with a small cot, a toilet, and a washbasin without running water. The small, barred window was up high under the ceiling. This was the worst since no one in our family had ever been locked up for anything. I felt like an outcast, so ashamed.

That evening as I lay on the cot, covered with an old army blanket and a lumpy pillow behind my head, I felt like a kitten that in Malchow we had stuffed into a sack and tied up with a rope so there was no escape before we drowned the kitten in the lake since there were too many to be fed. I was nineteen years old in 1948, but I had never felt so small, so alone and forsaken.

The following day I was sentenced and taken to juvenile facilities. My sentence was to spend three months there, and in addition, I was going to be on probation until my twenty-fifth birthday. The huge building I was taken to looked like a school from the outside. A tall fence surrounded it, and the gate was guarded. The smell was awful in there. There were girls of all ages. Some were underage prostitutes. Others just had no other place to be. Many of the younger ones were war orphans. Hearing their stories made me feel sad again, guilty over being part of the Nazis. Depression set in. I felt like a real lowlife. I had trouble eating and sometimes chewed on my fingernails so much they bled. Yes, I was a whore, I decided, a dirty whore.

It did not take long for my survival instinct to kick in at the juvenile facility. I followed orders and did as I was told. Also, I stayed away from troublemakers. Soon I was assisting the teachers with the caretaking of the younger kids. The teacher let me stay in her living quarters, and I did not have to take meals that were served on long tables with the other girls. I think I was thought of as an employee by most of them. This made my three-month confinement go by fast, and I enjoyed being needed. When I left, I considered returning as caretaker.

Most of all, being locked up for three months made me really stop and think about who I was and what I was doing with my life. I had made so many mistakes, but I was determined to do better. Upon my release, I found a room for rent. Now I had to go about building my life again after having fallen down in so many respects.

The war may have been over, but Berlin was still a war zone. This was especially true in what was called East Berlin, the Eastern Zone. The Russians did not bother to do any rebuilding, and thus nothing was repainted or kept up. Bombed buildings were never repaired, just left in that sorry state. The east was a constant reminder of the war, while the Allies worked hard to transform West Berlin into the fine city it once was. Separation between the east and west broadened as time passed. The division was really final when the Berlin Wall was erected.

Besides finding a new room, a job at a sewing factory appeared when I learned about it from an employment office. What a blessing this turned out to be. It was certainly what I would later look at as a life-changing moment, one that headed me in the right direction after so much turmoil and craziness in my life.

My boss, Mr. Behling, was a well-known designer in Berlin. I learned things that helped me understand the construction of designer dresses. I wasn't allowed to actually work on a sewing machine because I had not been formally trained and had no degree. At the time, those were the laws in Germany. But I was able to do handwork, and while doing that, I also answered the phones. During several seasons, I was allowed to help with the dresses for the new showings. And since I was a perfect size, as Mr. Behling noted, I was also the one to try them on while they were being constructed. I made several friends working there, and we went swimming, dancing, to the movies, and did winter sports together.

Ruth, one of the girls who worked with me, became an especially good friend. In the spring of 1948 while the flowers bloomed and soft rain made them grow, I reluctantly agreed to attend a party Ruth invited me to. She had lived in South America for a while and spoke Spanish fluently. I knew that several soldiers of Latin American descent were gathering in her house almost daily. She said there would be guitar music and that there was one man in particular, Merardo, that she wanted me to meet. I went, and she introduced me to what I thought was the handsomest man I had ever seen. He was very polite and seemed to be a gentle man as well. When he played guitar and sang, it seemed like it was just for me, and he sang himself into my heart that very evening. Two of the songs were called "Bésame Mucho" ("Kiss Me a Lot") and "You Belong to My Heart." I did belong to his heart from that moment on.

Soon Merardo and I were a steady couple and decided to live together. Once again I was wary of having sex with a man whom I was not married to. But being with Merardo felt like we were married, and I truly believed that this time, the third time around, would truly be a charm. Perhaps I was being naive again, but I sorely wanted a man to love me, and Merardo showed me so much love.

Merardo knew a German family that was renting rooms. Mr. and Mrs. Matke had a large apartment, and sometimes there were as many as four young people living with them. They were an elderly couple, and after Mr. Matke died, his wife made a living renting the extra rooms. She was like a surrogate mother to us. Her advice was always good, and we spent many happy hours around the kitchen table drinking delicious American coffee and playing the Canasta card game.

After a while, I was able to obtain a permit for my parents to return to West Berlin since they had lived there before. Just about that time, a room became available at Mrs. Matke's, and I rented it for my parents. They were so grateful to me for having made it possible for them to live in the west. This was a dream for most Germans living in Communist East Germany. Helping my parents, having a good job, and now loving Merardo made me feel better about myself. Finally, I was turning my life around as I left my years as a teen behind and became a twenty-year-old.

During the blockade of Berlin in 1949, Merardo was on full alarm, and therefore we were not able to see each other a great deal. At first, there were some scary hours. All of us in the west-occupied zones feared that our supplies would be cut off. Everyone was relieved when, several hours after the complete closing of the border, American planes supplied the large city with everything we needed. We called it the *luftbrücke*, or bridge through the air. It lasted more than 450 days, more than a year, and life went on without interruptions in our daily routine. Thank goodness for the Americans. They saved us.

Merardo and I spent all our free time together. On weekends, we visited clubs with friends or watched American movies. Since the Cold War was on, we got to see many famous entertainers from the US that came to entertain the troops. We even had the chance to see Sugar Ray Robinson in a championship fight. The German contender was well liked by the crowd, but he lost to the much-better black fighter. The mostly German crowd became very unruly at the decision. They booed and threw bottles and other stuff toward the ring. I was ashamed of my fellow citizens. I also felt embarrassed when Sugar Ray had to take cover under the ring to protect himself, but worst of all was hearing the racial slurs being shouted at the black man. But then I remembered how I had shouted "Jew" at kids at school we didn't like to get them to leave. Was I any different than those German fans?

What happened also reminded me of when in 1936 Jesse Owens had been booed by people and chastised by Hitler when the American runner won the Olympic races. I thought what he had done was right and now I was condemning the same thing. This made me understand that I still had a lot to learn, so much to learn.

During the evening hours, Merardo and I took long walks or visited with friends. We didn't have any worries and got along well with each other. One Sunday evening after dinner with my parents, when we were alone in our room, Merardo asked, "Honey, how you would like to live in the US?" Live in the US? This was almost everyone's dream, and I quickly answered, "I would like that very much, and I am sure I will make you happy." We held each other so tight, and that evening our lovemaking was extra special because now I knew that our being together had been like husband and wife just before it occurred.

I knew Merardo adored me, and I was sure I was in love with him. The following day, I went to the American consulate to apply for a visa. At that time, each country had a set amount of people from each country that were allowed to emigrate to the US. A number system was set up, and a person had to wait until his or her number was called. Sometimes, it could take years. America was the place of hope for a democratic new life that everyone longed for.

Since my parents liked Merardo from the start, all of us spent many an evening together playing cards. Later he was invited to family activities like parties at Heinz's parents' house. Everyone respected him, and family members were anxious to talk with him. He was always the center of attention. I never felt they were looking down at him and can only guess that they, like many Germans, wanted to make up for their failures, or at least make an effort to get to know what had once been the enemy. For me, I loved Merardo first and because he was a minority a distant second. But once again, the thought that maybe my being with him showed I was no longer a filthy Nazi who hated minorities came to mind. It had to since I so wanted to lose that Nazi identity that had caused me to hate and hate and hate some more.

My parents knew Merardo stayed with me until he had to be back at the base late at night or early in the morning, but we never talked about it. It was 1949 now, I was twenty years old, and still the talk about "the birds and the bees" with Mother had never come up. But just being with my parents and helping them along a bit was quite calming and permitted a bit of forgiveness for my troubles with the miscarriage and the troubles with Frank leading to my being locked up.

All appeared well, and then a shocker occurred when Merardo's orders to return to the US came across quite suddenly. There was very little time left for us, and when he tried to put in an application to marry me, he was told there wasn't enough time to take that route. The only other was to proceed through regular immigration channels, and we knew that it would be months or maybe even years before we could see one another again. Saying good-bye was hard for both of us, and I cried for days after he left, but love letters across the ocean kept us in touch. I tried to keep busy with work, but still, I couldn't help getting lonely, and I began to lose hope. Was I about to encounter another "Jonas" debacle where I was abandoned? At least this time, my letters weren't marked "Addressee Unknown" but instead answered with Merardo's loving ways.

The consulate took several months to inform me that my number to emigrate to the US had come up. The memory of Jonas's betrayal was still on my mind, even though I was sure that Merardo really did love me. Hadn't he been very sincere all along? As the weeks passed without any progress at the consulate, my parents started preparing me for the possibility that maybe a move to America was not in my future.

While I waited and waited as the year turned to 1950, and then waited some more, some good news came our way. An order had been passed that the government employees that had been let go had to be rehired because the political reason for their termination had been in violation of their contracts. Father was elated, and it was only a matter of time until he was finally working once again. This permitted him some self-worth, and I noticed that he smiled again, something missing for a very long time.

My parents suggested that it was time for me to think about a future in Germany. They thought it would be a good choice to start learning the banking business. How little they knew me. There was no way I could picture myself working in an office all day. But it had been many months since Merardo had left, and they were worried about me. I kept putting them off, believing that one day I would be joining him in America.

Temptation to forget Merardo occurred one day when I felt especially lonely. A friend of mine asked me to join her and her boyfriend for an evening on the town. We went to a nightclub, well known because of colorful, dancing waters on the stage, and telephones at each table. It was sort of a tourist attraction, with people of all nationalities. Soon after we arrived, we had a call to our table from a German man named Gerhard. After we talked a while, he asked if he could join us at our table, and we invited him over. I found out he was an attorney doing his internship while living with his parents. After we talked on the telephone almost daily, we started dating. Sometimes he invited me to watch him in court where he was a judge in training. His knowledge of the law impressed me. We got along well and had a good time together, and when I introduced him to my parents, they liked him very much. I still loved Merardo, but not seeing him for such a long time was hard on me.

When I received the long awaited letter with an appointment date for an interview at the consulate as the year turned to 1951, I was so happy that I didn't notice my parents' sadness. No one was going to put a damper on my excitement. Gerhard knew then that I was not going to be in his life much longer. He did not give up hope though. He kept thinking that I might come back and stayed in touch with my mother for years after I was gone.

I visited the consulate for interviews, medical examination, and all the other formalities needed to emigrate to the US. One large obstacle was my criminal record from the incident with Frank where I was locked up for hiding him during his AWOL escapade. I requested a full pardon. My parents were my witnesses at the hearing, and they testified that I had been underage at the time and that I was completely under Frank's control. My hands were trembling when it was time for a decision, but then a US commissioner granted the pardon much to my relief.

During one of the personal interviews at the consulate, I was questioned for an extralong time by a new embassy official named Mr. Restum. But rather than focusing on my crime, Mr. Restum, blonde and blue-eyed just like proper Aryan was supposed to be, wanted to know if I was aware that by marrying a US citizen of Mexican descent, I could experience much hardship in America. I knew from other applicants who were also leaving for the US that only one personal interview was normally given, yet I was asked by the same interviewer to come to the consulate again and again. One day, he showed me an article in *Life Magazine* headlined "The Forgotten People." It was about Mexicans that were living in poverty along the border in the area where El Paso, Texas, Merardo's home, was located. I never mentioned this to my parents because I knew they were already trying to make me change my mind. I wasn't going to do so no matter what, and the interviewer made me more certain than ever that I wanted to be with Merardo.

When the visa finally came through, the time had come to leave on my new adventure. I had a smile on my face a mile long. My parents invited some friends over, and we had a small party. I could tell they were both happy and sad since they hated to see me go. To them, America seemed as far away as the moon, and they wondered if they would ever see me again.

When the day arrived for my trip, Mother and Father took me to the airport so I could fly to the country that not so long before had been an enemy of Hitler's Third Reich. Growing up, I couldn't have imagined such a thing since even to think about that would have caused me to be a traitor to Hitler. Now a few short years later, I had disavowed him as my god, turned my back on the swastika and the Nazis, and was headed for what I had read was called the land of the free. I certainly wasn't free, but I hoped to be someday as my wounded soul experienced the new adventures in America.

While we waited for me to leave at the airport, I remember Father's last advice was "Stay busy so you won't get homesick." True to our family's reserved fashion, there were no tearful good-byes. Just a quick hug, some nervous small talk, and off I went. Part of me was terrified at the thought of flying to another continent. I had wanted a more loving hug and some reassurance that everything was going to be the way I had planned and that I would find happiness. I knew they wished me well, but it must not have been easy to see their daughter move so far away and into uncertainty.

It was my first time to fly in an airplane. It was not a jet plane but one with four propellers. Before long, I got terribly airsick and remained so for the rest of my flight. My face was almost the color of the green suit I was wearing, and I must have been in bad shape because the flight attendant put an oxygen mask on me. She came to ask me in English every few minutes how I was doing and whether I needed anything. I answered her back in English, and that was the end of my talking German for a long time. Nothing helped me to feel any better until we landed at the international airport in New York City. By the time I transferred to a bus that would take me to the domestic airport, I was feeling better and even exchanged a few words with other passengers.

The view of New York City was not what I had expected. From the bus we took to the national airport, I could see buildings were covered all over with graffiti, more than I had ever seen in all my life. It was disappointing, but I hoped things would be better once I got to El Paso. No matter; finally being in America made me smile so much. I was finally in the United States. I had to pinch myself to believe it.

During the continuing flight, sickness overcame me again. But when one of the engines started smoking, and I saw small flames erupting from the wing, I was certain I was going to die. Perhaps this would be my ultimate punishment for my bad deeds as a Hitler Youth, a supporter of Hitler the monster who orchestrated the worst mass murder in history through burnings, gassings, starvation, shootings, and other atrocities. Maybe the god who must hate me was going to end it all for me. Maybe He was upset that I said "Jesus is a Jew. Jesus is a Jew. Jesus is a Jew" to Mrs. Pabst. This was contrary to a prayer I said when I was only four, "Dear God, I am little, my heart is pure. No one but Jesus may live in it." Later, I heard that some mothers changed the prayer to read, "Dear God, I am little, my heart is pure. No one but Hitler may live in it."

The airplane staff assured us that everything was under control and that we would land at the next airport that was only seconds away. In the condition that I was in, I did not care. I just wanted to die. The plane made an emergency landing, and we were delayed many hours. I don't remember where we were, just that the land, as far as I could see, was totally flat with one thimble-looking mountain in the background.

To calm everyone and to provide some nourishment, we were given some sandwiches on bread that tasted like cardboard. Other passengers were so kind and came up to me to ask how I was feeling. It surprised me how friendly everyone was. I was in the land that everyone I knew dreamed of coming to, and I could hardly contain my feelings. I hadn't seen Merardo for more than six months. I wondered. Did he change? Does he still love me? Do I still love him? What about the guilt that was still embedded deep within me? Could I discover a new life that might set me free from all the guilt and shame I felt?

CHAPTER ELEVEN

Station: El Paso, Texas (1952–1960)

As the airplane hovered over the city of El Paso, my stomach was full of butterflies. Here I was twenty-three years old and about to land in Texas, a state I had only seen on maps. That same year, 1952, was one when the United States Senate ratified the peace treaty with Japan, *The Diary of Anne Frank* was published, there were eight million refugees inside the West German borders, and war hero General Dwight D. Eisenhower was elected president of the United States.

Previously I had wanted Adolf Hitler and Germany to destroy the US and all its Allies that were trying to keep my beloved Nazis from restoring Germany to its rightful place as a country of honor, one that dominated the world, and perpetuated a master race that would rule for centuries to come. At Hitler Youth meetings, I had pledged allegiance to helping this occur, to being devoted to my god Hitler while looking the other way when there were clues that Jews and others were being tortured and killed in inhuman ways. The guilt I felt over behaving as I had was still imprinted inside my belly, but now I had a chance to discover a new land with a new husband and new people. But this made me feel shaky, and my breath was short as the plane's tires skidded to a halt on the runway. I was in America, for how long I did not know, but I was finally in America, the land of many people's dreams and my own.

The first surprise occurred when I realized the airport was miles away from the city. The second occurred when I was hit by a wall of hot air. It was past midnight, but the heat was almost unbearable. When I entered the terminal, my eyes scanned the small crowd, but Merardo was nowhere to be seen. Had he given up on me when my plane was delayed? Was he going to stand me up like Jonas, having had a change of heart? Didn't he love me anymore?

A third surprise happened when I noticed that I was just about the only white person standing near the luggage area since everyone else was dark-skinned, Mexican, or Mexican American I guessed. I heard no English being spoken as families embraced each other while I stood along knowing no one. It was hot and stuffy, and my wool suit with velvet trim made me feel even hotter. I had chosen it to look good for Merardo, but now I looked foolish among all the others who wore short sleeves.

After my luggage was by my side, I felt lost since Merardo was still nowhere to be seen. My face was all sweaty, and I finally left the luggage area and walked into the lobby. Merardo did not have a telephone, so I decided to find a taxi to take me to him. Twenty-three dollars was all that I had left over from the plane fare that Merardo had sent to Berlin. Would that buy me a way to his house in the taxi?

My face must have made me look like a lost child, both from the hot temperature and from worry. I searched my purse for Merardo's last letter with his return address on the envelope. There was a white man with wavy hair similar to Merardo's standing next to a taxi, and he looked at the envelope. I had been practicing my English for some time, and I understood that he was asking me if I wanted to go to the address. I nodded, and then he shook his head and put my suitcases in the taxi trunk.

During the bumpy ride, the driver asked me where I was from. I told him that I had come from Germany to be with my fiancé, and from then on he was very nice. He had been stationed in West Germany, he told me, and he had even remembered a few German words. As the meter came closer and closer to $23, the areas we drove through were getting shabbier and shabbier even though it was dark. The streetlights made it possible for me to see, and El Paso was unlike any city I had ever seen. We drove past apartment houses with the stairwells on the outside, and the gentle wind was blowing the drapes, tied in knots, outside the windows. Finally, we stopped in front of an apartment building. What a sight. From the streetlight in front of the building, I could see the cracked walls in need of paint. The driver asked me to wait while he went in to take a look. The streets were mostly deserted at this time of the night. Only cars were passing, and they seemed huge compared to the ones I had seen in Germany. When he returned, the driver said that my fiancé had moved out, but someone in the building had given him a new address. It wasn't long until we came to an area that he said was called the city projects.

At least this place was an improvement over the other neighborhoods we had passed. The buildings looked new and were built out of brick. There was even some landscaping outside. The driver stopped and again asked me to wait. My legs were trembling, and I was biting my fingernails as I waited to see what was going to happen. What if Merardo had changed his mind and didn't want me anymore? What would I do alone in America with no money and no one I knew?

After a few minutes the man returned, followed by Merardo and a dark-haired woman I assumed to be his mother. In my excitement I could not help noticing how much darker he was than I had remembered. But I found out later that living in the hot Texas sun changed everyone's color. He was dressed in a white shirt and slacks, and his hair had grown longer. I had never seen him in civilian clothes before. He introduced me to his mother, Vicenta. Then he hugged and kissed me and explained that he was told at the airport that the plane was not expected until the following morning. With that, he paid the nice taxi driver some more money and held my hand as his mother kept saying hello to me.

Vicenta walked slightly bent over. But her wrinkled face had a kind smile. That first evening, while she was fixing some food for us, she kept asking me things, and I did not understand a word she said. She spoke very little English, and I spoke no Spanish.

The two-bedroom apartment was sparsely furnished, but it seemed new and clean. Everything was built in concrete without wood trim anywhere. A few days later, I found out the reason for the seamless construction. Merardo explained that Vicenta had come from Mexico with Merardo's older brother and her brother when she was very young. She supported herself by cleaning houses, mostly for white people. Merardo was born a few years later in El Paso. Vicenta had worked hard all her life, raising the two boys without a husband. The oldest had succumbed to TB while Merardo was in the army. Vicenta was a religious woman and never missed mass. A small Bible was her constant companion as it had been for Tante. She asked if I had one, and I said

I did not. God may still have been chasing me, but He had not caught me yet.

Even though Merardo appeared excited and happy to see me, he seemed a little distant. Was it just my imagination? I wondered. We settled down and talked for a while, and later when we were alone, as he was holding me, he suddenly asked, "Have you been true to me while I was gone?" I asked him, "What are you trying to say?" He went to a cupboard and came back with a letter. He did not want to show me the letter, but finally, he did and when I read it, it said that I had not been true, that I had seen other men. It was signed "a friend." Tears began to slip down my cheeks, but then I noticed there was something familiar about the handwriting on the envelope. The address was written in the same handwriting as the letter, and there was a return address in Germany. All at once I realized who this letter was from, and I shouted out, "My mother wrote this!" Merardo jumped back when I said this, and then I explained that she had written it hopefully to make him not want to be with me anymore. I told him I was so sorry he had received the letter, but that what my mother had written was false. She and Father wanted me to stay in Germany, and so she wrote the letter. Later, she admitted that Gerhard, the lawyer who liked me in Germany, had a hand in the deception, and for months, I was so mad at her for what she had done. Luckily, Merardo seemed to understand, and when he held me in his arms, everything seemed to be okay.

Of first importance was what to wear in the new, hot climate. When I opened my suitcase, Merardo and Vicenta looked at me like I was an idiot. I had brought fancy dresses, gowns, and cocktail dresses, and worst of all, two fur coats. None could be worn in sweaty El Paso. They thought I was crazy when I said the first thing I wanted to do was go to the post office and send all my wardrobe back to Germany. But they took me, and I did. What a bad start I had; such a dumb girl I was.

For the next weeks, homemaking was my goal, and I ventured out to get to know the stores in the area. At first, it was fun to decorate my first home, but Vicenta soon put a damper on my shopping sprees. She had always been very poor and saw no need for what she called fancy things. Vicenta felt, for instance, that if there were three people in the household, there was no need for a complete set of dishes. It was the start of many an argument in the house over my extravagance. Merardo was always in the middle, trying to please both of us. In all fairness to Vicenta, the money we, or mostly I, spent was the money that was sent to her by the army as Merardo's dependent. She could have used it for herself, but instead gave it to her son. I'm sure sometimes, in our eagerness to be right, things were said out of anger or because we did not understand each other. After all, our conversations were in English and Spanish, languages that did not fit together well.

A few days after I arrived in El Paso, another big surprise occurred one evening when we entered the apartment. When I turned on the light, what seemed like thousands of roaches scurried all over, trying to find any cracks to hide in. I let out a scream that could be heard for miles as Merardo and Vicenta tried to calm me down. They did but not much.

I later found out they were called German cockroaches, but I had never seen them in all my life. I wanted to call an exterminator, but Vicenta said no. She didn't seem too much bothered by them. I knew I had a major cleaning job for the next few days as I was determined to exterminate every cucaracha, as she called them, from our apartment. But then, a few mornings later, when I turned on the small oven, to bake some biscuits, I looked down toward my feet, and there were roaches all over, escaping from the heat. I jumped and screamed while realizing I had overlooked another breeding ground.

Two months after my arrival in El Paso, Merardo and I were married. The ceremony was performed by a justice of the peace, with only a couple of Merardo's friends and Vicenta as witnesses. Later there was a party at a cousin's house. Even though it was a nice celebration, everything, especially the food, was very strange to me. By then I missed the German cooking and couldn't get used to the spicy chili that we had for many meals. I enjoyed the music even though it was unlike the music back home. Everyone spoke Spanish except the younger high school age kids. And there were plenty of kids, running around like wild people with no discipline. I never did remember all their names, but they sure were having fun.

Finally marrying Merardo made me feel better, and a bit more secure since now I did not think he would send me back to Germany if he was angry or Vicenta told him to. Deep inside, I also felt that being married to a minority meant the Nazism in me had been cleansed a bit since now I loved a minority instead of hating them as before. I wished others that knew me as a Nazi knew this had occurred, but they were

URSULA MARTENS AND MARK SHAW

back in Germany, and there was no way to tell him what had happened. Many times I looked at the small wedding band on my finger and felt good and determined to be the best wife I could be to the man who had brought me to America.

The delight I had in being in this new, strange land was lessened when I noticed the way people, especially white people, looked at Merardo and me when we were in stores or on the sidewalk, wherever. The Latinos in the area looked at me in a strange way, like I was from the moon, and sometimes I saw people shake their heads. But it was the white people who were the worst. When we were in a store, the white salespeople looked at us funny, like we had done something wrong. The same happened in restaurants. We had long waits, and when we were finally served, often our plates were slammed down on the table by the white waiters or waitresses. I knew Merardo was not the problem; it was me, and here I was experiencing the same sort of discrimination, racial to be more precise, that I had imposed on others in Germany while growing up. Like the Jews, the sick, the elderly, the gypsies, the refugees, all of them, I was now hated by those who thought I was stupid to be with a non-white person. The tables had been turned, and now I had to try to understand why people hated me for only one reason, because of my color, or lack thereof, and because I was mixing with someone who wasn't white. This confused me, made me wonder how white people could be prejudiced against other white people. To them I was what they called white trash, a step down, different somehow, a lower class. This reminded me of the days when Germans in my area of the country looked down on Germans from other areas like they were outcasts. Now I was an outcast.

When I sat on the bed in tears one night after I felt some people had made fun of me, I wondered whether this was payback for how I had treated those Jews and others in Germany. Was this god who Vicenta and Merardo worshipped showing me what it felt like to be hated? I finally assumed this was true and that I deserved everything that was happening to me. I was the strange one, I was the one that everyone despised, the one who should be cast aside or perhaps put in a camp so I would not contaminate the people around me. These uppity people felt they were a master race of some sort, and I was the outsider, the one who should be exterminated. When I talked to Merardo about this, he told me not to worry or let it bother me, but I was embarrassed for him and for me. On the other hand, I was ashamed of being German especially with those who hated what Hitler and the Nazis had done. Often I would lie and say I was Swedish.

Merardo had graduated from high school and was proud to have served his country during the Cold War and the blockade of Berlin. He had been somebody there, a successful boxer and a baseball pitcher on his battalion team. He had been respected and well liked, and he had many friends. Strangers on the street would call out to him with some encouraging comment on a fight or a baseball game. Now, back home, reality hit hard. He was still a Mexican, and things hadn't changed from him being looked upon by whites as a second-class citizen. He was one of the first non-whites to be hired by the gas company as a meter reader, and he did his job well. Still, when he asked a year later to be transferred to a better paying job, with more chances for advancement, he was told that he was lucky "his people" were even hired.

When we decided I needed to begin work, I saw an ad for jobs as a seamstress. Arriving at the jeans factory, I lined up with the many other women who wanted a job. A white woman with red hair walked outside. She wore a cotton sewing smock, and it had pockets full of swatches of fabric. She looked around and then began pointing at people to come into the factory. I couldn't believe it that she pointed at me, and I quickly walked inside where they hired me on the spot without even knowing if I had experience. Later, I became friendly with the supervisor who hired me. When I asked her why she had hired me over almost one hundred more experienced workers, she answered, "Look around. What do you see? Almost everyone is Latino, right? You wonder why we hired you."

I answered that I did not think that it was fair. "I am from New York," she said. "And for a long time there it was the Irish that were on the bottom of the pole. In every part of the country, it's another race. There's always someone on the bottom. That's just the way it is, and you or I can't change a thing about it."

When she said this, I wondered, *Now, I am with more people who are at the bottom whereas in Germany I was on top as an Aryan example.* None of this made any sense, but at least I understood better what it felt like to be singled out. I hated it that I was picked because I was white. That was not right, but I needed the job. So I kept quiet. It didn't take long before I was a forelady with good responsibilities. Merardo was very happy about that, but it still bothered me. Here I had been hired because I was white, a reminder that Jews were not permitted to work in Germany because they were Jews. No Mexicans or Mexican Americans were hired because they were Mexican or Mexican American. Stereotypes all around, but now I was favored because of my color, or lack of color really. This was very strange and made me think more about how I had treated others in Germany. I was so sorry about that, but I had no one to tell that I was sorry since I saw no Jews in El Paso.

Also, here I was in the country that I had believed to be fair and free of discrimination, and I found that even good people made derogatory remarks when they thought they were safe among their own people. I had left the Nazis in Germany, but some of their ideas were alive and well in Texas. For instance, police conducted sweeps through all the cities and towns where they stopped people, especially young women and asked for papers. How this reminded me of what had occurred in Germany when Jews endured the same treatment. *Perhaps at some point, women might be required to wear a yellow star,* I thought.

If the woman did not have proof of working through a work certificate and ration book, she was harassed, and police immediately determined that she was a prostitute. She was taken to jail or somewhere where she had a VD test, and all this was entered on her record. Such discrimination was a shock to me, and I hated it when Merardo's friends were picked up for no reason. But I was lucky since I had a job, and I was white, so I was left alone by the white authorities. This despite Vicenta believing I was a "stupid German girl," as she told Merardo and others.

Sometimes I had to remember what my mother always said, "Wenn man sein Bett gemacht hat muss man darin liegen"—"You lie in the bed you make." I did just that, and overall things went pretty well most of the time. There were so many new things to discover, like the huge grocery stores where you could buy anything. My school English wasn't too bad, but I had a hard time finding certain items, like spices and other specialties. I missed the German delicatessen and the fresh butter. Sometimes I opened butter wrappers to smell the butter, but it smelled awful to me. Since my mother-in-law spoke little English, she was of no help.

As time went by, we started to become very uncomfortable with each other. It made being with her awkward. She talked to me in Spanish, even though I couldn't understand what she was saying, and often I thought she sounded angry. Her bedroom was next to ours, and the wall shared a heating vent meaning she could hear everything from the next room. This certainly didn't add to the pleasure of our lovemaking.

A few months later, in the middle of 1953, when I found out that I was pregnant, Merardo and I were very happy. So was Vicenta, but she decided to move back to her old neighborhood. We were relieved, and Merardo and I got along much better by ourselves. I did not have to feel guilty anymore on Sunday mornings when Merardo accompanied her to church, and she would ask why I was not going. Back in Germany, to please Merardo, I had attempted to take lessons at a Catholic church and had talked to a priest about converting to Catholicism but I just couldn't do it. After Hitler, I had sworn to myself never to follow anyone blindly or believe in anything before studying the facts of it. I had too many unanswered questions, and the priest became frustrated with me. Such things as the Triune or the Holy Spirit or the Immaculate Conception, any real concept of any one god, meant nothing to me, and I figured I was going to be an atheist for life. Since Hitler had let me down, I didn't want to trust a new god and be let down again. I was better off, I believed, with no god. Vicenta and Merardo could not understand this, and even they could not persuade me to go to church and worship. This was despite my always recalling that time when the man on the train when we were fleeing from the Russians saying to me, "God bless you and your family," and my replying, "God bless you." I still did not understand why I had done that, but I didn't need God now, so I pushed Him aside.

Six weeks before the delivery date, I stopped working. The girls at the factory gave me a baby shower. I knew I was going to miss them. That weekend, Merardo and I were busy getting the room ready for our little baby. It was a lovely room, painted in soft green, and a pale salmon. Everything was just perfect, the little dressing table, the bassinet with a lacy skirt around it, and the chest of drawers full of baby clothes. Mother had sent me a whole layette for the baby. German baby clothes were so much more practical, yet they had blankets to wrap up the baby tightly so as not to be able to free the legs to kick and move freely. What a way to start life.

The next Monday, a bright sunny day in 1954, while cleaning the rest of the apartment, my water broke. When Merardo came home for lunch, he called the doctor, and within minutes, I was in the hospital. Even though there were no complications, I screamed my head off. I was scared, unprepared, and I kept recalling Evie's terrifying delivery. Hours later, our tiny daughter Maria was born, but I didn't get to see her until much later. She was six weeks premature and needed to be in an incubator for several days. To me she was a beautiful baby, with an olive color, just perfect. After a week, we took her home, and I learned how to take care of the little preemie. Every two hours, or less, she would wake and cry. I had pumped my breast milk while she was in the hospital so I was nursing and supplementing my own milk with formula. Sometimes I was so tired that I fell asleep feeding her while she continued growing ounce by ounce.

I hated it that I could not show the affection for Maria that I felt I should have, but I was never one to show much emotion. This was totally acceptable in German, and thus I never felt that anything was missing in my life. There was never any explanation for this; it was just the German way. No explanation was necessary.

After a few months as 1955 appeared, it became more and more difficult to survive on Merardo's salary. I was now twenty-six. Vicenta came during the week to babysit Maria while I was there. Slowly we saved money, and with the help of Merardo's GI loan, we were able to buy a small two-bedroom house. Relatives offered to add a room for Vicenta. They knew of Merardo's difficulty in making two women happy. Her room had a separate entrance, which allowed us our privacy. The cousins just showed up one Saturday morning with material and several helpers and started construction. I was very grateful to them. They showed me how to put a finish color stucco coat on the house, and we were able to finish the job under their expert supervision. Merardo did the front landscaping, and we planted small trees in the backyard. It was a very small, simple house, but it was ours. This made me feel special, and I sent pictures to my parents to show them everything was all right. I had forgiven Mother for writing the untrue letter and hoped she and Father might visit one day to see us and their grandchild. Maybe Evie could come too and the two children might play together.

The year 1956 brought television into our home. How excited we were when we purchased our first set. At first, the few available channels broadcast only a few hours a day. From the beginning, I was very much interested in watching the news. Especially the news about the rest of the country and the world. That's when we knew about the civil rights struggle that seemed to be occurring mostly in the southern states. At first, I did not think that it was something that should concern me a lot. After all, the laws had been changed, and rightly so. Laws had to be obeyed, and that was it. There was no doubt in my mind that what had happened in Germany had been wrong, very wrong. But the new laws did not concern me, and so I did not pay much attention to what was occurring even though some of the television images of police beating black demonstrators reminded me of the rail yard beatings of Jews that I saw. Later, my not caring as much as I should have bothered me because I realized that I was still not sensitive to how other people were treated. I was still caught up in my own world, and that disappointed me.

At the same time Maria was born, my gray tabby cat Mitzie had kittens. While living at the projects, I had found her as a furrow kitten that was living with others off the trashcans. It was her first litter, and she was just as scared as I had been. Her first two kittens were born right on my lap while I was sitting on the sofa. I hurriedly got a towel to put under her, and when we got up the next morning, she had a total litter of six. I had fixed a nice box for them, but the mother decided she wanted to keep her kittens in the baby carriage. We'd remove them, but that's where we found them again every morning. Finally, we put the carriage in a closet at night. This made Merardo, me, and even Vicenta laugh. We needed some laughter in our lives.

Having a child was like a dream. When I held Maria, I just kept looking at her face and touching her to make sure she was real. I was a mother now, and I was determined to hold her and hug her and kiss her and not be like Mother, who rarely did any of those things. I had a precious gift, and I spent every moment I could with Maria as she began to grow up.

I could also show love in another way. After we bought the house, I was able to have my first dog Nicky. Later on, a black cocker spaniel named Toby became his companion. I always rescued pets from then on, and I remember all of them fondly. When I was a kid, I thought about becoming a veterinarian and while I gave no thought to this now, I still loved the animals from the days of Siegi and Heine.

Through the GI bill, Merardo was able to go to school. He learned to repair automobile bodies and fenders, but after graduation, he wasn't able to get a job in that field. Becoming discouraged because he wasn't getting ahead as he had planned, it became harder and harder to live with him. He started going out with the boys on Friday nights. At first, I didn't mind. It gave me a chance to have some time to myself, and when he returned home, he was always very amorous. But then he started drinking heavier, and on weekend mornings when I wanted to take Maria to the park or for a ride, he was too sick to get up. Thinking if we had another baby things would get better, I became pregnant. Janet was also born premature. She was over eight weeks early and had to be in an incubator for five weeks. When we finally took her home, she weighed barely five pounds. I did have my hands full with her. If only I would have been more relaxed instead of having to do everything perfectly. Why wasn't I able like other mothers I knew to just enjoy my babies? Why did I feel burdened by the responsibility of it all? What was wrong with me?

Supportive neighbors lived close when we moved into the house, and I became friendly with the women. I felt welcome amongst them. Most of these Mexican American women had small children of their own. I guess few people can resist the innocence of children. Maybe they realized that even though I was a foreigner in an interracial marriage, I was trying hard to make things work. This made me feel better, that I was somehow being more accepted even though I was different. I had certainly learned that people were just people, but so many others did not feel this way.

Hurt did come my way when I realized that little Janet got more attention because she was the *guerra*, the light one. Because Maria was darker skinned, people referred to her as India, or Indian, as if that meant she was less. As a mother, I never thought of my children as interracial. They were just my children, and I cared for them both the same. One's color favored me, and the other favored her father, and that was all there was to it. Perhaps this made me pay more attention to Maria because she was being discriminated against like I had when I first came to El Paso. All because of color, stupid color, or a lack of color. More discrimination, but this time, it was because one child was darker than the other. This made me stop and think again about how I had at one time thought a girl I didn't like had to be a Jew just because I didn't like her. Now my older child was being thought less of just because she was not the color people thought she ought to be. How shallow this thinking now appeared to me to be, but I had been the shallow thinker when I was younger.

Despite trying hard as the years passed from 1957 to 1959, my relationship with Merardo did not get any better. My nerves were frayed to the point of my being edgy all the time, my husband was drinking, and the situation with my mother-in-law wasn't the best. I wasn't really homesick, but perhaps I was in denial, a trait I acquired early in life. It was my way of not having to deal with feelings or even acknowledge them. On top of everything else, the large payments on the house put a financial burden on us as did Merardo's spending money on his drinking.

Finally, we had to rent out the house and move into a cheaper apartment. This move was my idea, and maybe I should have let Merardo make these kinds of decisions. But I had been in charge all along to make the important decisions, something that caused me to lose respect in his eyes, to make him feel less important. I think he knew I just couldn't look up to him any longer as a husband or head of the household. I sensed he was happy when I left him alone. Sometimes we didn't talk anymore, and I used the excuse of taking care of the children. Merardo was becoming a stranger to me, and me to him.

Things got so bad that a few months later, I suggested a divorce. After thinking it over, Merardo asked me to give him another chance. He said he would move to Los Angeles, find a good job, and try to make a new start for us. I agreed; the girls and I moved back into the house since we could afford it now, and Merardo left for LA. The year was 1960.

After he was gone for several months, I felt confused about what to do. I still cared for Merardo, but I wondered if I might find someone else to be with me. Temptation occurred when a guy I knew at work asked me out to a movie. I had told him about the problems I was having with Merardo, and he was very supportive. A neighbor took care of the children that evening. When we returned from the movie, I asked him in, and we talked and cuddled some. I realized the next morning that I was playing a dangerous game, that this had been the wrong thing to do. This wasn't for me. I had two children to consider, and I decided right then that I was going to follow Merardo to LA. The children missed their father, and yes, I missed him too. I sold the house and shipped our furniture to LA.

URSULA MARTENS AND MARK SHAW

During the days before the move, I was confused again as to whether leaving El Paso was the right thing to do. It was almost as if I was searching for something, something new and fresh by leaving, but I did not know what it was. Memories of the Nazi days were still in my mind, and I wondered if I would ever lose the stink of what I had done. I still felt dirty in some ways and was hopeful that being in California might cleanse me somehow. Maria and Janet were my responsibility, and I wanted a new life for them and for me. LA would be our new home, our new chance at some sort of freedom, freedom from the demons that still haunted me from my days as a Hitler Youth leader.

CHAPTER TWELVE

Stations: Los Angeles, California (1960 and Beyond)

Railroad stations had certainly played a major part in my life, and now a new station in life awaited us on the west coast. We did not take the train but traveled by car when Merardo came for us. The trip was long and tiresome, but I was certain that we were going to get ahead and build a better life for the children and us. I had heard exciting things about Los Angeles, about the terrific weather and the beautiful surroundings, a place that everyone I talked to thought of as desirable. Perhaps a white woman like me would not find people who were prejudiced. Surely this would be so.

What we did not take into consideration was that a recession was occurring in 1960. We also did not consider that living with our two daughters in a metropolitan city was a lot more costly. For a while, we lived in an old house made of wood with my sister-in-law and her son. Then we rented a duplex close to downtown before moving to Lincoln Heights. The sale of our El Paso house barely paid for the shipment of the furniture and covered only the first month's rent on an apartment. After looking for weeks to find work, Merardo found a job in a factory, assembling oil filters for trucks. It was not what he wanted to do, and it did not pay much.

While in the army, Merardo had been a rather good and popular boxer. He came home one day from work and told me he wanted to give boxing a try to earn some money. I knew the sport was dangerous, but I thought it might boost his self-esteem, so I agreed that he should give it a try. He trained hard and put his whole heart and energy in it. After several three-round exhibition bouts, he was entered in a six-round preliminary fight at the once famous Olympic auditorium. He lost, but the newspaper wrote about him, saying he was promising. But apparently he was not good enough since he was never offered another bout. This hurt his ego tremendously, and he was sad for many days after that.

One day, I got up enough nerve to visit the Holocaust museum in Los Angeles, but after I went, I was sorry that I did. To see the awful images, to hear the cries of anguish made me shake all over. How could I have had such blinders on? I wondered. How could I have been part of the death machine? I walked out so weak that I nearly fainted. I just kept asking, "Why, Why?" all the way home. I wanted to shout, "I'm sorry, I'm sorry, I'm sorry!" to someone, but I did not know who to shout it to.

On the bright side, one day while walking with the children, I saw a sign that said "Clothing Factory, Help Wanted. Experience Needed, Assembly and Handwork." The following morning, I left the girls with my husband's cousin and walked back to where the Fashiontime factory was located.

By this time, I was thirty-one going on thirty-two, and my appearance had changed quite a bit over the years. I felt I was pretty, and many Latino men took a long look at me since I was white. I still had the blond hair, and I always tried to dress well since I had a good figure and never a weight problem. Once my sister had said to my mother that I had good legs, and I still felt they were good even at thirty-one or so.

A sign at the foot of the stairs pointed upward alongside a message that told anyone looking for a job to go to the office. I did and was greeted by a secretary. Her smile was pleasant as she handed me an application. Before I finished filling it out, a tall man walked up to me and asked me to step into his office. He was about my age, nice looking, and he introduced himself as Mr. Aaron Gold, the boss. Two other men in suits were sitting beside him. I figured they were his partners or worked for him. I was a bit fearful of the tall man while noticing a European accent. I was sure his name sounded Jewish. He asked me to have a seat, inquired about my experience, and where I was from. Since I was still ashamed, for many reasons, to say I was German, I started to tell him I was Swedish. But somehow this man's nice way made me tell the truth. By doing so, if he was indeed Jewish, I knew there was no chance I would get the job.

Before I could answer, Mr. Gold said, "Herman, hand me the application." He did, and then Mr. Gold said, "You are from El Paso, but your last name is Mexican, and you definitely have an accent. Where are you from originally?"

I hesitated to answer and instead held my breath for a minute. My palms were all sweaty as I tried to think of what to say. Finally, with a lump in my throat, I said that the name on the application was my married name and that I was from Germany. The moment I said this, all three men hit their hand on the desk scaring me. "German, I knew it," Mr. Gold said, and I figured my chances of a job had been killed. But then one of the men said, "We are from Europe too," and I knew for certain that I was now sitting across from three Jewish men, one of whom was smoking a cigar. Imagine that, me with three Jews, ones who were now smiling and talking to me in a friendly way. Immediately, my brain flashed back to the beaten Jews I had seen in the railway yard and to those who were carried off the trucks who looked like bundles instead of human beings. I suddenly felt so ashamed and wanted to get up and leave before they asked me to go or said bad things about what the Nazis had done to their people. If I told them I was a member of the Hitler Youth, I knew I was a goner.

When Mr. Gold said, "Tell us a little bit about you," I left out any mention of Hitler Youth or my belief in Hitler as a god. I told them about leaving Germany to marry a GI, my days in El Paso, and how I ended up in LA. The men stared at me, making me very nervous, but I went on to tell them about my experience as a seamstress. Then to my shock, instead of dismissing me as expected, Mr. Gold showed me around the factory. It consisted of two large rooms upstairs with about seventy-five sewing machines, and a pressing, finishing, and shipping department downstairs. I saw women of all nationalities, including blacks, running the machines with great speed.

Aaron then, to my amazement, introduced me to several German women and I relaxed, knowing that my nationality wasn't going to matter. He told me I was hired as a forelady, meaning I would be in charge of all the machine operators. I started working the following day. My experience in the Berlin garment industry and the jean factory in El Paso made it easy for me to fit right in.

Being accepted by a Jewish man caused confused feelings. I still felt guilty over what I had done in Germany, but now this man had not held

URSULA MARTENS AND MARK SHAW

that against me. Somehow I felt as if I had been directed to meet him, to find a Jew who was not angry or hated me. What was directing me was still a mystery, but landing at this plant seemed meant-to-be, and I somehow knew that I was supposed to be there. Was there some higher power guiding my path? I wondered. If so, why, after my inexcusable conduct with the Hitler Youth?

With my extra income, Merardo and I were able to rent a larger house, and Vicenta arrived from El Paso to take care of the children. Little Maria had started first grade, and Janet was three years old. They were growing so fast. We had started calling Maria Cookie since she was always pointing from her highchair to the cookie jar, saying, "Cookie, cookie." While Cookie was at school, Janet stayed home with Vicenta, her Abolita (the Spanish name for Grandma). Abolita took as good care of her as only a granny can.

To show I was a hard worker, soon I was opening the factory in the morning and was the last employee to leave in the afternoon. I enjoyed working for Mr. Gold, who by this time had told me to call him Aaron. We became a good team, as I learned all the phases of assembling a ladies garment at a certain price.

As time passed, Aaron and I talked a great deal about our lives in Europe. His father had a mill, just like Wilhelm's family, but he explained that while he spoke German and other languages, he was not German but Czechoslovakian. When the war broke out, he was not sent to a concentration camp, but many in his family, including his mother and father, uncles, aunts, and cousins, had been. When Aaron told me they had all died in the camps, I wept and wept some more. How guilty I felt that I had been a part of the machine that sent these people to their deaths. I was so ashamed, and one night I beat my fist against a wall since I was so upset.

The reason, Aaron said, that he was not sent to a camp was because family friends had hidden him and his three sisters when the Nazis came to take his parents away. He told me that he had decided that he was not going to be one of the Jews who simply gave up and went along. When he could, he helped hide his sisters so they could not be found, and then he joined the underground and fought against Hitler and the Nazis wherever he could.

One night when we had time to really talk, Aaron, the same age as my sister Evie, told me how he and some of his friends had been captured by the gestapo. My brain almost exploded when Aaron described how he had been tortured by being beaten badly. He said he was strung up by his arms and legs while his body, stomach toward the floor, was suspended in the air upside down for hours on end while the thugs and goons attempted to gain information from him. When I saw the scars on his back where they had beaten him, I felt so sorry, so sad for him, more sorry and sad for him than for me since I still had to block away feelings that what I had thought were the best days of my life when I was in the Hitler Youth were in fact the worst days of my life. I was so ashamed since I felt that way. How had I been so crazy? How had a whole nation of Germans been so crazy? I knew that if I had been older, say eighteen, I would have killed people like Aaron. Imagine that. My gut hurt, my head hurt, I hurt all over. Ashamed. Yes, this is what I felt now that I heard that someone I felt so close to had been tortured by the Nazis, by my Nazis. This jolted me more toward reality; this hit me hard, and I laid awake at night thinking about all this and what it meant.

Aaron, a serious man who did not easily laugh, who was set in his ways, who had a soft but distinctive voice, who had trouble expressing himself and thus used song lyrics to tell me how he felt, did not tell me how he escaped from the Nazis. I think he wanted to talk about all that, but I believe he did not want to hurt me and make me feel bad so he did not. While I was crying, Aaron tried to make me feel better by telling me that many Germans had hid Jews, had helped him and also his sisters so they could survive. He was very thankful to them, and I could not help but recall that perhaps my grandfather had also helped men like Aaron since he had stood tall against Hitler and his Nazis. More and more, I had realized that people like Grandfather, and like Aaron, were true heroes when before I had thought they were cowards and traitors. Perhaps this was the first part of my awakening, my true understanding that at some point I had to forgive myself too for what I had done since Aaron wanted to forgive me as I needed to forgive my grandfather.

On another occasion, Aaron mentioned in his humble way how when his sisters were safe and out of danger, he worked again for the underground. His skill at different languages came in handy, and he said he worked for the Allied intelligence until the war was over. Then, as I looked into the eyes of this man, this Jew, that I was more and more

URSULA MARTENS AND MARK SHAW

respecting each day for both his friendship and his confiding in me, he said that because special attention was given to orphaned children, his sisters were one of the first to leave Germany since they had relatives in America. They were permitted to board ships, and Aaron was their guardian to start life over in the new land. He told me he had married since this was the right thing to do.

Aaron knew that at a certain age, a child had to join the Hitler Youth. It was painful to talk about the past, and so we didn't, but he knew what the Hitler Youth was all about and what they had done throughout the war. I had a feeling he wondered what I had done as a leader, but it didn't seem to matter to him since he was so understanding about what had occurred when I was just a kid growing up in Germany. Sometimes I had nightmares where I was raising my right hand and saying "Heil Hitler" and thinking "Ursula, you are in America now, and you can get in big trouble for doing that." Then I would wake up and be relieved. I never told Aaron about the nightmares. They were so real.

I also blocked out and never told Aaron about the terrible things I had seen after the war, including the Jewish girl I saw in the ration line in Schwerin. If I had told him, I think he might have thought I was guilty of sending someone to the KZ, Konzentrationslager, our name for the camps where I thought they sent people who were antigovernment and whom we called antisocials. But Aaron knew enough to know that I had a hard time by faulting myself for what I had done. He knew that without knowing specifics. When I had learned of the atrocities on radio broadcasts and in the newspapers after the war, of the terrible gassing of Jews in the camps, of the mass graves at Auschwitz, of the thousands of pounds of gold from teeth that were found, the horrible stories, I wanted to crawl in a corner and hide; I didn't want to deal with it, didn't want to accept it, because I felt so guilty. I was just one of the Germans who gassed Jews, I thought. One of the ignorant ones who said, "I did not know." This was the only excuse, but it was not much of an excuse really. Before, I thought if people were punished, they deserved it. Now I knew they had not deserved it; they were just punished. This was wrong I knew, so wrong.

More and more I realized how little I had in common with Merardo when comparing him to Aaron. He was a "take charge" kind of person, and there was little he did not have some knowledge about. I didn't admit it to myself then, but I was falling in love. Besides being attracted to him in a sexual way, I thought he was a very smart man, the first intelligent man I had met like my father. I loved to just listen to him talk about different things, politics, business, sports, whatever it was. I could listen for hours. This made him rather mysterious at first, but as I got to know him, that was attractive to me even though he really wasn't my type. I liked men with brown eyes and brown hair, and he was definitely German-looking.

Meanwhile, Merardo and I had really tried to work things out, but my feelings for him were gone, and our discord didn't add to the children's contentment. I saw an ad in the newspaper placed by a divorced woman with two children "looking for the same" to share her house. It sounded like a great opportunity, and I called. Her name was Mary, and after I met her and her daughters, I decided to make the move. When I came home in the latter part of 1961, I told Merardo about my decision, explaining the arrangements I had made with Mary and how she had agreed to watch Cookie and Janet while I worked. Merardo was furious and started yelling at me. It was a good thing that Vicenta had taken the children to visit a neighbor she had befriended. I was in the bedroom gathering some clothes to pack when he came into the room, pulled them out of my hand, and threw them on the floor. He reminded me of an animal that had been hurt and was going crazy. One moment he pleaded with me saying, "Please don't leave me! I'll do anything to work things out," and the next moment he said angrily, "You are nothing but a whore and you are a liar and a cheat."

I had never seen him act so violent, and I was scared. He pushed me around roughly and used language I had never heard him use before. When I didn't give in to his raving, he threw me on the bed and forced himself on me. All the while, I felt guilty and awful and certain that it was entirely my fault that I had driven him to this very unacceptable behavior. I could not sleep that night and I felt out of control, full of despair, sad all around. The next day, after I packed our clothes, Merardo had calmed down enough to drive the children and me to Mary's house.

Outwardly, the children seemed to be okay with our move. At least, I thought they were. They kept busy with their new friends and the dog Tippy. The house had a huge yard for them to play in. Maria started school in the new neighborhood, and during the day, Janet went on Avon calls with Mary. I was lonely without a man in my life, but I

URSULA MARTENS AND MARK SHAW

knew Merardo and I had nothing more to share. Hopefully he would forgive me as time passed since I was so thankful for his bringing me to America in the first place.

Aaron found out about the move when I gave him a change of address. He was helpful by giving me some time off every afternoon to be settled and to spend some time with the children. He also continued to tell me more about himself, especially what it meant to be a Jew. I told him I had never known Jews in a direct way, and this surprised him. One day, he said, "You know I am a Zionist, at least that is what I tell people, and many people don't even know what that is." He also said that Americans didn't want to know what happened; some didn't believe anything had happened to the Jews. They just wanted to ignore all the torture and death. It did not faze them because they had not been there and seen the atrocities that had occurred.

But then Aaron added something so important that I would never forget it. He said that most people who hated Jews had never met one, never talked to one, like me. This made me shiver since this was so true. I had hated Jews even though I never knew any, really knew them. I just went by what I was told, that they were bad and dirty and could not be trusted. I recalled being so happy when the Crystal Night had occurred and all those Jewish shops had been destroyed even though I did not like to see the crystals broken in the streets. But I was made to hate Jews, and so I did without any questioning. The guilt I felt over that could not be measured. It filled my whole body and soul.

Aaron said that many people hated Jews since they had had one bad experience, and then instead of being upset with that Jew, they decided they hated all of them. But he added, "The people with the extreme hate, the ones who hate so much like the Nazis, they for sure have never known a Jew at all." He said again, "it is so easy to hate someone you do not know" and that "Once you know someone and their family and so on, then it is not so easy to hate." I realized Aaron was right, and it made an impact on me causing me to rethink everything I thought about Jews and how I had become a Jew-hater. I also began to read everything I could about the Jewish faith so I could talk with Aaron some more about things that really bothered me, things I did not know anything about. When I told him about the discrimination I had seen in El Paso, he was not surprised. "Prejudice is everywhere," he said, "there are just different forms of it."

When I read more about what had occurred with the Nazis and Jews, I started to use the word *Holocaust* more. I had heard that word before but had never really understood it or didn't want to. It was a terrible word, but after a time, I could use it and talk about it with Aaron. Little by little, I began to understand what monsters Hitler and the Nazis had been. And I had been a part of that. Shame on me.

Other words I now knew were *genocide* and *Final Solution*. Slowly I educated myself more about what had occurred while I was wearing blinders. Sometimes I tried to tell myself that my youth had caused me to look away when the atrocities were occurring, but that was just an easy excuse. People, especially Grandfather, tried to open my eyes, but I did not want to see the truth.

Without realizing it, I began to think about Aaron and Wilhelm at the same time. It wasn't only that both of their fathers had been millers, but this did permit me to blend them together somehow. A dream I had caused me to wake up in a cold sweat when I somehow saw the two facing off, each with a rifle in his hand. I wasn't sure what that meant, but it bothered me for some time.

One evening, after work, Aaron offered to give me a ride home. I was thirty-three years old, but I still hesitated because we would be all alone. But he was my friend more than my boss now, and so I accepted. Then we stopped in the park, and after eating some sandwiches and laughing at some stories, he put his arms around me and drew me close to him. A million thoughts ran through my mind as this tall man with the good looks and light-up smile moved closer to me. Was it really possible that Aaron, this Jewish man, was going to care for me, a person who had once been a Hitler Youth leader, one who had hated Jews like him? Goose pimples ran down my arms, and suddenly I was cold even though the day was hot. Now I waited as his eyes met mine, and he moved even closer, so close I was betting he could hear my heart beating faster and faster.

Suddenly, so sudden it startled me, Aaron kissed me. I did not resist but instead felt the warmth of his lips as my body shook with passion. Tears flowed as well, and then while he wiped them away, he said the magic words I would never forget for the rest of my life, "Don't cry, Ursula, everything is going to be all right. Surely you must know I have cared for you for a long time."

A Jew caring for me, imagine that after all that I had done, including being a cheerleader for the Nazis. My brain was frozen with a thousand thoughts, and yet I grabbed on to this man who was holding me like I had never been held before. It was a true miracle, yes, a true miracle, and all my sadness poured from me in tears that wet Aaron's shirt and caused my eyes to redden. I almost couldn't catch my breath. It was unthinkable to be cared for, even perhaps loved by a Jewish man, one whose parents had been killed by the very Nazis that I had worshipped. Later, I would try to describe the feelings I had had at that moment in the park to people, but I never could. I felt so light, like a thousand demons had left my body, all the ones I had stored up over the years deep inside my soul.

This was the reassurance I needed, someone to believe in me, to forgive me, to just care for me, and I felt relief for I loved Aaron so. From that moment on, there was no turning back for me. I was alone with my two girls, but I was sure that Aaron would be there if I needed support. That day in the park was the start of a relationship that carried me to the highest highs, to some sort of enlightenment I never knew could possibly exist. The passion between us was strong, but we were also the best of friends. We were truly soul mates. For the first time in my life, I thought I had found someone I could look up to, someone who was there for me, and with whom I could share my thoughts and feelings. There was no doubt in my mind that Aaron felt the same. I think the differences in our backgrounds brought us only closer together. Aaron was able to judge me for who I was and not what I had been. I, on the other hand, was only too glad to have a chance to right, on a small level, some of the wrongs that had been my thinking years before. This permitted me self-forgiveness since Aaron had forgiven me for being someone who hated Jewish people like him. It is hard to imagine how this made me feel, but perhaps *clean* is the best word. The dirt had finally been washed away, thanks to Aaron.

Aaron was not very explicit in talking about feelings of love, but once, after we had made love, he said, "You know, I heard a song this morning and for the first time paid attention to the words. They kind of describe me. The song was 'What Kind of Fool Am I?'" This was his way of telling me that he had never felt as deeply for anyone before me.

Of course, Aaron was married, and my mind was confused about that since I did believe in the institution of marriage. He told me he and his wife were together for their children but that they were more friends than married couple. I believed him because I wanted to believe him. Was I being used again? I did not think so. But if I was, then okay to that since somehow my being with him and loving him made me feel cleaner than I had ever felt before. But no excuses were offered because I could not see that any were necessary. We were in love. That is the only excuse I can give.

Whenever we could find the time, Aaron and I spent it with each other. The first few months, we packed a picnic basket for the park or found a secret place whenever Aaron could be with me outside of work. I had never experienced lovemaking like I did with Aaron. He was a passionate lover, and I was only too eager to please him. But he pleased me back, a sign that we really had true love.

When the girls were in school, I moved out of Mary's house and rented an apartment closer to work and within walking distance of where Aaron lived. He visited often, and the children got to know him better. I had brought them up to never hate anyone, to never feel like people were different, to always have respect for every person they met. I made sure of this since I wanted them to never be like I was when I was a child.

I never asked Aaron much about his home life, and he didn't say too much about it. It was like he had another life, and I did not want to know what that was like. We always spent Friday nights together. It didn't matter what date it was on the calendar. I knew that sometimes it wasn't easy for him to walk away from his family, and I suspect that he often ate two meals so as not to hurt feelings. What he told his wife he was doing on those Friday nights I do not know, and perhaps it was selfish of me to never ask. Being in the arms of a loving Jew was so unreal, so unexpected, so special, that I did not want to think about anything else but being with him and making him happy.

By this time, around the late part of 1962 or early 1963, I learned how to drive and had bought a car with Aaron's help. Almost every weekend, the children and I went on outings. Sometimes we visited cities surrounding LA and went to the beach. Other times, we went to the mountains in the wintertime or horseback riding in the park. These times were so special, and I felt unbelievably blessed that life could be so good. Nothing was going to spoil this, I decided, nothing. Even when the Watts riots took place in 1965, and I was so scared when buildings were burning and I thought my home might be, I still could cope because I was stronger as a person than I had ever been. This did not mean the riots kept me from recalling the same sort of racial tension in Germany between the Nazis and the Jews as now poured out into the streets of LA when the blacks and whites hated each other. Hate is hate, I knew from experience. Only the faces change.

In 1970, I was finally financially able to return to Germany for a visit with my parents. They had moved to Frankfurt after Father was reinstated in his old job. It was vacation time for the girls, and they stayed with their father and his new family. I was so pleased he found someone to share his life with.

This time, with the help of medication, I was able to enjoy the flight without getting airsick. My parents, whom I had kept in touch with through letters and phone calls, greeted me at the airport, and we were very happy to see each other again although not too much emotion was showed. My grandparents had both died days from each other the year before, and there was little news from the relatives and friends in the east zone. It was still the time of the Cold War, and we knew their living standard was low. Mother sent many a care package with food and other necessities to our relatives in the east.

Evie and Heinz had been reunited and were now living in Lüneburg. The city was located in the district where Heinz had been captured at the end of the war. He had been reinstated as a schoolteacher and was now working at the Johanneum, a prestigious boy's school. Wolfgang now had a baby brother, Rolf. They did not live far from my parents, and we went to visit them. It felt strange to be back with everyone speaking German, but it did not take long to feel at home again. Being with Evie was special, but for the first time, we were both adults, and I wish I had talked to her more about life and feelings and more deep things. I also noticed while I was visiting her that there were now two distinct Germanys. One, the west, was living; the other, the east, was dying.

I was eager to tell my parents about Aaron but not sure of how they might feel about him. I should have known better since one discussion with Father in particular was about blacks in Germany. The West German government was building housing for African students at the time. I asked Father, "Why is it necessary to build separate housing?" Angry, he replied, "You cannot seriously expect Germans to live under the same roof with Negroes, do you?" This was in keeping with his belief that blacks didn't have the same brains as whites. They just couldn't match the German brain, he believed.

I realized then that the past hadn't taught Father anything. I don't think he was a real racist. He just thought Negroes were inferior meaning his mind-set was still that of a Nazi with no understanding of equality. I dropped the subject, especially since Mother dutifully agreed with him. This made me recall that I had never seen a Negro until there were black soldiers. That was quite a shock.

A few days later, I read an article in the newspaper about the difficulties black students were having trying to rent rooms from Germans. The writer said that even though some people were willing, they were afraid to encounter the wrath of their neighbors. I met friends of my parents that voiced similar concerns. They were still missing the good old days and how he (meaning Hitler) would not have let certain things happen that were going on in Germany now. Like the freedom that they thought young people abused, they complained about there being no order anywhere. My visit was a short one, and I knew that arguing would have caused a rift in our relationship especially if they had known about my love for Aaron. How much I had learned from him, how much better I felt about myself by being in his loving arms.

Before leaving, I finally decided to tell only my mother about Aaron because I knew where Father stood on matters of morality, and I did not know how he would feel about him being Jewish. Slowly, I told my mother the story, and her face was ashen as I proceeded along. As a mother, she could not help but realize that from my feelings about Aaron, we were very much in love. She was concerned though with where the relationship was going to lead us. Over and over she asked me, "But is he ever going to marry you?" I could not answer her truthfully, and so I did not.

Weeks later, after I had returned to LA, I received a letter from Father in his excellent handwriting. It was the only one Father ever wrote to me in all my life. In it, he said, "Dear Ulli, I was most disturbed by your mother's telling me about your affair with a married man who is also your boss. I wonder what made you fall this low. I totally disapprove of this relationship, and I trust you will come to your senses and break it off. This man, as you must know, is living a lie." The letter was very painful to me, but I did not take heed, even though I knew deep in my

URSULA MARTENS AND MARK SHAW

heart Father was right. But I could not help myself, and I never even wanted to. Somehow I began to understand Aaron as a gift to me, a blessing, a man who had opened my eyes to so many things that I had never considered before.

When I sat in the park and thought about it, Germany was the home of so many disappointments and America had brought me freedom despite some hard times. And Aaron was part of that search for freedom. That is for sure.

Several visits to Germany would occur later, but one day, after my second visit, I had returned from walking our small dog, Daisy. It was late evening, and when I opened the door to the lobby of the building, a Western Union deliveryman passed by me. I knew at that moment that something had happened to Father even though he had been in good health since his heart attack the year before. On my door, I found the telegram from Mother advising me of Father's death. I felt sadness and concern for Mother, and the tears flowed that evening so much that Aaron's shirt was all wet from my crying on his shoulder. Even though we were very busy at work, Aaron insisted that I take time off to attend the funeral in Frankfurt.

As I viewed Father's body before the funeral that was to be the following day, I was overcome by a feeling of great loss not only because he was gone but because I realized I had never really gotten to know him. I remembered him as the father that took care of me and the man I thought could answer all my questions as a child, but what had been his dreams, his thoughts, and his innermost feelings? I knew we disagreed on some things, but I knew he was not an unreasonable man. We had talked a little on my visit the year before, but because he had his first heart attack, I didn't want to upset him in any way. I always felt much respect for him, but I knew very little of him on an adult level. Now, I would never again hear him recite famous poems or excerpts from Shakespeare's writings, something he enjoyed.

Many old friends came to the funeral. Father was eulogized as a sincere, honest man and a good friend. The speakers said he was a proud man, with high moral standards, a man who would be missed by anyone that knew him. No mention was made of his being a member of the brownshirts, the Nazis, and being in charge of the trains, many of them headed for concentration camps that led to the death of millions of Jews. No, this part of his life was wiped away as if it had not occurred.

And he had never taken responsibility for his actions, the ones like I saw in the photographs in his desk that showed Jews being shot or literally starved to death before being gassed at terrible places like Auschwitz and Ravensbrück. Father had probably directly sent people to these places through his actions as a stationmaster. Why he was not tried as a war criminal was always unknown to me, but he was a criminal nonetheless, just like I was. We were both guilty, guilty as charged.

After the ceremony, some of the closer friends and family gathered in Mother's apartment. It was almost a party atmosphere, and it saddened me. I wanted everyone to talk about the man that had just made his transition. I had hoped that maybe the people there could fill some of the gaps of what I did not know about Father. Did I feel the need for something deeper, more spiritual perhaps? I was not sure yet couldn't find in my heart the answer to these questions especially about the spiritual part even though I had begun to think more about such things in America. Mother tried to make everything as comfortable as possible. "Sei tapfer"—"Be brave, don't show emotions." This was like our family motto.

Two days later, Mother, Evie, and I took my father's ashes to his final resting place. I traveled back to LA. My mother gave up their large apartment and rented a smaller one in the suburbs. It would be only a year later when Evie called to say that Mother, who missed Father dearly, had taken an overdose of sleeping pills but would live through it. Evie was quite angry and never quite forgave Mother for this attempted suicide. Neither she nor I had learned how to be supportive, how to show love. All we knew from our screwed-up German upbringing was that attempting suicide wasn't an accepted way of dealing with grief and depression. In later years, when we wanted to talk about it with Mother, it was quite uncomfortable for the three of us, so we just let it be. Since Evie was not able to forgive, their relationship stayed somewhat strained to the end.

After Mother's cry for help, and despite their differences, Evie found an apartment in Lüneburg across the street from where Mother lived. Even though they were not too close, she was happy with the move, happy to have at least one daughter nearby. She made many new friends and continued her bridge playing that she enjoyed so much.

Did I really have a chance to be a daughter? A good daughter? I knew my parents only in my youth and on my few visits to Germany.

We talked but mostly about comfortable topics. When I was a child, I must have caused my parents many a small headache. I was the little whirlwind, but to them, the little whirlwind must have turned into a full-blown storm with what I put them through while they were alive. It seemed like I was always doing something wrong. "One doesn't do such a thing," I heard Mother say to me quite often. But why would I even try, when I always felt that Evie was the good one, pleasing Mother and Father more, the one that excelled in every area? I was only a good worker, a good housecleaner who would maybe make some man a good wife. I had dreams but didn't voice them often, and when I did, I was put down. For instance, when I had mentioned going to a colonial school I wanted to go to and said I would plant carrots, slice them, and use them for payment, the idea was laughed at by my grandfather.

Father and Mother had a habit of saying "One day you are going to stand by my grave" and regret such and such. Alternatively, Father had this version, "You are going to stand by your mother's grave, and regret the things you've done." But my biggest regret is that, though I honored and respected my parents' memory, the word *love* was not in their repertoire. I thought love was something that happened on a film screen, something you could dream about. I often wondered if I really loved my parents, if I really did, but of course I did. I know without a doubt that I respected them a lot. In Germany I was taught, and learned well, how to hate, but no one taught me to love. Only through Aaron was I now learning about this, about true love in every sense of the word.

The year after my father died, Mother came to Los Angeles for a visit. She and Aaron liked each other from the start. He took us to dinner several times, and we went to the theater or saw shows. Over the years, I think Mother had grown to be more open in her views. With television and books she read, she could not help but change some of her beliefs in terms of racism and other related issues.

During the early times of my relationship with Aaron, I was grateful for every moment I could be with him, but a relationship built on deceit is bound to fail. This is a lesson I did not learn right away, and I certainly regretted being with a married man when I knew that was wrong. Loving Aaron brought me both the deepest pain, when I realized he would never leave his wife and children, and the highest ecstasy, when he held me in his arms and loved me all over. But all too soon, I became restless and started finding faults. We went from breaking up to making up over and over. My working for him didn't help matters, or maybe I just stayed because I was desperately clinging to hope, trying to avoid the final break.

This had to come, I knew that, and finally it did when Aaron told me that his wife was pregnant. An emotional agony I had never experienced before welled up and spilled out into a wracking, sobbing cry. With each wave I let out another, and I have no sense of how much time passed with me lying curled up on the sofa sobbing, Aaron sitting on the edge in front of me, rubbing my shoulder and back. I always wondered if Aaron's wife had tried with whatever means to save her marriage. I couldn't blame her for that.

She also had learned that Aaron was having an affair when some telephone bills had too many calls to a number that she traced to mine. And Aaron told me of an incident that hurt me very much. At work, we took up collections to buy Christmas presents for the bosses. This had been the custom for many years before I started working there. As the forelady, I was asked to purchase these gifts, toys for the bosses' children. One day Aaron's wife gathered all these gifts and threw them in the garage, telling Aaron she would not tolerate any Nazi stuff in her house.

Now, the relationship was over, I was sure of that, and even though later we would try to rekindle it when his marriage was over, that did not work out. But a few months after it ended, I sat in a park and reflected on what the love affair with Aaron, a Jewish Holocaust survivor, had meant to me. Above all, even above the love he had shown me, above the understanding, above the listening to me pour my heart out over so many things, I had learned the most important lesson of my life, the lesson of forgiveness. Despite my having been a Nazi through membership in the Hitler Youth, despite my having been a contributor, an enabler to Hitler, his storm troopers, his executioners, his killers of more than six million Jews, Aaron forgave me for my conduct, for my terrible mistake. Seeing this forgiveness in Aaron's eyes was such a gift, such a special gift.

Best of all, because he could forgive me, I could somehow forgive myself, somehow live with what I had been, live with having hated so much, live with terrible decisions that I had made as a youngster growing up believing that Hitler was indeed God. In essence, Aaron Gold had set me free, permitted me to experience freedom in the land of the free, and I would love him for the rest of my life no matter whether I ever saw him again or not. He was truly my savior, and his saving me would lead to finally discovering the god who had been chasing me all my life.

———————————

Many experiences would highlight my life path over the following years, each adding to the learning process for one who had been transformed from a girl who hated during her youth to a woman who had discovered love and forgiveness as the adult years continued on. More and more, the nightmare of what had occurred, the guilt I felt over turning in the man Jacob with the trick dog Wanda, Grandfather getting beaten by the Russians when he would not tell them where I was, the time I stood by and did nothing when the Jews were being attacked by dogs and beaten by soldiers in the railway yard, the rape of my aunt by Russian soldiers, and even the fact that Aaron had been tortured and his family exterminated began to disappear from my mind-set since I realized that the youthful Ursula had never intended to cause harm but instead had been duped like millions of others. When I looked in the mirror, I was finally not disgusted with myself, having come to terms with who I had been and now who I was. Aaron had been a true savior, sent to me and me alone.

Each experience I had also was a step in the right direction toward a spirituality that marked a new attitude toward others, a new feeling of peace and goodwill toward all who crossed my path. In effect, a new Ursula Martens had been born, with the old one dead and buried. This enabled me to deal with a marriage to an African American man that blew hot and cold and then cold, the raising of two daughters complete with all the ups and downs mothers experience while loving them dearly, and the attempt at reconciliation with Aaron when he decided his marriage was over. This wasn't to be since the same spark that had brought us, the Jew hater and the Jew, together, simply wasn't as bright as it had been. But neither of us would ever forget what we shared, a true love bonding us forever. When I visited him one last time, I noticed a slab of salami hanging in his kitchen. He had told me before that during the war, he had always kept a piece of dry salami with him until someone gave him another piece so he would never go hungry. This brought back so many memories of our talks together and our times together, and I knew that Aaron would always be in my heart.

While reflecting one day on where I had been, and where I was, I realized that there was never a time when there wasn't prejudice and racism around me. In Germany, I learned to be proud of who I was, to the point of being sure that as a German, I was better than anyone else in the world. Everyone was aware of the blue eyes, the blond hair, and even the head measurements that were the norm for the true Aryan. I learned that Catholics were different, and later in the Hitler Youth, I was taught to look down on any religion. When I was about thirteen, there had been a Catholic girl at my school who had the misfortune of coming home pregnant from a retreat. The Lutheran children, me included, gave her a very hard time. She insisted that she had not done anything. We thought it very funny to suggest that maybe the Holy Ghost impregnated her. We teased her so much that her family decided to send her away for good. We had run her out of town. I don't remember her name, but her face I remember perfectly. The shameful, miserable look she wore constantly was still burned in my mind. When I did think of her, I thought of how people did not need to segregate themselves by race or religion. What I had, and what many still have, is a collective chip on their shoulder, which tells us to hate, to kill anything that's different. What a strange philosophy for billions of people to adopt especially when each of us is unique.

While living in Germany, titles were also important, and if you had a uniform to go with your title and swore allegiance to the swastika, then you were better still. People were even suspected of not being true Germans if their name didn't sound German. When Evie started dating Heinz Zielinski, her husband, I remember his name being questioned in our family. Was he really German since Zielinski sounded Jewish?

During my reflections, I realized that when I arrived in the USA, I thought I would leave all that different stuff behind me. I figured I was going to be part of a land that was free, where many different races were living together, and the law applied the same way to everyone. I had hoped that I was coming to a new beginning, a new life, but I learned that prejudice is universal and plays no favorites.

For many years, I was ashamed of having been a Nazi. But talking with Aaron made me realize that because of my upbringing, my young mind didn't have a chance; all I knew was to follow orders. In effect, my innocence of youth had been stolen, my dreams stolen; I was never taught right from wrong and, more important, to think for myself. That meant never questioning, never objecting, never refusing to do something even though I had an inkling, a feeling, it might be wrong. Yes, I was like a robot, indoctrinated, brainwashed really, and when this occurred with no spiritual foundation to counteract what I was being told, I was used, molded, and taught never to fight back against authority. When Hitler and his boys said "Jump," I jumped, and no one made me see that I was part of a collective force intent on taking over the world and while doing so, exterminating millions of Jews.

Much of my own prejudice, I realized while contemplating where my life had taken a wrong turn, was class prejudice. A person's *kinderstube*, or standing, was most important to me while growing up. Then in America, I heard whites call blacks niggers. I heard people say, "Blacks are taking good jobs away," "Persians are moving into our choice living areas," and "Latinos bring crime." Ignorance was the poison, and that poison infected me when I was young because to me, as I was taught, all Jews were bad and had to be punished.

When I was married to the black man, we were stopped several times for no reason. After a blond LA policeman with a short haircut told us to get out of the car, I had flashbacks to how the gestapo arrested asocials in Germany. Growing up, I was taught, ordered really, to call officers Uncle Policeman and to not be afraid of them. Now in America, this cop scared me to death because I could tell he hated my husband because he was black and me because I was white and with a black man. Another time, we were stopped, and when my husband could not produce his driver's license since he had left it at home, the white officer asked him to step out of the car, handcuffed him, and put him in the patrol car despite our pleas that we were on the way to the hospital to see a sick child. The officer saw the balloons and flowers on the back seat, but he was going to show this black man who was the boss. When we finally got to the station to post bail, my husband had been strip-searched and booked. This was humiliating to him, and to me, especially since no charges were ever filed.

All these thoughts were in my mind when Mother visited to celebrate her eightieth birthday. We had good talks and reconciled any ill feelings that either of us had with our mother-daughter relationship. When she finally died, I felt we had reached an understanding and that she knew

I loved her very much. She appeared proud of me, especially regarding the business success that had come to me over the years.

With her passing and continual thoughts about what a new person I had become through my love affair with Aaron, I began to really try to understand myself for the first time in my life. I started reading self-improvement books, watched all of doctors Deepak Chopra's and Wayne Dyer's television programs, and listened to their tapes. They talked about how to meditate with purpose and power and how to reap the benefits of their teachings. All this was very new to me, but this was the start of daily meditations, something I had never done before.

Then, without warning, it happened, *it* meaning a path to God that I could have never imagined. This spiritual journey began when a friend named Mike asked if I could pick him up at the Agape Church, the International Center of Truth, the next day. Spirituality really held no interest for me, but I was a bit curious to see what this part of Mike's life was like. I parked across the street as agreed and watched as people emerged from the warehouse-type building. The first thing I noticed was the racial makeup—the group was made up of all colors, and all ages, some in their Sunday best, and others dressed casually, even in shorts. They seemed to all take time to hug each other, to talk, and to smile, a true sign of friendship.

If I had any doubts this was to be a church for me to attend, another friend named Herb mentioned this New Thought church during a lunch. The next Sunday, I walked in at 7:00 a.m. sharp ready to see whether the god who had been chasing me my whole life had chased me here.

The service at a branch of the Church of Religious Science, not affiliated with Scientology or Christian Science, began with soft piano music. Instantly I was able to totally relax and feel as if I was transferred into a blissful state of mind. As I sat in the silence, calmness settled upon me. It was as if I completely stopped thinking about specific things and just floated peacefully inside myself. After a while of music, a leader whom I later learned was called a practitioner read a few pages of inspiring words. Then, with the lights dimmed, everyone was quiet for about twenty minutes.

I didn't remember ever having felt so peaceful. After the lights were turned on, I noticed the doors to the sanctuary that had been closed were opened to let more people in, and the room filled to capacity and more. As I looked around, I could see the high ceiling full of wires, but the side walls were decorated with all sorts of inspiring artwork. This day was called Choir Sunday, and I was overcome by the beautiful music and the inspirational songs. Words from the minister, Dr. Michael Beckwith, resonated with me even when he quoted from the Bible, the book I had avoided all my life like it was poison.

Later, I learned that in less than ten years, the membership had grown from ten people to over five thousand, but that first Sunday was like nothing I had ever experienced before. A new frontier had been opened to me as I encountered something that had been missing my whole life, releasing emotions in me that I did not believe I could feel.

Certainly my heart and mind were like virgin soil waiting to be seeded. The church message involved with the science of the mind was a correlation of the laws of science, opinions of philosophy and revelations of religions applied to human needs and the aspirations of all. The teachings of the founder, Ernest Holmes, who was fond of saying, "We are Christians and more," came very natural to me. He quoted extensively from philosophers, religious thinkers, and teachers such as Buddha, Jesus, Moses, Homer, Plato, Einstein, Augustine, and Gandhi. I liked the openness of all this teaching, the chance to think for oneself, something I have never experienced growing up in Germany.

I took lessons, talked to other seekers, and read many books, including those by Meister Eckhart, Emerson, Howard Thurman, Carl Jung, and many other New Thought writers. A whole new way of life had opened up to me, and more important, I was open enough to finally understand that having a spiritual foundation in my life was a must. For it to have come through unconventional means, the Agape Church, one practicing science of the mind, was perhaps unusual, but more important, a higher power had influenced this part of my life leading to curiosity and enlightenment.

During the orientation to Agape Church (*agape* means unconditional love), many lessons were learned. As part of the training, I had to write about my early life, including time with the Hitler Youth. I started crying while reading and barely finished, but I did finish. As I dried my eyes, several students came up to me to tell me how they had appreciated what I had to say and how brave I was for saying it.

In an effort to explain my feelings over the transformation that had occurred in my life, I wrote a poem:

I have my eyes to SEE the beauty that surrounds me.

My ears can HEAR the roaring of the sea.

I FEEL the softness of a baby's hand and SMELL
the earth of the rain-soaked land.

And, oh, the sense of TASTE!

Without it would food not be a total waste?

But in the autumn of my life, I found a sense that
takes away all struggle and all strife!
It gives me everlasting peace, and now I know true happiness.

The sense of GOD is mine at last, and
all my darkest days have passed.

Imagine me, the Jew hater, the one who believed Adolf Hitler was my true god, writing such words. Through the trials and tribulations of a life that swept across Germany to Texas and California, a young girl disillusioned with who she had been and yearning to cleanse herself had found that by emptying herself, she had become whole in the hands of a loving god who had guided her soul to a promised land. Yes, the stations along the way had permitted learning and growth, and I could finally look in the mirror, through the love of Aaron and the teachings of a new church, and be at peace with who I was. In essence, I had found the healing I had been searching for, had a new identity, and thus was no longer the lost child who worshipped Hitler and the Nazis. Instead I had become a loving person who loved everyone and was devoted to helping others wherever possible. A higher spirit far greater than any I could have ever imagined had washed me clean through two of the greatest human emotions possible—love and forgiveness. I even got a license plate with the letters "Gdisall," God is all. God is for sure, I decided, and I see Jesus, Buddha, Krishna, and others as true wise men that I could learn from.

In effect, I had finally traded in *Mein Kampf* as a bible of sorts for a real Bible; I had chosen the cross instead of the swastika as my symbol of life. God had chased me, and God had finally won. I had a broken heart over the breakup with Aaron but a cleansed heart as it was meant to be. No longer was I in denial. I had faced my demons and shut them in a closet never to return. Regrets over my conduct would surface from time to time, but regrets don't measure up to guilt unless we let them do so. The redemption I had sought was complete. Very much so.

During one of the seminars at the church, I was asked to write what they called, a Declaration of Spiritual Reality. Here is what I wrote with perhaps the final line the most important in terms of the spiritual journey I had experienced during my transformation, my awakening from being a person of hate to a person of love:

> I deeply believe that this beautiful earth on which I live and the awesome universe that surrounds it is created by one power, one presence, one infinite Spirit.
>
> This Spirit, that I lovingly call Mother/Father/God, manifests itself in everything that exists, and we are surrounded by its infinite intelligence. The highest god is my innermost god; therefore, I am a perfect incarnation of God. All the highest attributes of the Spirit are mine, including free will and self-choice. I live in the present and strive daily to be godlike in every way.
>
> I know without a doubt that the kingdom of heaven is mine, for I live by the law of the universe. This truth will be revealed to everyone, and love will guide us all toward peace. Through my thoughts, I align myself with the Higher Being and can effectively transform my experiences of distress into ones of comfort and harmony; I accomplish this through meditation, mind treatments, and affirmations. It is the same process of creative fertility the farmer uses to grow his crop.

The nourishment of the mind is my deepest faith. It empowers me to unite with the divine mindland to realize the power of the spoken word. My life will not be ended upon my death, for my soul will make a transition to a different sphere and will continue to expand forever. I am dedicated to living my life to its fullest potential. My understanding and love for God will guide me to be the best human I can be. Not only do I love my immediate family but all mankind. I do not judge anyone, and I will forgive those who have wronged me.

My heart and my mind are evolving toward a deeper understanding of the principle of life, and each day I strive to bring about a deep understanding among people of different color and race. Through love, understanding, and an open mind, I am bringing this to pass.

I have my eyes to *see* the beauty that surrounds me. My ears can *hear* the roaring of the sea. I *feel* the softness of a baby's hand and *smell* the earth of the rain-soaked land. And, oh, the sense of *taste*! Without it would food not be a total waste? But in the autumn of my life, I found a sense that takes away all struggle and all strife!

It gives me everlasting peace,
and now I know true happiness.
The sense of *God* is mine at last,
and all my darkest days have passed.

My church experience, the spiritual growth I had experienced, prepared me for a special blessing, a special love that I could never have expected. This came from another angel of mercy as well, a Jewish woman named Ruth whom I met after I became friends with Judy, her mother. Judy had been born in Poland and then sent to Siberia by the Russians for slave labor where she had to cut wood in freezing temperatures. But she survived, I learned, through a strong determination not to let the Nazis steal her life away.

What a brave woman she was. Ruth had been born at Bergen-Belsen, one of the camps used to house people after the war. She was a big supporter of Israel, even had a house there. She and I talked about many things together, and I felt a comfort level with her as I had with Aaron. One day she totally surprised me by asking if I would read some special prayer words at her son Eric's bar mitzvah. I wasn't even certain what happened at a bar mitzvah, so I stammered a bit before answering yes. Then I started reading about what a bar mitzvah meant, that it was a rite of passage for boys turning thirteen to adulthood. At the event, the boy would become a man because he could read from the Torah, a privilege only given to adults.

Since the ceremony was so sacred, the very heart of Jewish tradition, I could not believe that a former Jew hater like me was going to be part of this age-old ceremony. When Ruth showed me the passage she and Eric had selected from a small book, I read it a hundred times over so I would get it right. Goose pimples pockmarked my arms when I did; there was something so strange about reading the words, words I could never have imagined reading in a thousand years.

When I sat at home and really thought about what was happening, I cried and cried some more. Aaron had taught me that most of those who hate Jews never even knew one and how right he was. Now I had known him, and his loving heart, and now first Judy, and then Ruth had shown me love despite knowing my terrible background. Talk about forgiveness; talk about love. I was simply overwhelmed by the kindness and mercy shown to me as the day approached for the bar mitzvah.

That evening, I put on my best clothes and entered a temple for the first time in my life. It was beautiful, all colorful, and bright. This, I was sure, was the same kind that had been burned by my fellow members of the Hitler Youth during the war. What a shame that had been, I now realized.

When I looked around and knew that most everyone else attending was Jewish, I could not believe my eyes. Here I was surrounded by people like the ones I hated during my early years. According to Ruth and Judy, many were Holocaust survivors, and I wondered which ones were which. I was so nervous, shaking like a leaf and so scared that my hands were all sweaty. Part of me kept hoping the ground would open up and swallow me so I could keep from reading.

When Eric read from the Torah, words attributed to Moses, tears filled my eyes. What a beautiful boy, man, he was. Judy had invited me to watch him play basketball for the high school team. He was such a shy young man, but he played so well, and I cheered for him when he scored. Later, when Ruth's husband died, I went to the shivah at her house, another Jewish tradition. For several days, friends and relatives visited, and I ate Jewish food that I could have never imagined eating. Sitting with Ruth's friends and eating with them, I could hardly breathe at times; I simply felt like this was a dream. When I lay in bed after the shivah, my heart was still pounding with the excitement of the day.

When Eric made a short speech about what the passage meant at the bar mitzvah, I teared up again. Was I really here? Was this my imagination? Could it be possible that someone like me was part of this, part of a precious Jewish rite of passage, so special to everyone sitting beside me and nearby? Did Eric know who I was, what I had been? Had Ruth told him? Maybe not, I thought, because he had held my hand tightly when we met that morning. Or maybe he did know, maybe everybody knew that I had been a Nazi.

As the time came close for me to read from the small paperback book they called a siddur, I continued wondering what these people might think of me if they knew who I really was, one of the Germans who gassed the Jews. I hadn't done that, but I would have thought about it, and thinking is sometimes as bad as doing. It was like the Nazis came and took away my brain and put in another one. One filled with hate.

When my turn came, I could almost not rise out of my seat. My legs were wobbly, and I thought I might fall. A hand reached out to steady me, a loving hand from someone I did not know, a Jew helping me, the former Jew hater. After I spoke in a very shaky way all choked-up with emotion, I sat down with a sigh of relief. But I still felt that people were looking at me, wondering who I was and why a German like me was there. I kept seeing eyes glued to me, or so it seemed, eyes that were looking right through me.

Afterward, as we mingled among all of Ruth's friends, her Jewish friends, Judy kept introducing me as "my best friend Ursula," and this made me shiver, made me so proud that she considered me a friend, the best friend of a Jew. We had never really talked too much about my Hitler Youth days, but she and Ruth had to know, like Aaron, that I was in the group. But they never brought it up, never asked questions, never threw it in my face, just treated me like a friend. After the dinner that they had, one where some people complemented me on my reading, I hugged Ruth with all my might, hugged my friend the Holocaust survivor and never wanted to let go. Later, I thanked her in a letter by writing, "This was both a closure and a healing for me. Thank you from the bottom of my heart."

During the Jewish holidays like Hanukkah and Yom Kippur, Judy asked me to go shopping with her at special kosher shops. Then she invited me to be at the special dinners where they served the delicious food. All her grandchildren were there, and I met them and hoped they would not be as stupid as I was when I was their young age. I hoped they would think for themselves, be independent unlike me who was like a lamb being led to bad things all around. But it was still the experience reading at the bar mitzvah that impacted me more than any other. I would never forget that day as long as I lived.

When I later learned that Eric had graduated from high school and then left for Israel to become a soldier never to return, my eyes welled up again since I realized that I had been part of such a spiritual experience for him at the bar mitzvah. When he had read from the Torah, from the Bible, I wondered if Tante might be smiling from above, Tante who always read her Bible in the train station while I played nearby.

During all my stations along the way that I had experienced, a new outlook on life had infiltrated my life. Through the love of Aaron, and the love of Judy and Ruth, love had replaced the hate in my heart, and I realized that people are just people and that prejudice against those who are thought to be different, those who have a different color of skin, or different racial heritage, isn't right. Hitler had said he would control me from "cradle to grave," but he did not. I was finally free, finally able to put the past behind me. I knew there would continue to be struggles, reminders of the old Ursula, the hater, but I was determined to love, to care for others, and to be one who would always embrace people who were called different as long as I lived.

Through my experiences with first Aaron, my spiritual growth, and then my friendship with Judy and Ruth, I was now more comfortable talking to Jewish people I encountered. Somehow I felt that this proved that I wasn't as bad as people who thought all Germans were bad thought I was. If Aaron, Judy, and Ruth accepted me despite my past, then I should like myself, I decided. Ruth and Judy even invited me to spend Jewish holidays with them. And I helped Ruth by knitting shawls and different-colored socks for Israeli soldiers. Imagine this occurring, many years after I had knitted socks for the German soldiers who wanted to kill the Jews, Jews like Ruth and her mother.

In one of his speeches touting how he was going to control German youth "cradle to grave," Adolf Hitler also said something like, "They will never be free, for the rest of their lives." Through the grace of Aaron, and the majesty of a Holy Spirit I never knew existed by a god I had resisted my whole life, I had disobeyed the führer. I was, after a life filled with pain, regret, and guilt, finally healed, and yes, most important, free.

Telling my story at age eighty-two seems okay now after years of having been too afraid to do so. All those years, I hid the truth with only a few chosen people knowing of my having been a Hitler Youth. This was my secret, something I hid away with all my regrets and pain and sorrow. I know there are still those who say, "Do you know Ursula is a Nazi?" There is nothing I can do about them, but I hope my story will be a beacon of light for those who show prejudice to others by whatever means they do so. People are just people, it's that simple.

Since the World War II, I was always afraid to speak up on social issues since I knew someone would drag up my Nazi past. But I have paid my dues and collected enough wisdom that now I wonder why people let hate rule their lives so much. Maybe the world just needs people to fear, but I am the eyewitness to where this can lead since I lived what happened. Hating is wrong, so wrong, and my hope is that my story will make people stop and think about how hate destroys, how it infects people, how it sucks all the good out of them.

Over the years, I have tried to make up for my mistakes by working with many minorities, including those from the Latino community. I have shown them respect and learned from them as they have learned from me. This mind-set has also been one I have used with people of all races that are part of Los Angeles, a city diversified as perhaps no other. With a smile, and a helping hand where necessary, my life has been directed toward love instead of hate. Hitler may have taught me the latter, but in the end, a higher power took over and taught me that love conquers hate. I had to learn this lesson the hard way, but at least I learned it.

EPILOGUE

As noted in the prologue, Ursula Martens's story is a wake-up call, a reminder, a chance to relive through her eyes what it was like for a young person to be blinded by a government leader who only wanted to use her for his own personal vendettas. Adolf Hitler certainly intended to control people, to keep them from thinking, to keep them from being free, and there is no doubt that he succeeded. Today, the target once again is anyone who is different, and people, especially children, are being brainwashed to believe that those labeled as troublemakers, in many instances, are the cause of society's evils, a distressing thought at the very least.

One must recall, as author Daniel Jonah Goldhagen wrote in *Hitler's Willing Executioners*, that the Holocaust, the extermination of people who were different and dirty, may have been orchestrated by Hitler and his Nazi thugs, but it was ordinary people who carried out the execution. Older Germans, and youngsters like Ursula, may not have pulled the triggers or screamed "Attack" to the dogs that then leaped at their Jewish victims, but they were a part of the Nazi regime responsible for the mass murders. Why? Goldhagen wrote, "[We must] acknowledge what has for so long been generally denied or obscured by academic and non-academic interpreters alike: Germans' anti-Semitic views about Jews were the central cause agent not only of Hitler's decision to annihilate European Jewry . . . but also of the perpetrator's willingness to kill and brutalize Jews."[5]

This sort of mentality fits perfectly with Goldhagen's belief that "ordinary Germans" were convinced that Jews "ought to die." He wrote, "Simply put, the perpetrators, having consulted their own convictions and morality and having judged the mass annihilation of the Jews to be right, did not want to say 'no.'"

Goldhagen's views fit perfectly with young people like Ursula who were told how Jews were dirty, bad, and nonhuman. Simply put, she and the millions of others brainwashed did not know any better, for they were forbidden to think for themselves but instead indoctrinated with hate, hate, and more hate. This permitted a mind-set to ignore the truth even though, as Ursula discovered as she grew older, she knew the truth based on people disappearing and never returning, the ugly photographs in her father's drawer showing the brutality of German soldiers toward the defenseless Jews, and confirmation of this having occurred based on what she observed one night in the rail yard. But she did not want to say no, could not say no, a disposition perhaps excused for the first three or four years when she was a Hitler Youth but inexcusable when she reached the age of fifteen and sixteen and should have known better. When the war was over, she knew this and the guilt and shame she felt was a direct result.

By understanding how Ursula Martens was treated by those attempting to control her mind, it is possible to prevent such occurring ever again by those who believe segregation of the races, in any form, or exclusion of those termed different is the answer to the problems of the world. Hate begets hate; it is as true today as it was when Hitler spread hate throughout Germany. And if people do not speak up, if people do not defend the rights of others who are being persecuted, the hatemongers will win.

German Lutheran pastor Martin Neimoller opposed the Nazis and paid dearly for it when he was imprisoned at the Sachsenhausen and Dachau concentration camps. Perhaps this caring man best summed up what risks, what dangers, are possible when prejudice rules. In his poem, "First They Come," he wrote:

> First they came for the communists,
> and I did not speak out
> Because I was not a communist.

> Then they came for the socialists,
> and I did not speak out
> Because I was not a socialist.

> Then they came for the trade unionists,
> and I did not speak out
> Because I was not a trade unionist.

> Then they came for the Jews,
> and I did not speak out
> Because I was not a Jew.

> Then they came for me,
> And there was no one left to speak out.[6]

URSULA MARTENS AND MARK SHAW

APPENDIX

Historical Preludes

CHAPTER ONE PRELUDE

Because she was only four years old at the time, Ursula Martens did not realize it, but she was the very person, the perfect specimen that Adolf Hitler was talking about in 1933 whom he intended to seduce as part of his new order, a master race designed to rule the world for centuries to come. But the seeds for what became the nearly eight-million-member Hitler Youth, one being Ursula, had been sewn many years before, after Germany was destroyed in World War I.

When it ended on November 11, 1918, in Western Europe and four years later in the eastern part of the continent, more than fifteen million of the seventy million people who had been called to military duty had been killed. The German invasion of Belgium, Luxembourg, and France was a trigger point for the conflict, and when the war was lost, Germany was made to pay, and pay dearly for its aggression. Under the terms of the Treaty of Versailles in 1919, the German government was forced to accept complete responsibility for instigating the conflict under what was later called the War Guilt Clause. Punishment included forced disarmament, considerable territorial concessions, and perhaps most damaging, the payment of more than thirty billion dollars in reparations. Those with math skills estimated it might take as long as seventy years, until 1988 or so, for the money to be paid.

Instead of providing closure to the German assault on world domination, the excessive punishment opened the door for one man to walk in and rekindle dreams of that domination. His name was Adolf Hitler, and despite sorely lacking any sense of an advanced education, and not even being German-born (he was Austrian), he saw an opportunity to seize power and lead the German people toward reestablishing Germany to its rightful place among the world's elite countries.

With bold strokes, Hitler joined the German Worker's Party within a year after the war had ended, and then one year later renamed that party the National Socialist German Worker's Party (NSDAP) or Nazi Party. In 1922, his eyes focused on establishing the first Nazi Party youth group, but any grandiose ideas were thwarted when he was incarcerated for treason at Landsberg Prison in 1923. During the year he was there, Hitler wrote the infamous *Mein Kampf* (*My Battle* or *My Struggle*), a bible of sorts laying out his clandestine plans for Nazi Party domination of the political and social elements of the German population. The book was originally called *Four and a Half Years Struggle against Lies, Stupidity, and Cowardice*, and in it, Hitler chronicled his political philosophy to the effect that the Aryan race was superior but threatened by interracial marriage. A more serious threat, he believed, was the Jews, the ones who were lazy and responsible for everything from modern art to pornography and prostitution. Regarding Communists, they wanted to take over the world, something that could not prevail since, as he wrote, "A hundred blockheads do not equal one man in wisdom." He also noted, "The great masses of the people will fall victim to the big lie than to a small one."[7]

By July 1926, the first formal Hitler Youth was formed with Kurt Gruber as its leader. In 1927, more than three hundred Hitler Youth marched in a Nuremberg rally, earning congratulations from Hitler. By 1929, the year Ursula Martens was born, the Hitler Youth had been anointed the only official youth group of the Nazi Party. That same year, the stock market crashed in America, an event far across the Atlantic from Germany that slid Germany and the rest of the world deep into the Great Depression.

During the next four years, Hitler took advantage of the difficult economic times to surge the Nazi Party into significant prominence. On September 14, 1930, the party shocked the electorate by winning more than 18 percent of the vote while seating nearly a fifth of the 577-member Reichstag government. By December 1931, when German unemployment had reached more than five and a half million, Hitler seemed firmly in control, but he could not defeat President Paul von Hindenburg in two presidential elections. Hitler would not give up, and a year later, the Nazis doubled their election totals, and the NSDAP was now the largest political party in Germany. Responding to the cries of the people supporting the Nazis, President Hindenburg appointed Hitler chancellor in a coalition government on June 30, 1932, just four months after he had spoken to a cheering Hitler Youth crowd estimated at seventy thousand to one hundred thousand at a rally in Potsdam, a Berlin suburb.[8] Only twenty thousand had been expected, and nearby factories were utilized to house the youngsters when fifty tents proved inadequate. The brown-shirted youths had come through villages, towns, and hamlets where they made their presence known with loud marching songs.[9]

Celebrations throughout the country occurred on a day people called the Awakening of Germany. Author Susan Campbell Bartoletti described a scene in Berlin: "At last, bugles blared, drums rolled, and the parade began. Hitler's followers sang Nazi songs as they marched straight-legged, goose-stepping in military style . . . Each marcher carried a flaming torch, creating a river of light that flowed through the center of Berlin . . . [When] they spotted Hitler standing on the balcony, [they] extended their arms in the Nazi salute and thundered joyously, 'Heil Hitler.'"[10]

Subsequently, several events occurred that impacted Ursula Martens. They included the burning down of the German Reichstag, blamed on Communists, the passing of the Protection of the People and State which suspended all civil liberties and permitted police to arrest people and put them in "protective custody," and the passing of an Enabling Law, a prelude to Hitler's dictatorship. In addition, there was a boycott against Jewish businesses and professionals and an election where the Nazis received more than 95 percent of the votes.

Against the backdrop of this history, little Ursula Martens came into the world. If Adolf Hitler would have known of her birth, he would have rejoiced for she was destined to be part of the collective group of young people so important to his dream for a Hitler Youth that could rule the world. By 1933, there were more than 3.5 million members. One more was on the way.

CHAPTER TWO PRELUDE

Those who opposed Adolf Hitler and the Nazis had a short life span. In June/July 1934, SS and gestapo operatives methodically killed anyone who attempted to interfere with Hitler's quest for power. Then death did the führer a favor when President von Hindenburg died. Immediately Hitler consolidated the offices of chancellor and president. Now he ruled both civilian life and the military as commander-in-chief.

A year later, compulsory labor service for youth aged eighteen to twenty-five was introduced. In September 1935, the Nuremberg Laws against Jews became official. It categorized people with four German grandparents as German or kindred blood. People were classified as Jews if they descended from three or four Jewish grandparents. One with two Jewish grandparents was labeled a *Mischlinge*, a crossbreed of mixed blood. Above all, the law excluded Jews from any citizenship rights while prohibiting marriage between Germans and Jews. Now there was no question as to who was Jewish and who was not providing the opportunity to restrict the rights of anyone deemed Jewish. If there was a question, one device used was called a nose measurer. Certain specifications were known regarding the perfect nose for an Aryan, and if someone's nose was too wide or perhaps too full, they were immediately discarded as a potential true German with kindred bloodlines.[11] Also discarded were those deemed too sickly to be part of the master race. Hitler emphasized this later when he said, "Anything that is weak . . . is choked off and dies. It is killed mercifully and pitilessly and that is the best thing for it. This is how the Good Lord has arranged nature."[12]

Certainly Jews were not permitted to be a part of the Hitler Youth. Candidates had to first pass a written examination detailing their knowledge of the Aryan race and political issues. More important, they had to provide absolute proof of racial purity in the form of an Ahnenpass, a signed and stamped official document indicating proper racial heritage. Once qualifications were met, the prospective Hitler Youth member stood with other candidates in a large hall as parents and leading Nazi officials looked on. The blood banner, allegedly having been dipped in the blood of the martyred youth Herbert Norkus, the son of a taxi driver killed by Communist radicals, stood at the front of the hall. The boy or girl, while gripping the banner with the left hand and holding three fingers in the air in Boy Scout fashion, repeated the sacred oath: "In the presence of this blood banner, which represents our führer, I am willing and ready to give up my life for him, so help me God." Trumpets then blared as a military band struck up tunes in accordance with Nazi folklore.[13]

In accordance with the credo that "Youth should be led by youth," meetings called home evenings were held in venues away from any parental interference. Many times the leaders were barely teenagers. Songs were sung, games played, and most important, propaganda read so that the youth digested enough information to become what they were supposed to be, good Nazis, with the boys earning the special award of a dagger inscribed with "Blood and Honor" on it. One special treat occurred when the youth were permitted to listen to Hitler radio broadcasts on special stations allowed by the party. Un-German broadcasts were forbidden. Author Bartoletti observed, "The Nazis knew what appealed to kids—uniforms, flags, bands, badges, weapons, and stories about heroes—they offered plenty."[14] Author Otto Knopp observed, "In the increasingly monolithic and disciplined Nazi society the Hitler Youth appealed to children's self-esteem and urge for recognition."[15]

By 1936, Hitler, with confidence that the Hitler Youth movement was on the rise, had completed his first act of aggression, occupation of the demilitarized Rhineland. He promised that was the end of his efforts outside Germany. More importantly, the new leader could enhance his worldwide pictorial as host of the Summer Olympics in Berlin. There he showed a glimpse of his racial prejudice by refusing to acknowledge the athletic prowess of black American sprinter Jesse Owens. Confidant Albert Speer said Hitler felt that "People whose antecedents came from the jungle were primitive; their physiques were stronger than those of civilized whites. They represented unfair competition and hence must be excluded from future games."[16]

A year later, the world waited to see what Hitler might do next. Secretly, he and his military team plotted the strategy they intended to impose toward eventual takeover of Europe and beyond. The first target was to be his native Austria, but this occurred in 1938 when

Ursula turned nine years old, just a year shy of when she could become a member of the Hitler Youth.

One man already captivated by Hitler's magnetism was the young, budding architect Albert Speer. In 1931, he had attended a Hitler speech expecting to listen to a "hysterical demagogue, a shrieking and gesticulating fanatic in uniform." Instead, he heard a man "candidly expressing his anxieties about the future," one whose "irony was softened by a somewhat self-conscious humor," one who spoke with a "hypnotic persuasiveness." By speech end, Speer, destined to become a close friend of Hitler's and part of Hitler's inner circle along with Joseph Goebbels and Martin Bormann, decided "Here, it seemed to me, was hope."[17]

CHAPTER THREE PRELUDE

Enamored by a new leader, Speer had become a member of the Nazi Party (#474,481 by his calculation). Hitler had seduced him, as he would later seduce Ursula, and never let go.

In 1934, an ad appeared in a German newspaper that read: "SA member, 30 years old, healthy to the core, looking for the mother of his children and keeper of his roost. Must be of pure heredity. Stately blond preferred, no dark-skinned shorty."

Simply put, this ad said, "No Jews need apply." Such was the mindset of Adolf Hitler, his Nazi comrades, and a continuing stream of Germans who were being told two important things: they, the German people, the true Germans, were the master race, superior to all beings, and two, the Jews were lowlife types who needed to be removed from the face of the earth. Aryans, the blond, blue-eyed Scandinavian types, were the replacements, and young Ursula Martens fit this description to a T. If there was such a thing as a target audience for being the perfect German, she was it.

As 1937 passed to 1938, Hitler Youth membership became mandatory for those aged ten to eighteen. Hitler wanted to be sure that children like Ursula would be part of it. But the remnants of the Hitler Youth had begun many years before when the concept of totalitarianism began to sweep through Europe. This meant control of a country by a single person or class whereby every aspect of rule was imposed on the people including those relating to the economy, freedom of speech and assembly, aspects of surveillance, and acts of violence to back up threats of repercussion when disorder occurred. Hitler and his Nazi Party leaders had achieved this total control based on seeds of discontent from those frightened by economic woes and other hardships. Author Jean-Denis G. G. Lepage wrote, "Hitler's Germany went even further. National Socialism was the most evil manifestation of megalomania in history. It claimed an absolute domination over every department of daily life and carried the development of state sovereignty and raison d'etat to a new extreme. From cradle to grave, a German man or woman would be part of the Nazi-controlled organization."[18]

This "cradle to grave" scenario was aimed directly at youth like Ursula. Hitler had stated, "The German youth of the future must be slim and slender, swift as a greyhound, tough as leather, and hard as Krupp steel . . . they will not be free for the rest of their lives."[19]

Being a member of the Hitler Youth was the first step, and this organization had a rich history, one triggered, of course, by the rise to power in Germany of Adolf Hitler. Born in 1889 the son of a little-known Austrian customs official, he served in WWI as a non-distinguished corporal before becoming a listless laborer who painted houses, and a failed artist. But author and Holocaust expert H. R. Trevor-Roper saw more in the Hitler mystique that soon captivated an entire nation and the world:

> The son of a petty official in rural Austria, himself of meager education and no fixed background, by all accounts a shiftless, feckless, unemployable neurotic living from hand to mouth in the slums of Vienna, [Hitler] appeared in Germany, as a foreigner, and, in the years of its most abject condition, declared that the German people could, by its own efforts, and against the wishes of its victors, not only recover its lost provinces, but add to them, and conquer and dominate the whole of Europe.[20]

Trevor-Roper added, "Further, he declared that he personally could achieve this miracle. Twenty years later he had so nearly succeeded that the rest of the world thought it another miracle when he was at last resisted."[21] Mindful of those who underestimated Hitler such as Sir Lewis Namier, who "endorses the account given him by a disgusted German official" who called Hitler "a mere illiterate, illogical, unsystematic bluffer and smatter," Trevor-Roper suggested, "And yet . . . could a mere adventurer, a shifty, scatterbrained charlatan, have done what Hitler did . . . starting from nothing . . . survived and commanded all of the dark forces he had mobilized, and, by commanding them, nearly conquered the whole world?"[22] Holocaust expert Gerhard L. Weinberg wrote, "With the skills, enthusiasm, and resources of one of Europe's most advanced and populous countries harnessed to these views and policies, [Hitler] not only transformed that society in a few years but

URSULA MARTENS AND MARK SHAW

unleashed a war that changed the entire globe, and, in the process, wrecked the nation he led."[23]

In April 1920, at the age of thirty-one, Hitler, a Catholic as a youth who remained so his entire life, had surged the NSDAP to prominence. It was then called the Nazi Party since the word *national* was pronounced "na-tsi-o-nal" in German.[24]

When the leader of the party became an honorary leader, Hitler took over in 1921, eight years before Ursula Martens was born. The Nazis used a newspaper they purchased, the *People's Observer*, to publish their extreme views. They also established the Sturmabteilung (SA) to serve as a parliamentary activist wing.

Author Jean-Denis G. G. Lepage wrote that Hitler had chronicled his "anticapitalist, anti-Semitic, extreme nationalist ideology in a 25-point program drawn up in February 1920 and reaffirmed in 1926." It included such manifestos as rejection of the Treaty of Versailles, the formation of a lethal national army, the demand that land formally controlled by Germany be returned, and classification of citizens by race including there being no citizenship for anyone of Jewish heritage.[25] Author Lepage believed "Hitler achieved unprecedented personal power by systematically promising anything to anyone, while making secret deals with anyone who could be of any use to him, no matter how much difference there was between secret promises and public official oratory." Lepage added, "The ideology was simple, even simplistic, and often contradictory, with emphasis on anti-Semitism, ultra-nationalism, the concept of Aryan racial supremacy, contempt for liberal democracy, and principle of unique leadership." Simply put, Lepage said, "The Nazi program was designed to appeal to everyone with a grievance of some kind . . . it was flexible movement aiming at aggressive action, a kind of religion leaning on blind faith, on irrationality, and exploitation of subconscious fears and basic instincts."[26] Regarding youth, author Bartoletti wrote, "Adolf Hitler admired the natural energy and drive that young people possess[ed]. He understood that young people could be a powerful political force that could help shape Germany's future. In his quest for power, Hitler harnessed their enthusiasm and loyalty." To this end, she then quoted Hitler, "I begin with the young. We older ones are used up . . . But my magnificent youngsters! Are there finer ones anywhere in the world? Look at all these men and boys. What material! With them I can make a new world."[27] Later, he would boast,

"They wear the same brown shirt. No-one asks about their background. And they all look as if they have come from the same mould. There are working-class children, middle-class children, children of employers and employees, of farmers and so on. But to look, they are all identical."[28]

With Hitler at the helm, a natural progression was the establishment of the Hitler Youth (Hitler Jugend, HJ, or HY for short). But as Lepage, Bartoletti and other historians point out, it was only one youth party in a long list of them that had been in existence since the early 1900s. This was true not only in Germany but across the globe with one example the formation of the Boy Scouts of America, founded in 1910. Italy had paramilitary Balillas, youth ages eight to twelve, and the Soviet Union the Komsomol or Communist Union of Youth, aged ten to fifteen.[29]

Preceding the Hitler Youth had been such groups as the Wandervogel, emphasizing the need for youngsters to disengage themselves from repressive values present in Germany at the time, the Jungstahlhelm, or young steel helmet, and the Jungdeutscher Orden, "an extreme-right antirevolutionary youth group with somewhat confusing ideology."[30] Hitler's values had their basis in all these groups, but he saw the opportunity to unite them all in a forceful manner during the time of Kampfzeit. Occurring during the years of 1925 to 1933, Kampfzeit meant "the heroic time of struggle,"[31] and Author Bartoletti wrote, "As Fuhrer, Hitler wanted to achieve Gleichschaltung or 'conformity,' in all aspects of Germany society. He began by eliminating all other youth groups except the Hitler Youth saying 'It is important to bring every member of the new generation under the spell of National Socialism in order that they may never be spiritually seduced by any of the old generation.'"[32]

Hitler's one-year incarceration in prison briefly prevented any youth group from ascending to the level the führer intended, but once he was free, the quest began to unite all the pro-Hitler youth groups into one. In April 1926, the name Hitler Jugend appeared for the first time, and two months later, the Hitler Youth was established by Hitler with Kurt Gruber as Reichfuhrer der Hitler Jugend, leader of the Hitler Youth. An ad had invited "all national-socialist-minded youth, aged between 14 and 18, regardless of their social class, whose heart suffered under the pitiful conditions of Germany, who wanted to fight the Jewish enemy, shame and suffering, and who wished to serve the cause of the Fatherlands to join the Nazi Youth League." The youth organization was separated into two groups, the Jungmannschaften, boys fourteen to sixteen, and the Jungsturm Adolf Hitler, boys sixteen to eighteen years old. The league was then positioned under the command of the SA, "early private militia of the Nazi Party." They were "young roughnecks" designated to "oppose rival political parties by force."[33]

In 1928, a rally was attended by more than 2,500 boys, but party leadership swayed, and even though party membership rose to thirteen thousand by 1929, the Hitler Youth was not as imposing a force as Hitler had hoped.[34]

Gruber fell into disfavor, but Baldur von Schirach, son of a former Prussian captain and three-quarters American, replaced him. He used the HY as a propaganda tool and swung the youth into action during 1930 and 1931. They, along with the SA, distributed pamphlets, marched in military-like rallies and large parades, and sung songs designed to appeal to those seeking a home for their distrust of the current Weimar regime. Author Lepage wrote, "The essential purpose of such manifestations was to display strength and physical force, to create a sense of power and feeling of unity, and show to all that the success of the Nazis was irresistible." So impressive was the display that the Weimar regime outlawed all "political uniformed militia, including the communist fighting squads, but also the Nazi SA, SS, and Hitler Jugend."[35]

Ursula Martens's fourth birthday in 1933 coincided with the rise of Hitler and the Nazis to power. By then, more than 850,000 people were party members, up from 600,000 three years earlier. Absolute authority was the byword as the system of government was altered as never before. Trade unions were prohibited, opponents of the Nazis were sent away to concentration camps, and the first plans were executed that would eradicate the Jews from the new German way of life. All political parties except the Nazis were forbidden. In effect, a totalitarian state was enacted. Schirach, as leader of the Hitler Youth, seized the opportunity to increase membership to more than eight hundred thousand youth by end of year. One year later, when Ursula turned five, the total was more than one and a quarter million.

During the process of what was known as Gleichschaltung, the elimination of individualism, Schirach achieved his goal, absorbing every youth group into the Hitler Youth. This was coordinated with the Nazi aim to eliminate any opposition to its policies and plans. One example of the means to do this was to require that any youth seeking to join a sport organization or earn a certificate had to be a member of the Nazi Youth. Similar pressure was then exerted on members of any youth religious group. Beginning in 1935, they were forbidden to wear "uniforms or insignias, hike or encamp in large groups, to fly banners, flags and pennants, or practice or receive instruction in sports." Such laws, along with pressure exerted through threats, forced the Catholic episcopate to order the breakup of all Catholic youth league organizations. Although the Pope objected to Hitler's tactics, he was ignored.[36]

Soon those aged ten to eighteen had no choice, since membership in the Hitler Youth was compulsory. This caused the membership roles to swell from nearly five and a half million in 1936 to more than seven million by 1938. Sympathetic Hitler Youth branches existed in far away countries such as Australia and the United States, where many groups believed strongly in Hitler's policies.

Ursula Martens was approaching ten years old when this occurred. The way had been cleared for her, and every other German youth, to be part of the exalted Hitler Youth, whether they liked it or not. What awaited her was indoctrination and, in many ways, a brainwashing. Hitler's "cradle to grave" control plan was moving forward at a lightning pace.

CHAPTER FOUR PRELUDE

As the decade turned from the 1930s to the 1940s, Adolf Hitler, despite promises to the contrary that he would not attempt to conquer neighboring countries, swept the swastika across Europe with blazing speed.

In quick succession, the German army attacked and then conquered Poland to trigger the start of the Second World War. Nobody, despite warning signs at every turn, realized it then, but the Third Reich was on schedule to take over the world, to spread Nazism and its master race to every city, town, and village on earth.

As Hitler's plans for domination escalated, his precious Hitler Youth flourished as he had intended. This was most evident regarding the educational angle he favored, one designed to produce strong minds and bodies dedicated to the führer and only the führer. To this end, from the first day students were in school, they were taught that the only way to greet each other was with "Heil Hitler." They then had to swear allegiance to Hitler, raise their arms in the Nazi salute, and use Hitler's name in their prayers and worship. To restrict the number of Jews who could attend schools, the Nazis passed the Law against the Overcrowding of German Schools with students being told that Jews "have no business being among us true Germans."[37] Subsequently, teachers were required to read *Mein Kampf,* and any teacher "with democratic views were either suspended from duty, forced into early retirement or sidetracked into insignificant jobs . . . when a school had won 90 percent of its pupils over to the Nazi youth movement, the HJ presented it with a banner . . . One school blackboard was imprinted with the words, 'All Calamities Come From Jews.'"[38] Former HY member Paul Stüben recalled, "Our headmaster stood up in front of the class in his Party uniform and announced, 'I must inform you that we have a Jewish girl in the class . . . You are no longer allowed to play with her, you may not do schoolwork with her, or have anything to do with her . . .' After a few days, the girl disappeared. We never saw her again."[39] To emphasize how much trouble those were who did not meet the test of a strong German, one school math quiz included the following information: "To keep a mentally ill person costs approx. 4RM per day, a cripple 5.5 RM, a criminal 3.5 RM."[40]

From 1936 on, any boy celebrating his tenth birthday had been required to register with the Reich youth headquarters. A formal investigation of the boy and his parents, one especially focused on whether he was of racial purity, was conducted. If the youth passed the test, he was admitted into the Deutsches Jungvolk (a subdivision of the HY). Initiation ceremonies were held on April 20, Hitler's birthday. Age groups were established to separate the boys, and various leaders, some not much older than the boys, were installed.

Those fourteen to eighteen were called Hitler's Boys, members of the Kern Hitler Jugend. Ranks included national youth leader, Hitler Youth leader, and Hitler Youth member. If one was a member of a Gefolgschaft, a military unit consisting of 150–200 boys, they had their own flag to fly high when they marched. Nationally, groups were formed with designated locations such as East Prussia, Brandenburg, Berlin, Cologne, and Hamburg. All along the line, every group was regimented, strict military hierarchy in place.[41]

Ursula Martens had her own Hitler Youth girls group to join. In December 1928, a year before she was born, Karl Gruber had created the Jungmädelbund (League of Young Girls), for girls ten to fourteen, and the Bund Deutscher Mädel (BDM, German Girls League), for girls fourteen to eighteen. Jutta Rüdiger, a leader in the German Girls League, outlined what goal the Nazis had in mind for girls like Ursula: "The organization would bring out in the girls character and the ability to perform, not useless knowledge, but all-around education, and an exemplary bearing."[42] Author Lepage believed, "The female organizations were intended to give girls and young women a sense of pride and self-worth, and produce political and racial conformity in the young so that they would go on as adults to have unquestionable loyalty and faith to the Führer, Adolph Hitler."[43] The "look," author Michael Kater said, was "to correspond with the beauty ideal of male adolescents and grown-ups . . . this ideal was of a woman who did not use lipstick or make-up, did not arrange or dye her hair—all the denigrated attributes of sick Weimar-republican city girls or French seductresses."[44]

Units, squads, and rank were utilized to separate the girls similar to that used for the HY boys. But Hitler believed boys/men were far superior to girls/women with the latter's duty to birth healthy specimens of Aryan baby boys. To make certain the girls/women were in top physical shape, various tests were provided regarding all sorts of athletic events. When the girls were ripe for birthing, they advanced to the Glaube und Schönheit, the Faith and Beauty wing of the Hitler Youth. The goal: to provide the perfect specimen of the proper Nazi woman. Only blue-eyed blondes need apply, but they also had to have "superior intellectual gifts and grace of mind and body." Membership fees were paid by parents, with instruction intended to "teach domestic handiness and foster-home-spun feminine charm." Many of the prettiest girls were chosen for an elite assignment. This involved becoming "companions" for many of the Nazi brass with the result to be a perfect Nazi who would help Hitler rule the world in future years.[45] Author Dr. Otto Knopp noted, "What about the girls? They . . . were taken in hand, drilled and comprehensively lied to. 'German lasses' were meant to be hard-working to the point of self-sacrifice, obedient and above all prepared for their roles as mothers of future soldiers . . . machines for producing human reinforcements."[46] Hitler had observed, "There is surely nothing finer than to educate a young thing for oneself; a lass of eighteen or twenty years old is as pliable as wax. It must be possible for a man to impose his stamp on any girl. Indeed, a woman wants nothing else."[47] His propaganda minister Joseph Goebbels agreed, saying in 1929, "It is the woman's task to be beautiful and bring children into the world."[48] To all the HY, a directive read, "You, ten-year-old cub, and you, lass, are not too young nor too small to practise obedience and discipline, to . . . show yourself to be a comrade."[49]

To emphasize the pomp and circumstance necessary for the Hitler Youth to be the hope of the future, flags abounded. One most prominent was a red and white striped flag. Imprinted in the center was a tilted white square with the swastika carefully positioned in the center. Such flags were considered to be holy in nature, and units swore an oath of allegiance to the führer on them. The cloth was never permitted to touch the ground, and when it was not being carried, it could not to be leaned against any object such as tree or a building. Medals awarded for separate achievements were not free but had to be purchased. Swastikas were imprinted on any number of items including rings and necklaces were available for purchase. Daggers, many of them designed by the führer himself, were hot items.[50]

Certainly no member of the Hitler Youth could ignore the importance of the Nazi salute. Much care was taken to properly instruct each boy and girl that they were expected to know how to salute similar to that of the Roman salute, one adopted by Mussolini in Italy for his Fascist Party. This meant that the boy or girl had to stand straight and at attention with the left hand positioned on the belt buckle. The right hand was then raised at what amounted to a forty-five-degree angle from the chest so that the arm was outstretched just above the shoulder. While clicking the heels in typical Nazi fashion, a strong, enthusiastic "Heil Hitler" was said in a loud voice. Failure to handle this important task properly was akin to sinning against the führer, a sin unforgettable in the eyes of those who worshipped him like a god.[51]

Author Michael H. Kater believed that these people included members of certain religious groups. He wrote, "To the racist Nazi 'German Christians' in the Protestant Church who thought that the Jewish Jesus really was a blond 'Aryan,' Hitler appeared as having been directly sent by God in order to save Germany."[52]

This was the same man of whom author and historian H. R. Trevor-Roper wrote, "Children were to him the merely continually replaceable (and therefore continually expendable) means of conquest and colonization."[53]

URSULA MARTENS AND MARK SHAW

CHAPTER FIVE PRELUDE

While the world looked on with fear and trepidation, Adolf Hitler and the Nazis began conquering country after country. Denmark, Norway, Belgium, the Netherlands, and Luxembourg fell like dominoes. In June 1940, the same month Hitler and Spain's Franco entered into a non-aggression pact, Paris was Hitler's. On June 23, Hitler toured the ancient city as the French looked on in horror.

On August 13, the Battle of Britain began when German Luftwaffe bombed airfields and factories in England. Hitler imposed a blockade of the British Isles, and during the final week of the month, air raids on London were a daily occurrence. But the British fought back, and within days, Berlin began to feel the strength of the English bombers. A month later, Hitler's forces assaulted the British with all their might. That same month, September, the führer signed the Tripartite (Axis) Pact with Italy, and most important regarding future events involving the United States, Japan. While war loomed large, Franklin Roosevelt was reelected president.

As the year 1940 ended, the Germans continued to bomb London while Hungary joined the Axis powers and the Greeks turned back the Italians. In the new year, German general Erwin Rommel began his assault on Tripoli as the Nazis invaded Greece and Yugoslavia. Both countries surrendered to the German invaders.

May of 1941 marked Deputy Führer Rudolf Hess's surprising trip to Scotland where nuances of peace were discussed. The Germans continued to bomb London, but the British bombed Hamburg. The mortal enemies traded sunken ships when first the Germans sunk the ship *Hood* and then the British sunk the *Bismarck* that had sunk the *Hood*.

The next month, June, saw Germany invade Russia as Operation Barbarossa began. In July, Soviet leader Josef Stalin called for a scorched earth policy as his country began to battle Hitler's forces. That same month, Hitler ordered the initial planning for what would become known as the Final Solution, the plan to extinguish Jews once and for all. August included Roosevelt and British prime minister Winston Churchill signing the Atlantic Charter. By September, every person of

Jewish heritage was required to wear a yellow star. Toward the end of the month, more than thirty-three thousand Jews were exterminated at Kiev.

On December 6, 1941, the Soviets launched a major counteroffensive against the Germans in Moscow. One day later, the Japanese bombed Pearl Harbor. The United States declared war on Japan on the seventh, and Germany declared war on the United States three days later.

On January 20, 1942, German leaders gathered at 56–58 A, Groben Street in Wannsee, a Berlin suburb. The conference held there became infamous since those attending were told of a master plan to be overseen by Reinhard Heydrich, the alter ego of Heinrich Himmler. This was the Final Solution, one approved by Hitler that would deport the entire Jewish population of Europe and French North Africa to German-occupied territory in Eastern Europe. Part of the plan was to use Jews for strenuous projects such as road building so they would die in the field. Anyone surviving would be killed regardless.

During this same January, Hitler remarked, "I don't see much future for the Americans. It's a decayed country. And they have racial problems and the problems of social inequalities . . . Everything about the behavior of American society reveals that is half Judaized, and the other half negrified. How can one expect a state like that to hold together—a country where everything is built on the dollar?" He also noted, "There is nobody stupider than the Americans."[54]

Reinhard Heydrich was assassinated by Czechoslovakian freedom fighters in Prague five months later, but by then mass gassings at Auschwitz had begun since Hitler believed that killing Jews with bullets was too expensive. By November, any plans to send the Jews to Eastern Europe evaporated when the Soviet Army surrounded Germany's Sixth Army at Stalingrad. Defeat was imminent.

As the war raged on, the Hitler Youth had been active in support of the führer. In August 1940, Artur Axmann had succeeded Baldur von Schirach as leader of the Hitler Youth. That fall, an edict from the National Youth Directorate had required all boys ten to eighteen to undergo target practice and terrain maneuvers. New camps were opened under Hitler's orders to provide three weeks of mandatory training since it was the intention for the Hitler Youth to play an even more important part in the fighting as the war progressed. Each of the boys and girls, including Ursula Martens, had taken the oath of obedience. There was

URSULA MARTENS AND MARK SHAW

also a pledge of allegiance: "I promise to do my duty in love and loyalty to the führer and the flag."

These were the same youth who author Michael Kater said "sang anti-Semitic songs with texts that sanctioned 'Jewish blood dripping from the knife.'" Later, he reported, members of the Hitler Youth were required "to watch Veit Harlan's film, Jud Suss (Jew Sweet), by all accounts the most anti-Semitic feature film ever made in Nazi Germany."[55] Youth were also bombarded with anti-Semitic books including *Der Giftpilz* (*The Poisonous Mushroom*) by Julius Streicher. His motto, "Educate the children to a healthy hatred."[56] An excerpt from this book featured an exchange between a student and his teacher after he is asked about how to identify a Jew. The boy walks to the blackboard and points to some sketches while saying, "A Jew is usually recognized by his nose. The Jewish nose is crooked at the end. It looks like a figure 6. So it is called the 'Jewish Six.' Many non-Jews have crooked noses too. But their noses are bent, not at the end, but further up. Such a nose is called a hook-nose or eagle's beak. It has nothing to do with a Jewish nose."

After noting that a Jew may also be recognized by their thick lips, often with the lower lip hanging down and that the look of a Jew is "sly and sharp," the student recites verse including the line, "If we are to be free from the Jew/and to be happy and glad again, then youth must join our struggle/to overcome the Jew devil."[57] Such comments caused editors Jeremy Noakes and G. Pridham to state, "Antisemitism was at the core of Nazi ideology . . . it expressed a vision of a cosmic racial struggle in which the Jews, representing the forces of darkness, were pitted against the Aryan forces of light, of which the German people were the standardbearers."[58]

This occurring should not have surprised anyone who had read *Mein Kampf.* Besides writing that young men's "whole education and training must be so ordered as to give him the conviction that he is absolutely superior to others,"[59] Hitler blasted the Jews at every turn. Discussing the "moral stains of the 'chosen people,'" he wrote, "Was there any form of filth or profligacy . . . without at least one Jew in it? If you cut even cautiously into such an abscess, you found, like a maggot in a rotting body, often dazzled by the sudden light—a kike!" Explaining his anti-Semitism, he proclaimed, "Hence today I believe that I am acting in accordance with the will of Almighty Creator; by defending myself against the Jew, I am fighting for the work of the Lord."

After noting the "blood-sucking" nature of Jews in commerce, he attacked young Jews' relations with others, writing, "With satanic joy in his face, the black-haired Jewish youth lurks in wait for the unsuspecting girl whom he defiles with his blood, thus stealing her from her people." Speaking directly to his dedication to saving girls like Ursula, he swore to prevent "the seduction of hundreds of thousands of girls by bow-legged, repulsive Jewish bastards." The intended goal: "In the interest of nation; that the most beautiful bodies should find one another, and so help to give the nation new beauty."[60]

By "new beauty," Hitler had meant a master race, one devoid of Jews. This required their becoming the chief enemy of the German people, the scapegoats for everything bad that had happened to the country. Hitler loyalist and friend Albert Speer, who became Hitler's chief architect during the war, reasoned that the führer had a special gift for being able to "unleash mass instincts" at meetings, an ability to "play on the passions that underlay the veneer of ordinary respectable life." To this end, he noted that to "compensate for misery, insecurity, unemployment and hopelessness" that ran rampant during the early 1930s, Hitler seized on the need by listeners for a time when "the personal unhappiness caused by the breakdown of the economy [to be] replaced by a frenzy that demanded victims." This led, he surmised, to the belief that Hitler "threw them the victims. By lashing out at . . . opponents and vilifying the Jews, [he] gave expression and direction to fierce, primal passion."[61]

To Ursula Martens and millions of other ordinary Germans, this passion would result in a look-the-other-way attitude as millions of Jews became the ones to blame for all of Germany's troubles, true lambs to the slaughter in a Germany destined to be a torture chamber. Despite there being a copy of *Mein Kampf* in the Martens's home, Ursula never read it. She should have.

CHAPTER SIX PRELUDE

Despite the propaganda being passed on the German people by the Nazi regime, the defeat at Stalingrad marked a significant turning point in Adolf Hitler's plan to rule the world. Fourteen-year-old Ursula Martens was never told in February 1943 that the German Sixty Army had surrendered. This downturn coincided with Ursula's fellow Hitler Youth members, all teenagers, officially becoming operators of antiaircraft batteries to defend the Fatherland.

Required allegiance to the Nazis by Hitler Youth did not prevent many Germans from deciding the Third Reich was not their Reich. Some parents objected to the motto "Führer, command—We follow," believing it was wrong to follow the seduction undertaken by the Nazis. To them, as author Klaus P. Fischer wrote, "The Hitler Youth was a state organization designed to indoctrinate young people in the mindset of the Führer, Adolph Hitler. Young people were deceived by a smokescreen of youthful idealism."[62] Author Daniel Jonah Goldhagen believed "the fidelity of the Germans to their genocidal enterprise was so great as to defy comprehension." These Germans, he noted, included the Hitler Youth. He related a story indicating that ordinary Germans, including those in the HY, had participated in the burning of a large barn near the town of Gardelegen where as many as five thousand Jews were trapped inside and killed.[63] Reports also surfaced that during roundups of Jews who were to be transported to the concentration camps, Hitler Youth officiated and helped control those headed for their deaths.[64] Parents were astounded to learn their children were being used for such purposes, but what could they do?

On the heels of the defeats in the Soviet Union, another defeat occurred for mighty Germany when the Allies overwhelmed German troops in North Africa, putting an end to domination there. All across Europe, German forces met resistance and defeat, but this did not keep SS Reichsführer Heinrich Himmler from ordering the liquidation of all Jewish ghettos in Poland. By fall and winter, when President Roosevelt, British prime minister Churchill, and Soviet premier Stalin met at Tehran, the noose was closing in on Hitler and his Nazi comrades.

Despite the defeats, confidant Albert Speer said Hitler was defiant, certain he could turn the tide: "He made himself believe in his ultimate victory. In a sense he was worshipping himself. He was forever holding up to himself a mirror in which he saw not only himself but also the confirmation of his mission by divine Providence." He added, "If there was any fundamental insanity in Hitler, it was [an] unshakable belief in his lucky star. He was by nature a religious man, but his capacity for belief had been perverted into belief in himself."[65]

Superior Allied airpower began to show dominance as bombs dropped on a daily basis in Germany, including those areas where Ursula Martens lived. Then, in June 1944, the D-day landings occurred at Normandy on the northern coast of France. Germany began a V-2 rocket attack on Britain, but American troops began to inch toward German soil after liberating such towns as Cherbourg, France. In July 1944, an assassination attempt on Hitler's life nearly killed the führer, but he escaped. A month later, Allied troops forged into Paris and liberated the city. When Athens was liberated as well, German military hero, General Erwin Rommel, committed suicide. By October, the last gassing of Jews at Auschwitz occurred. In December, the famous Battle of the Bulge occurred in the Ardennes, and within a few days, American general George Patton took the city of Bastogne.

Many German soldiers had been trained at a special school called Napola (national political institutes). These schools had been established in 1933 as a birthday present to Hitler from education minister Bernhard Rust. The purpose: to train an elite group of young men by restoring them to the principles invoked at Prussian academies. Admission priority was given to Nazi family members, Hitler Youth members, sons of those killed in battle, and sons of military.

Perfect Aryan bloodline was prerequisite and physical fitness superiority a must. As time passed, Heinrich Himmler fought to have the Napola students, the perfect political soldiers, placed under the control of the SS. He succeeded in this attempt and soon the Black Corps were in control. SS-style uniforms and ranks were introduced. Teachings included "Strong emphasis on developing soldierly spirit, physical courage, a sense of duty, simplicity, austere conduct, self-discipline, physical fitness, a sense of community, and readiness for service and self-sacrifice, focusing on forming a Nazi personality rather than intellectual development."[66]

Special units were an integral part of the Hitler Youth movement. To any casual observer, amassing nearly ten million youth into something akin to the Boy Scouts appeared to have been innocent enough, but in fact the Nazis had other ideas in mind. Author Jean-Denis G. G. Lepage wrote, "The HJ was not an innocent youth movement at all . . . the Hitler Youth was providing the Nazi Party with a new generation of believers with cannon fodder for war. It was government-dominated organization dedicated to making fervent Nazis, producing obedient citizens, and molding savage warriors for the Third Reich."[67]

To keep these "savage warriors," most of them barely teenagers, from harm, Nazi leaders decided to send certain young people to places of safety away from the large cities threatened by bombings. The official party line said the reason to send the youth to "places of safety" was to "protect [them] from risks to their health that might arise from frequent air-raid warnings . . . and also to ensure uninterrupted schooling and communal education." On September 27, 1940, Martin Bormann wanted to make certain there were no questions about the motives behind the action. His circular read, "By order of the Führer, however, there is to be no use of the word 'evacuation,' but rather of a 'dispatch to the countryside' of children from the big cities."[68]

Innocent to the point of blindness, Ursula Martens and her Hitler Youth comrades were being used for the führer's purposes. Taught to hate, taught to torture, taught to kill. Young and impressionable, they never had a chance.

CHAPTER SEVEN PRELUDE

On September 25, 1944, all males between the ages of sixteen and sixty had been called to serve in the Volkssturm (home guard). Those Hitler Youth who had sworn allegiance to the führer and offered to give up their life for him were now going to risk it.

In a last ditch effort to stave off defeat, V-1 rockets had been launched toward London. But opposition was strong there and everywhere as the Allies pushed forward toward defeating the führer. In Warsaw, Poland, the Polish resistance had attempted to liberate Warsaw from German occupation. They hoped to fight for only a few days until the Soviets came to their aid. During the first battles, the Poles controlled several areas of the city, but the Soviets did not push forward as early as the resistance had planned. The saga lasted for more than sixty days, and the resistance was finally crushed. More than fifteen thousand brave souls were killed, but worse, between 150,000 and 200,000 civilians died in the violence. By January 1945, the Soviets finally broke through and liberated the city.

Two years earlier, when the Germans had suffered the huge losses in Russia, a new division of the SS was organized. It was called the Twelfth Panzer Grenadier Hitlerjugend Division, the SS-HJ. Inducted into this special force were Hitler Youth born in 1926 meaning the troops were teenagers just seventeen years of age. Each was carefully chosen, with many having received the Hitler Youth Achievement Medal for outstanding service. The best of the best were chosen as boys joined in the excitement of potential combat for their beloved führer. Author Susan Campbell Bartoletti observed, "New SS-HJ recruits were supposed to be volunteers, and most boys joined willingly. But others were tricked or coerced. In some instances, the SS told the boys to sign papers to verify personal information. Afterward, the boys discovered that they had signed themselves into the SS."[69]

By April 1944, more than twenty thousand youngsters belonged to the SS-HJ. When the troops were catapulted into battle after the Allies landed in Normandy, their commander, Kurt Meyer said, "The magnificent young grenadiers look at us with laughter in their eyes.

They have no fear. They are confident. They have faith in their strength and the will to fight."[70]

During the ensuing fighting, the Hitler Youth in the SS-HJ, ones just two years older than Ursula Martens, distinguished themselves. Allies had once called this unit the Baby Milk Division, but the youth held their own in combat. But in the end, defeat was at the doorstep, and losses amounted to more than eight thousand of the SS-HJ. Later, Hitler would reward many of those youngsters who fought with presentation of the Iron Cross. For those in the Hitler Youth, any chance of defeat was a crushing blow. They had given, as required, their heart and souls to the führer, to their homeland.

One prayer they uttered, based on the *Lord's Prayer,* read, "Adolf Hitler, you are my great Führer. The name makes the enemy tremble. The Third Reich comes, thy will alone is law upon the earth. Let us hear thy voice and order us by thy leadership, for we will obey to the end and even with our lives. We praise thee. Hail Hitler." Dr. Otto Knopp observed, "In the Hitler Youth belief in the Führer replaced trust in the Heavenly Father."[71]

Mottos were an essential part of the Hitler Youth code. Examples included, "Live Faithfully, Fight Bravely, and Die Laughing" and "We were born to die for Germany." For girls such as Ursula, one motto was "Be faithful, Be pure, Be German."[72]

Perhaps it was Baldur von Schirach who best summed up what he believed was the duty of the Hitler Youth: "We do not need intellectual leaders who create new ideas, because the superimposing leader of all desires of youth is Adolf Hitler." He then added, "Your name, my Führer, is the happiness of youth, your name, my Führer, is for us everlasting life. He who serves Adolf Hitler, the Führer, serves Germany, and whoever serves Germany, serves God." To this end, his military training officer Helmut Stellrecht stated, "As the years progress, we want to reach a point where German boys hold a gun with as much assurance as a fountain pen."[73]

Later, while on trial for his crimes, Schirach admitted guilt for serving a leader that author Dr. Otto Knopp called the Great Seducer: "I believed I was serving a Führer who would make our people and its youth great, free, and happy. Millions of young people believed this with me and saw their ideal in National Socialism. Many died for it. It is my fault that I brought up the youth for a man who was a murderer millions of times over. I believed in this man; that is all I can say in my defence."[74]

To those such as Ursula Martens who was one of these youth, Hitler was the everlasting life, the one who held the promise of great things for Germany. Each day those in the HY hoped that their sacred führer could turn the tide and lead Germany to a stunning victory.

CHAPTER EIGHT PRELUDE

To ease discomfort among the German people that the war was being lost, Adolf Hitler's voice was heard on the radio throughout the country on January 30, 1945. The people's savior told the listeners to hold out until the very end. Less than three weeks later, destruction of Dresden spelled doom for the German troops.

In February, what was dubbed the Werewolf project began. Its intention was to train Hitler Youth in the art of sabotage. On his fifty-sixth birthday, Hitler appeared outside Berlin to pin medals on Hitler Youth defending bunkers there. Ten days later, May 1, 1945, he killed himself. In a voice shaking with sad emotions, the announcer on the Reich radio station reported, "We have heard from the Führer's headquarters that our Führer, Adolf Hitler, has died at his command post in the Reich Chancellery, fighting to his last breath for Germany against Bolschevism." Author Otto Knopp wrote, "It was the last lie of the regime."[75]

Hitler's cowardly act occurred on the heels of Nazi defeats far and wide. Soviet troops had captured Warsaw, Poland, and then liberated those incarcerated at Auschwitz. Allied troops seized Cologne, and Soviet troops captured Danzig. President Roosevelt died in April knowing that the Germans were being defeated. Harry Truman replaced him.

On April 21, the Russians overran Berlin. Seven days later, Mussolini was captured by Italian opponents and hanged. One day later, the Americans liberated Dachau.

On all sides, the inevitable was apparent. Germany had lost the war. On May 7–9, unconditional surrender terms were signed at the American headquarters in Rheims and at the Soviet headquarters in Berlin. Herman Goring, Hitler's henchmen, and arguably the second most powerful man in Germany, was captured by Allied troops. Heinrich Himmler committed suicide.

Despite knowledge that all was lost, author Daniel Jonah Goldhagen noted how ordinary Germans, including young boys in the SS-HJ, purposely killed Jews. He wrote, "Jewish survivors report with virtual unanimity German cruelties and killings until the very end. They leave no doubt that the Germans were seething with hatred for their victims." He then added, "To the very end, the ordinary Germans who perpetrated the Holocaust willfully, faithfully, and zealously slaughtered Jews."[76]

These Hitler Youth who were supposed to be part of the Werewolf project were never told their mission was a last ditch effort to turn the tide of the war. The elite group was formed in April 1944 based on an idea conceived by Minister of Propaganda Joseph Goebbels. Acting in guerrilla fashion, as commandos of sorts, the troops would fight to the end to undermine Allied efforts as the war wound down. World War II historian Otto Knopp wrote, "Children and young people, predominantly, were to wage a pitiless guerilla war as partisans behind the enemy's back . . . Acts of sabotage against the Allies were planned, as was action against 'German traitors.'" The operative words to be used, Knopp stated, was "The Werewolf is here. Anyone who surrenders will be shot."[77]

More than five thousand soldiers were recruited, drawn mainly from the SS and the Hitler Youth. Training occurred, but it never reached the point where the Werewolf outfit could pose a military significance for the Allies. Nevertheless, in later years, an outgrowth of the Werewolf project was called neo-Nazism. One symbol/variant was known as the werewolf.

Author Klaus P. Fischer summed up the feelings of many who had witnessed the grand plan Hitler had for the youth of Germany: "Nazi indoctrination was able to miseducate and misuse a whole generation of young people, a generation that, on the whole, felt happy and empowered under the Third Reich, but one that also came to realize, in the words of one former young man, that they were 'used up and destroyed as a generation by Adolph Hitler.'"[78]

CHAPTER NINE PRELUDE

Ursula Martens's beloved Germany was now in shambles. Across the country, destruction appeared at every turn. The Allies had won the war, and Germany was now theirs. Forever, May 8, 1945, would be known as V-E (Victory in Europe) Day. On June 5, the Allies divided up Germany. Ursula was now property of a new master.

By July 1, American, British, and Russian troops occupied Berlin. In August, two atomic bombs were dropped in Japan by the Americans. By midmonth, the Japanese had surrendered. World War II came to an end. More than one hundred million military personnel had been mobilized. It was the deadliest conflict in history with estimates that more than seventy million deaths occurred. Of this, some five million German military died, among them many of the Hitler Youth. Many of those who surrendered at the end of the war to the Allies were barely teenagers. Allied soldiers could not believe that they had been fighting against such youth. After the war, the HY was disbanded by the Allies and faded away. Some thought was given to prosecuting the youngsters for war crimes, but none were ever charged.

For those who had been Hitler Youth members, their childhood had been robbed from them. To show dedication, they had to sever interest in any other youth organizations and even in areas of interest reserved for kids growing up. Author Jean-Denis G. G. Lepage believed the Nazis had a definite game plan for separating these youth from parental control. He wrote, "In the long term, the Nazis intended to reduce the role of parents to their unavoidable biological function. Relegated to the background, parents often had trouble keeping their brown-shirted sons and daughters in line." He added, "Children were encouraged to criticize the convention of their parents' generation and think of themselves as the hope of the future. 'Youth must be led by youth,' and 'Youth is always right' were slogans frequently used."[79]

True to his belief, the Hitler Youth became pawns to be played after war broke out. Immersed in paramilitary exercises, they were being trained to become soldiers without their even realizing it, since for many the organization was full of fun, hiking, boating, running, and singing.

Most never knew the true reason for their being required to become Hitler Youth. They looked upon membership as a privilege, a duty, one encased in loyalty to the führer.

During the first part of the war, responsibilities had included door-to-door solicitation of scrap metal, bottles, and paper. These were recycled to help with the war. They also collected blankets and warm clothes, even furs. When soldiers became sparse, they leaped into action to replace those immobilized. Three million girls, ones the same age as Ursula, worked sixty-hour weeks in factories around Germany. Others worked at postal outlets, assisted the wounded in hospitals, and became cheerleaders who visited railroad stations for departing soldiers who needed a boost of their spirits from a pretty girl.

When bombings increased, evacuation under the program called Kinderlandverschickung had been initiated. This had required youngsters to leave Berlin and Hamburg and move to the safety of the countryside. By April 1942, more than 850,000 boys and girls had been sent to safety.[80]

When the Germans began to invade Eastern Europe, Hitler had seen a perfect chance to use his vaunted Hitler Youth as substitute teachers in Poland and the Western Ukraine. More than thirty thousand girls and boys were involved. Back home, Axmann, the leader of the youth, bragged that more than a million boys were now certified sharpshooters. This expertise came in handy for many of the youngsters when they were drafted into the military auxiliary forces. Instead of wearing their Hitler Youth uniforms, they now wore standard issue army uniforms and carried government-issued weapons. Author Lepage wrote, "As the war progressed, the youthful loyalty of the HJ members was ruthlessly exploited."[81]

With the war winding down, and Germany on the losing end, the Hitler Youth had become more involved in combat. As part of the Volkssturm, teenagers Ursula's age became Hitler's fighting force along with old men drafted into the fight since those aged in the middle were already fighting or dead. By 1945, Hitler Youth were what author Lepage said was "the backbone of the Volkssturm." They were part of antitank battalions and carried automatic weapons like soldiers twice their age. Girls the same age as Ursula operated antiaircraft guns and shot Panzerfausts. Author Lepage wrote, "The HJ fought fanatically because they believed [Reich Minister of Propaganda] Goebbel's propaganda that the Russians would kill them anyway."[82]

During April 1945, more than six hundred fifteen- and sixteen-year-olds fought hard to save the Wannsee Bridge in Berlin believing reinforcements were on the way. They weren't. Hitler Youth also protected Hitler's bunker. A few days later, Hitler awarded some Hitler Youth the Iron Cross, the youngest just twelve years old. One soldier serving to protect Munich's Maximilian Bridge, to the amazement of Allied soldiers who captured him, was ten. He and his fellow youngsters had been equipped with Panzerfausts, but they were too scared to fire them against the onrushing Allied opposition.[83] Author Dr. Otto Knopp noted, "Film taken by US Army cameras showed the fear on the faces of the young German soldiers taken prisoner. They looked like confused and helpless children."[84]

These brave child-soldiers were being captured as prisoners of war about the same time Hitler committed suicide. Many of the youth were taken to the liberated concentration camp of Dachau. One eleven-year-old recalled, "To our left and right soldiers mingled with concentration camp inmates, the latter wearing the vertically blue and white striped suits which hung on figures so thin. It was impossible to believe that these people could still speak, let alone walk." He added, "During the first few moments after entering the compound, I thought the former inmates were going to tear us to pieces. Astonishingly enough, they just flanked the way where we went, but never a word was uttered, never a hand raised against us." Author H. W. Koch wrote, "For this Hitler Youth already at the age of eleven a world had collapsed . . . the boys and girls [were] thrown together by crisis, by stark, naked fear, and by the belief in their country . . . they were worthy of a better cause than that which their Führer had to offer."[85]

By the calculations of Dr. Otto Knopp, more than one-third of those German youth born between the years of 1921 and 1925 were "slaughtered on the battlefield or fell victim to the Allied bombing on the home front . . . Of all the males born between 1919 and 1928, nearly 1.9 million lost their lives in action." His assessment: "Hitler cheated their youth. Indeed many were victims and perpetrators. Hitler Youth were involved in almost all the atrocious measures initiated in the eastern territories by the Gauleiter [party leader of a Nazi regional branch] and SS . . . in the final chaotic weeks of the war. HJ members sometimes had to take part in the shooting of Jews."[86]

Despite their fighting to the end, the HY could not save Hitler. His desire for a thousand years of rule had come to an end. Like millions of other Germans, Ursula Martens had awakened to realize their führer had not kept his promises. What to do now was a question with few answers.

CHAPTER TEN PRELUDE

Two years after the war ended, the year Ursula Martens turned eighteen, Germany was only beginning to understand what lay ahead. Berlin was divided, east and west as people attempted to regroup while living in an occupied country.

From late July to October 1946, representatives from the Allied countries, the USSR, the USA, the United Kingdom, France, and Canada, negotiated a peace treaty in Paris with the defeated countries of Italy, Bulgaria, Finland, Romania, and Hungary. Under the agreement, signed on February 10, 1947, each was permitted to be a sovereign nation with membership in the newly formed United Nations. War reparations were imposed on the defeated countries but perhaps most important was language requiring that "[Signatories] should take all measures necessary to secure to all personals under (its) jurisdiction, without distinction as to race, sex, language or religion, the enjoyment of human rights and of fundamental freedoms, including freedom of expression, of press and publication, of religious worship, of political opinion and public meeting."

Despite these safeguards for human rights, in February of 1948, the year Ursula turned nineteen, the Communist Party, with support from the Soviets, took control of the Czechoslovakian government. This rule would continue for nearly four decades. Reaction to the sudden turn of events caused consternation among the Western powers, a prelude to the Cold War. Quickly the Marshall Plan, named after US secretary of state George Marshall, was created. It provided a method for reconstruction of European countries through billions of dollars of foreign aid. Instead of being punishment-oriented, it was a futuristic plan to help defeated countries gain some sense of economic stability. The plan also was designed to keep Soviet influence from spreading beyond its borders as it had done in Czechoslovakia, Hungary, and Romania.

Tensions between the eastern and western blocs raged, resulting in the Berlin Blockade. It began in June 1948 and lasted almost a year. The trigger point was the Soviets blocking the Allies' access to road and railroad routes to West Berlin. The Soviets' aim was to control passage of goods to West Berlin permitting them to, in essence, control the entire city area by selling their goods to West Berliners with no choice in the matter if they wanted to survive.

The response was direct and active. To thwart Soviet efforts, British and US air force pilots flew more than 275,000 flights. More than thirteen thousand tons of needed supplies, including food, clothing, and fuel were airlifted to the thankful Germans. Finally the Soviets realized their plan had failed and the blockade was lifted.

A year later, in 1949, the Federal Republic of Germany was established. West Germany, as it was called, evolved from eleven states in three zones occupied after the war by Britain, France, and the United States. Bonn was designated the capital. The Soviets, who controlled the fourth zone, called their area of ownership the German Democratic Republic.

When the Koreas, North and South, aimed their guns at one another in 1950, Ursula Martens's West Germany homeland became embroiled in debate. Some felt it should be armed to thwart any possible invasion by the Soviets. By then Germany was partner to Europe's Coal and Steel Community, the six-nation (Germany, France, Italy, Belgium, Luxembourg, and the Netherlands) international organization designed to create a common market for coal and steel. It was a prelude to the European Union.

The proposal was to establish the EDC (European Defense Community), with each member, including West Germany, to contribute armed forces to a larger force that would defend every EDC country. West Germany's forces would be overseen by the EDC with the other countries independent of such oversight. But the idea was nixed by the French Parliament and never took effect. Instead, under the auspices of the WEU, the Western European Union, West Germany was permitted to rearm with WEU regulating the size of the West German forces, ones only to be used in defense not for aggressive actions. Allied forces continued to occupy Berlin as before.

For Hitler, words he had spoken to Albert Speer in 1936 were indeed prolific. After gazing outside a bay window of his dining room, Speer said Hitler told him, "There are two possibilities for me: To win through with all of my plans, or to fail. If I win, I shall be one of the greatest men in history. If I fail, I shall be condemned, despised and damned."[87]

Years passed before West Germany was permitted to be a sovereign nation. It would join the Northern Atlantic Treaty Organization (NATO) and finally be steadfast on the path to economic and political stability. For a girl like Ursula Martens who was turning twenty-one in 1950, there was much to consider. Was she to stay in West Germany the remainder of her life and be part of a country whose motto was "Enigkeit und Recht und Freiheit" ("Unity and Justice and Freedom"), or would her thoughts lean toward leaving her homeland for another far, far, away?

Whatever choice Ursula made, she was certain to wrestle with the demons as to the extent of her responsibility regarding what had occurred during the war. This included knowledge that while the bait used to lure her into the Hitler Youth was a bit softer than that used to lure boys, one directed toward a girl's interest in fashion, looking good, "communal singing, enacting fairy tales and theatrical plays, and performing puppet shows,"[88] the Nazis had nevertheless forced her into HY service.

Author Michael Kater believed there were two theories regarding the responsibilities of girls and women during the war. One absolves them based on the girls being dominated by male superiors who took advantage of them forcing the girls "by biology and circumstances into roles they did not want to play and even to the status of victims." The other is much harsher, with Kater writing, "Women were just as responsible as men for the rise of Hitler before 1933 and for what happened in the Third Reich thereafter." He added, "Even though women could not fight at the fronts and usually did not murder Jews, they supported their men in these actions, either directly, by sharing their Nazi beliefs and giving the men active support, or indirectly, by remaining silent yet giving tacit approval to anything political or military their men might be up to."[89]

How Ursula Martens felt she measured up to these standards of guilt, or lack thereof, would shape her for years after the war. Certainly she had much to consider, such as how she had supported her beloved Wilhelm, an HY leader like her.

CHAPTER ELEVEN PRELUDE

For a young woman of twenty-three haunted by the ghosts of war and deep regret over having been a leader in the Hitler Youth that supported a führer responsible for millions of deaths, including six-million-plus Jews, arrival in the border city of El Paso, Texas, in 1952, was to be a new awakening.

Consumed with guilt, and overridden with the hope of starting a new life in a new country, Ursula Martens was dropped into a cesspool of agitation where Mexicans, Mexican Americans, and Americans were attempting to live side-by-side despite cultural differences that were much like those Ursula had experienced in Germany where those of Aryan descent had shown disdain for anyone not foreseen as part of the Nazi master race. Discrimination, bigotry, racial prejudice, and the belief that certain sects of people were different would rear their ugly heads again in some sort of a mirror image of the calamity that had been triggered by Adolf Hitler and his belief that those judged inferior should be sent away, avoided, or dealt with harshly.

The city Ursula encountered was positioned on the Rio Grande across from its Mexican counterpart, Ciudad Juárez, Chihuahua, Mexico. Its roots existed as far back as 1598 when Spanish explorer Don Juan de Oñate Salazar had arrived. Through the years leading up to the fifties, El Paso had dealt with a reputation as a lawless border town, but when Ursula arrived, the city had modernized despite racial tensions between Anglo-Americans and non-whites. In fact, during the 1950s and early '60s, one bone of contention was simply identification; no single name had emerged as to what to call the non-whites. Some thought the name used should be Spanish-speaking people, others suggested Latinos, Hispanics, Chicanos, or simply Mexican Americans.

When World War II ended, GIs like Ursula's attempted to blend into the new social standings, but everyone was uncomfortable with everyone or so it seemed. Being a border town, El Paso was highly influenced by what was occurring in Juárez where lawlessness ran rampant. Since El Paso's economic strength depended on the Spanish-speaking people of Juárez, Spanish was the spoken language throughout much of the city. But according to sociologist Dr. Clark S. Knowlton, "the reigns of political and economics always rested securely . . . in Anglo/American hands." This caused, he believed, at least during the 1950s and '60s, "a silken soft, cushiony pattern of prejudice and discrimination [that] always existed [to] subtly emphasize the superiority of the Anglo/American culture. The Mexican-American who conforms [was] rewarded, the one who [did not] was excluded from most possibilities of social mobility."[90]

Tension between the minority whites who were leaders of the city despite the minority status, those new residents after the war, and those of Mexican descent flourished as Ursula Martens began her new life in El Paso. If it was struggling with these issues at the very heart of its population, the Deep South as a whole had more problems to bear. Although the Civil War had been over for nearly a hundred years, equality among blacks and whites was unknown in many areas of Mississippi, Alabama, and the like. Separate restrooms and separate drinking fountains for people of color and those of noncolor continued to exist as did restaurants where blacks were forbidden to enter. Certain hotels turned away blacks, and discrimination existed based on a caste system that dropped blacks to the bottom ring of society. They were still looked upon as being different, in some sense dirty, the same terms Ursula and her Nazi sympathizers had used to describe the Jews, the sick, the mentally ill, and others of a minority status.

By 1948, recognition of the deep division between blacks and whites in the military had caused President Truman to issue an executive order. It read, "It is hereby declared to be the policy of the President that there shall be equality of treatment and opportunity for all persons in the armed services without regard to race, color, religion, or national origin." A half-decade later, equality in the military had been improved, but the question of whether a black youth could be admitted to a school dominated by whites still lingered as prejudice against blacks reared its head at every turn.

During her days in El Paso, as she attempted to understand her new American society, Ursula was an eyewitness to racial tension first born of the monumental May 1954 *Brown v. Board of Education* Supreme Court decision that declared segregation in public schools unconstitutional. Whites in the Deep South were inflamed by the thought that their kids might be dumped into schools with black children. In August 1955,

Ursula learned about the despicable killing of fourteen-year-old Emmet Till who, while visiting family in Mississippi, was kidnapped, brutally beaten, and then shot for allegedly whistling at a white woman. When an all-white jury acquitted the two white men, the case became a cause célèbre of the upcoming civil rights movement.[91]

Four months later, a tailor's assistant named Rosa Parks boarded a bus in Montgomery, Alabama, after an exhausting day at work. She took a seat near the "black section" of the bus. Three more blacks joined her there, but when a white man needed a seat, the bus driver ordered the blacks to move to the rear. The three black men reluctantly moved, but Parks did not. Threatened with arrest, she stood fast. The bus driver called the police, and Parks was arrested, sparking legal action that would be decisive for years to come. As author David Halberstam wrote, "Parks [had] continued to sit. In so doing, she became the first prominent figure of what became the Movement."[92]

By *movement* Halberstam meant the civil rights movement, and in the coming years leading up to 1960 and beyond, Ursula Martens witnessed a crusade to rid the United States of racial discrimination similar to that of those who attempted to overthrow a Nazi regime that persecuted Jews and other minorities just as Rosa Parks had been persecuted. The only reason: color or ethnic heritage, nothing more.

Parks's distress, and the ensuing legal battle, brought to the forefront a man Ursula had never heard of, Dr. Martin Luther King Jr. She watched as Reverend King and his Southern Christian Leadership Conference, along with other civil rights pioneers, slowly cut away the smoke screen of racial prejudice in the Deep South. He attacked the hatemongers as being shameless bigots, an attack similar to that leveled by those who finally stamped out the hatemongers who existed among the Nazi regime.

URSULA MARTENS AND MARK SHAW

CHAPTER TWELVE PRELUDE

When television began to bring the civil rights movement to her eyes in 1956, Ursula had a window in her living room to what was occurring throughout the Deep South as blacks and whites clashed on a daily basis. Ursula thought she had escaped such prejudice when she left Germany, but without warning, its ugly nature had appeared right at her doorstep.

By 1960, racial tensions were at a boiling point in Los Angeles, Ursula Martens's new home. Like El Paso, the City of Angels was a melting pot of multiple racial origins with the most contentious being the battle between blacks and whites, each attempting to solidify a position of strength.

When Ursula arrived in LA, she continued to watch with interest events in other parts of the country. Since she had come from a land separated by racial prejudice, she noted struggles by the Little Rock Nine, a group of Arkansas black students prevented from attending Central High School. In 1961, Ursula learned that several freedom riders, each attempted to test new laws prohibiting segregation on public transit, had been attacked by angry mobs. October 1962 brought to her attention the case of James Meredith, a black student hungry for an education at the University of Mississippi. When violence erupted, President John Kennedy ordered five thousand federal troops to keep the peace.

The year 1963 was marked with more violence. Ursula watched as fire hoses and police dogs were used by police to quell black demonstrators in Birmingham, Alabama, a reminder of the days when dogs attacked defenseless Jews in the German railway yards. On June 12, NAACP field secretary Medgar Evers was gunned down. Two months later, Dr. Martin Luther King Jr. gave his famous "I Have a Dream" speech before two hundred thousand people during the March on Washington. Eighteen days later, four young black girls attending a Sunday school class in Birmingham, Alabama, were killed when a bomb blew up. Two months, later, Ursula watched with horror the news that President Kennedy had been assassinated.

Even though President Lyndon Johnson signed the Civil Rights Act in 1964, tensions continued to escalate when, one month later, members of the Ku Klux Klan, ones with beliefs similar to the Nazis Ursula had supported, were held responsible for the deaths of three civil rights workers in Mississippi. In February 1965, black nationalist Malcolm X was murdered. In March, black demonstrators marching in support of the voting rights were attacked by police using whips, clubs, and tear gas, another reminder for Ursula of the days when Nazis had clubbed Jews to death.

In August, racial upheaval arrived at Ursula's doorstep after a white California highway patrolman stopped a black man on a motorcycle over suspicions he was driving drunk. Soon, an angry crowd gathered, and rocks and other objects were thrown as racial epitaphs were shouted at the officer. When the black man, his brother, and their mother were arrested, the Watts riots began. In all, thirty-four people were killed, more than two thousand were injured, and nearly four thousand were arrested. Extensive looting and property destruction added to the melee causing forty million dollars in damage. Police chief William Parker added to the tension when he labeled rioters as "monkeys in a zoo," another reminder of the type of language used to label Jews during World War II.

Author Gerald Horne believed "the revolt led to a wrenching and agonizing reappraisal of race relations." He quoted social scientist H. Edward Ransford as concluding "that the civil rights movement itself spoke more to the interest of a 'middle class . . .' with 'rising expectations for full equality,' while the revolt revealed a 'very different population— one whose members are intensely dissatisfied, feel powerless to change their position, and have minimum commitment to the larger society . . . for them, violence is a means of communicating with white society."[93]

Throughout this violent period of American history, Los Angeles became a focal point for civil unrest. By the middle of the 1960s, when Ursula Martens reached her midthirties, she was seeking more from American life and from life in general than could be found in the streets of LA. What she was seeking was still a mystery to her, but soon surprising events began to occur providing some enlightenment as to what lay in store for the former Nazi Youth leader.

ENDNOTES

[1] Hitler quoted by W. F. Connell in *A History of Education in the Twentieth Century World* (New York: Teachers College Press, 1980), 258.

[2] Klaus P. Fischer, *Nazi Germany: A New History* (New York: The Continuum Publishing Company, 1995), 354–55.

[3] "Hate in the Mainstream," Intelligence Report, Issue 142 (Summer 2011), 4

[4] Seth David Chernoff, *Manual for Living: Reality* (Boulder: Spirit Scope Publishing, 2010), 267.

[5] Goldhagen, *Hitler's Willing Executioners: Ordinary Germans and the Holocaust*, 9.

[6] Ruth Zerner, "Martin Niemoeller, Activist as Bystander: the oft-quoted Reflection," in Marvin Perry and Frederick Schweitzer, eds., *Jewish-Christian Encounters over the Centuries: Symbiosis, Prejudice, Holocaust, Dialogue* (New York: Peter Lang, 1994), 327–340.

[7] Adolf Hitler, *Mein Kampf*, trans. Ralph Manheim (Boston: Houghton Mifflin Company, 1943), 211.

[8] Susan Campbell Bartoletti, *Hitler Youth: Growing Up in Hitler's Shadow* (New York: Scholastic Nonfiction, 2005), 13.

[9] H. W. Koch, *Hitler Youth: The Duped Generation* (New York: Ballantine Books, Inc., 1972), 55.

[10] Bartoletti, *Hitler Youth: Growing Up in Hitler's Shadow*, 16–17.

[11] Koch, *Hitler Youth: The Duped Generation*, 60.

[12] Guido Knopp, *Hitler's Children* (London: Sutton Publishing Limited, 2004), 115.

[13] Bartoletti, *Hitler Youth: Growing Up in Hitler's Shadow*, 25, 24.

[14] Ibid., 27.

[15] Guido Knopp, *Hitler's Children*, 12.

[16] Albert Speer, *Inside the Third Reich* (New York: MacMillan Publishing Company, 1982), 73.

[17] Ibid., 16.

[18] Jean-Denis G. G. Lepage, *Hitler Youth—1922–1945: An Illustrated History* (Jefferson, NC: McFarland & Company, 2008), 3.

[19] J. Noakes and G. Pridham, eds., *Nazism: 1919–1945* (Exeter, Devon UK: University of Exeter Press, 1991), 417.

[20] H. R. Trevor-Roper, ed., *Hitler's Table Talk, 1941–1944: His Private Conversations* (New York City: Enigma Books, 2000), xxii.

[21] Ibid., xii.

[22] Ibid., xxi.

[23] Ibid., x.

[24] Lepage, *Hitler Youth—1922–1945: An Illustrated History*, 9.

[25] Ibid., 9.

[26] Ibid., 10.

[27] Bartoletti, *Hitler Youth: Growing Up in Hitler's Shadow*, 7.

[28] Knopp, *Hitler's Children*, 20.

[29] Lepage, *Hitler Youth—1922–1945: An Illustrated History*, 11.

[30] Ibid., 16.

[31] Ibid., 19, 20.

[32] Bartoletti, *Hitler Youth: Growing Up in Hitler's Shadow*, 32.

[33] Lepage, *Hitler Youth—1922–1945: An Illustrated History*, 21.

[34] Ibid., 22–23.

[35] Ibid., 25.

[36] Ibid., 30.

[37] Bartoletti, *Hitler Youth: Growing Up in Hitler's Shadow*, 41–42.

[38] Knopp, *Hitler's Children*, 53, 116.

[39] Ibid., 57.

[40] Noakes and Pridham, eds., *Nazism: 1919–1945*, 439.

[41] Lepage, *Hitler Youth—1922–1945: An Illustrated History*, 34–35.

[42] Ibid., 37.

[43] Ibid., 37.

[44] Michael H. Kater, *Hitler Youth* (Cambridge, MA: Harvard University Press, 2004), 83.

[45] Lepage, *Hitler Youth—1922–1944: An Illustrated History*, 39.

[46] Knopp, *Hitler's Children*, x.

[47] Ibid., 78.

[48] Ibid., 78, 63.

[49] Noakes and Pridham, eds., *Nazism: 1919–1945*, 421.

[50] Lepage, *Hitler Youth—1922–1945: An Illustrated History*, 69.

[51] Ibid., 62, 66, 70.

[52] Kater, *Hitler Youth*, 22.

[53] Trevor-Roper, ed., *Hitler's Table Talk, 1941–1944: His Private Conversations*, xl.

[54] Trevor-Roper, ed., *Hitler's Table Talk, 1941–1944: His Private Conversations*, 74.

[55] Kater, *Hitler Youth*, 64.

[56] Knopp, *Hitler's Children*, 121, 133.

[57] Noakes and Pridham, eds., *Nazism: 1919–1945*, 543.

[58] Ibid., 521.

[59] Hitler, *Mein Kampf*, trans. Manheim, 411.

[60] Ibid., 59, 65, 325, 412.

[61] Speer, *Inside the Third Reich*, 17.

[62] Fischer, *Nazi Germany: A New History*, 347.

63 Daniel Jonah Goldhagen, *Hitler's Willing Executioners: Ordinary Germans and the Holocaust* (New York: Alfred A. Knopf, 1996), 367–368.

64 Kater, *Hitler Youth*, 65.

65 Speer, *Inside the Third Reich*, 357.

66 Lepage, *Hitler Youth—1922–1945: An Illustrated History*, 95.

67 Ibid., 97.

68 Knopp, *Hitler's Children*, 183.

69 Bartoletti, *Hitler Youth: Growing Up in Hitler's Shadow*, 131.

70 Ibid., 133.

71 Knopp, *Hitler's Children*, 56.

72 Ibid., 135, 141.

73 Ibid., 15.

74 Ibid., 37.

75 Ibid., 67.

76 Goldhagen, *Hitler's Willing Executioners: Ordinary Germans and the Holocaust*, 371.

77 Knopp, *Hitler's Children*, 274.

78 Fischer, *Nazi Germany: A New History*, 354–355.

79 Ibid., 82–83.

80 Ibid., 124.

81 Ibid., 128.

82 Ibid., 155.

83 Koch, *Hitler Youth: The Duped Generation*, 154.

84 Knopp, *Hitler's Children*, 240.

85 Koch, *Hitler Youth: The Duped Generation*, 158–159.

86 Knopp, *Hitler's Children*, xi, 279.

87 Speer, *Inside the Third Reich*, 101.

88 Kater, *Hitler Youth*, 81.

89 Ibid., 71–72.

90 Clark S. Knowlton, *Changing Patterns of Segregation and Discrimination Affecting the Mexican Americans of El Paso, Texas* (prepared for the Annual Meeting of the Southern Sociological Society, March 31, 1967).

91 David Halberstam, *The Fifties* (New York: Random House, 1993), 432–41.

92 Ibid., 540–45.

93 Gerald Horne, *Fire This Time: The Watts Uprising and the 1960s* (Charlottesville, VA: University Press of Virginia, 1995), 40.

INDEX

E

East Germany, 154, 187, 241
EDC (European Defense Community), 242
El Paso, Texas, 159-60, 162-64, 166, 169, 173, 175-76, 178-79, 183, 198, 244-45, 247, 251
Eric, 68, 201-3
Europe, 72, 179, 213, 215-16, 221, 229, 237
Evie (Ursula's sister), 29-33, 35-38, 43-46, 48-50, 65-67, 69-71, 76, 79, 88-89, 105, 120-24, 131-33, 142, 149, 190-91
Evie's wedding, 108-9

F

farms, 41, 79, 85, 107-8, 115, 118, 132, 136
Father (Willie), 29-39, 47-50, 53-57, 63-66, 70-72, 74-76, 78-79, 81-82, 117-27, 129-30, 132, 135-36, 141-43, 158-60, 187-91
Final Solution, 184, 225-26
First World War, 39, 104
Fischer, Klaus P., 229, 236, 249-51
forgiveness, 18, 157, 192-93, 198, 201
France, 72, 74-75, 78-79, 209, 230, 241-42
Frank (GI), 149-53, 157, 159
Frankfurt, 81, 187, 189
Frau Lorenz, 72
freedom, 175, 188-89, 215, 243
führer, 55, 60, 65, 68-70, 73, 76, 106-7, 119, 204, 212-13, 218, 221-33, 235, 238-40, 244

G

German Girls League, 58, 222
German soldiers, 63, 117, 124, 204, 206, 230
Germany, 18, 38-40, 49-50, 58-60, 62-

63, 65-69, 79-81, 111-13, 149-51, 162-70, 178, 187-91, 209-11, 216-18, 233-38
German youth, 204, 216, 220, 239
goal, 165, 219, 222-23
God, 35, 59, 81, 120, 143, 160-61, 165, 170, 192, 196, 198-200, 213, 224, 233
Gold, Aaron, 177-81, 183-89, 191-94, 196, 198-99, 201-4
Goldhagen, Daniel Jonah, 205, 249, 251
grandfather, 64, 85, 104, 110-11, 113-14, 118-19, 131, 136-37, 180, 184, 191, 193
grandmother (Omi), 35, 59, 64, 85-86, 92, 104, 109-11, 113, 118, 130, 139
Grete (Ursula's aunt), 109
guilt, 18, 20, 135, 137-38, 143, 149, 161-62, 183, 193, 199, 204, 206, 243-44
gymnasium, 34, 90
gypsies, 25, 43, 56, 167

H

Hajo (pet), 89
Hanns (coworker), 71
hate, 17, 25, 60, 65, 113, 119, 138, 143, 157, 160, 183, 186-87, 191, 194, 202-6
hayloft, 74, 131
Helga (best friend in Schwerin), 73-74
heroes, 80, 213
Heydrich, Reinhard, 226
Hindenburg, Paul von, 210, 212
Hitler, Adolf, 17-20, 38-39, 49-50, 59-63, 67-72, 75-79, 81-83, 110-11, 119-21, 125-26, 159-62, 203-6, 209-30, 233-36, 249-51
Hitler Jugend, 218-19
Hitler's Boys, 222
Hitler Youth, 18-19, 49, 61-63, 68-70, 87-90, 113-15, 135-37, 178-81,

N

napolas, 88, 105, 230
NATO (Northern Atlantic Treaty
    Organization), 243
nazi Party, 17, 36, 38, 55, 59-60, 64,
    118, 129, 209-10, 215, 217, 219,
    231
New Thought, 196-97
NSDAP (National Socialist German
    Worker's Party), 209-10, 217
nuremberg, 49, 55, 58

P

Pabst (schoolteacher), 25-26, 160
Panzerfaust, 106, 113, 137, 239
Paris, 74-75, 225, 230, 241
peace, 61-62, 68, 76, 88, 166, 193,
    198-99, 225, 247
photographs, 39, 76, 78, 190
pictures, 36-37, 50, 58, 61, 68, 77, 79,
    83-84, 114, 148, 158, 171
Poland, 69-70, 84, 200, 232, 235, 238
police, 58, 62, 148, 153, 169, 172,
    246-48
porcelain, 62-63, 65, 129, 132, 140
poster, 61
prayers, 59, 160-61, 221, 233
prejudice, racial, 18, 150, 213, 244,
    246-47
Pridham, G., 227, 249-50
prison, 109, 116, 127, 130, 136, 139-
    40, 142, 218
propaganda, 18, 125, 135, 213, 239

R

rabbits, 41-43, 74
railway, 122, 124-25, 178, 193
rallies, 55, 58, 210, 219
rape, 114, 116-17, 124, 193
realschule, 34

refugees, 87-88, 115, 122, 126, 131,
    135, 167
Reich, 59, 62, 70, 104-7, 229
religion, 25, 31, 35, 59, 194, 197, 217,
    241, 245
Restum (embassy official), 159
Rhineland, 49
Rolf (Ursula's cousin), 85-86, 187
room, cold, 54
Rosenfeld, 35
Russia, 69, 78, 87, 117, 129, 142, 232
Russian army, 120-21, 123, 127, 130
Russian soldiers, 114, 116-19, 123,
    127, 130, 136, 140-41, 193
Ruth (Ursula's coworker), 154, 200-204

S

SA (Sturmabteilung), 38, 217, 219
Schirach, Baldur von, 219, 226, 233
Schubert, Wilhelm, 90-91, 103-5, 107-
    8, 110-11, 114, 118, 126, 130,
    137-39, 147, 184
Schwerin, 53-55, 59, 65, 67, 70, 73,
    78, 80-81, 89, 108, 112, 118,
    120-22, 126-27, 131
shivah, 202
Siegi (best friend in Karow), 40-43, 45-
    46, 126-27, 172
Soviets, 226, 232, 241-42
Spanish, 155, 164, 166, 169, 244
speeches, 7, 38, 59, 61, 82-83, 214-15
Speer, Albert, 214-15, 242, 249-51
SS, 63, 73, 76, 97, 212, 219, 230, 232,
    236, 240
SS-HJ, 232-33, 235
swastika, 20, 37, 55, 117, 159, 194,
    199, 221, 223

T

teachers, 18, 25-26, 34, 42, 88, 120,
    142, 154, 197, 221, 227

URSULA MARTENS AND MARK SHAW

Teterow, 46-47, 50
Third Reich, 11, 20, 59, 65, 81, 159,
    221, 229, 231, 233, 236, 243,
    249-51
Torah, 13, 201, 203
Trevor-Roper, H. R., 216, 224, 249-50
Twelfth Panzer Grenadier Hitlerjugend
    division, 232

U

United States, 17-18, 160, 162, 220,
    225-26, 242

V

Vicenta (Merardo's mother), 164-67,
    170-71, 179, 182

W

Wanda the Wonder Dog, 55-56, 193
war, 18, 67, 73, 77-80, 82, 86-88, 106-
    8, 111-14, 116-17, 121-28, 135-
    36, 140, 179-81, 225-26, 235-45
weapons, 89, 106, 113, 118, 213
Weimar regime, 219
werewolf project, 235-36
West Berlin, 141, 147, 155, 241-42
West Germany, 142, 163, 242-43
Wilhelmshorst, 129, 131-33, 147, 149
Witkatitz, Heine, 41-45, 53, 172
World War II, 15, 18, 20, 204, 237,
    244, 248

Z

Zielinski, Heinz, 88-89, 105-6, 108-9,
    114, 142, 187

Made in the USA
Las Vegas, NV
27 February 2021

18684096R00152